Teaching Academi...
Higher Edu...

Universities into the 21st Century

Series Editors: Noël Entwistle and Roger King

Teaching Academic Writing in UK Higher Education

Theories, Practices and Models

Edited by

Lisa Ganobcsik-Williams

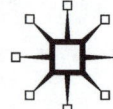
First published 2006 by
PALGRAVE MACMILLAN
Houndmills, Basingstoke, Hampshire RG21 6XS and
175 Fifth Avenue, New York, N.Y. 10010
Companies and representatives throughout the world

PALGRAVE MACMILLAN is the global academic imprint of the Palgrave Macmillan division of St. Martin's Press, LLC and of Palgrave Macmillan Ltd. Macmillan® is a registered trademark in the United States, United Kingdom and other countries. Palgrave is a registered trademark in the European Union and other countries.

ISBN-13: 978–1–4039–4534–9   hardback
ISBN-10: 1–4039–4534–9   hardback
ISBN-13: 978–1–4039–4535–8   paperback
ISBN-10: 1–4039–4535–7   paperback

This book is printed on paper suitable for recycling and made from fully managed and sustained forest sources.

A catalogue record for this book is available from the British Library.

A catalog record for this book is available from the Library of Congress.

10   9   8   7   6   5   4   3   2   1
15   14   13   12   11   10   09   08   07   06

Printed and bound in China

Contents

Part I   Starting Points for Theory and Pedagogy

List of Tables and Figures

Tables

Figures

Acknowledgements

I thank Lisa Ede, Jacqueline M. Labbe, Andrea A. Lunsford, Mary R. Lea and David Morley for responding to early drafts of the proposal for this book. I am grateful, too, to Suzannah Burywood at Palgrave Macmillan for her enthusiastic guidance. I also thank Jeremy Treglown for co-organising with me the March 2001 Warwick Writing Programme conference 'Teaching Writing in Higher Education', from which some of the chapters in this volume originated, and I express my gratitude to the Royal Literary Fund and to the Arts Council, England, for their generous sponsorship of this conference. Many thanks are also due to Ray Land, former Director of the Centre for Higher Education Development at Coventry University, and to my colleagues at CHED and at the Centre for Academic Writing. Penny Gilchrist, Jon Morley and Mary Deane deserve special thanks for their work on the manuscript preparation. I also thank Frances J. Ranney for helping to clarify terminology. Finally, and most importantly, I thank my family for all of the support they have given.

Grateful acknowledgement for permission to reproduce copyright material is extended for: the extract from Gary Day (2004) 'Opinion', *The Times Higher Education Supplement*, 30 January, p. 15; the extract from Josep-Anton Fernandez and Jan Marsh (2002) 'Frustration to Fun', *Thinking Writing: News from the Writing in the Disciplines Project*, Spring, pp. 3–4; reprint, in full, with minor editorial amendments, of Mary Jane Curry (2003) 'Skills, Access, and "Basic Writing": a Community College Case Study from the United States', *Studies in the Education of Adults*, vol. 35, no. 1, pp. 5–17; the extracts and table 7.1, in revised form, from Theresa M. Lillis (2001), *Student Writing: Action, Regulation, Desire* (London: Routledge), pp. 132–59, 164; and Table 1, in revised form, from Theresa M. Lillis (2003), 'Student Writing as "Academic Literacies": Drawing on Bakhtin to Move from Critique to Design', *Language and Education*, vol. 17, no. 3, pp. 192–7.

Series Editors' Preface

This series is designed to fill a niche between publications about universities and colleges that focus exclusively on the practical concerns of university teachers, managers or policy makers, and those which are written with an academic, research-based audience in mind that provide detailed evidence, argument and conclusions. The books in this series are intended to build upon evidence and conceptual frameworks in discussing issues which are of direct interest to those concerned with universities. The issues in the series will cover a broad range, from the activities of teachers and students, to wider developments in policy, at local, national and international levels.

The current pressures on academic and administrative staff, and university managers, mean that, only rarely, can they justify the time needed to read lengthy descriptions of research findings. The aim, therefore, is to produce compact, readable books that in many parts provide a synthesis and overview of often seemingly disparate issues.

Some of the books, such as the first in the series – *The University in the Global Age* – are deliberately broad in focus and conceptualisation, looking at the system as a whole in an international perspective, and are a collection of integrated chapters, written by specialist authors. In other books, such as *Research and Teaching: Beyond the Divide*, the author looks within universities at a specific issue to examine what constitutes 'best practice' through a lens of available theory and research evidence.

Underpinning arguments, where appropriate with research-based conceptual analysis, makes the books more convincing to an academic audience, while the link to 'good practice and policy' avoids the remoteness that comes from an over-abstract approach. The series will thus appeal not just to those working within higher education, but also to a wider audience interested in knowing more about an organisation that is attracting increasing government and media attention.

NOËL ENTWISTLE
ROGER KING

List of Abbreviations

ACT	American College Testing Service test (US higher education entry examination)
A Level	Advanced Level (UK higher education entry examination)
CCC/CCCC	College Composition and Communication (US journal and conference)
CCUE	Council for College and University English
DfEE	Department for Education and Employment (in 2001 the Education section became the Department for Education and Skills, DfES)
EAP	English for Academic Purposes
EARLI-SIG Writing	European Association for Research on Learning and Instruction Special Interest Group on Writing
EATAW	European Association for the Teaching of Academic Writing
EFL	English as a Foreign Language
ELLs	English-Language Learners
ESL	English as a Second Language
ESOL	English for Speakers of Other Languages
ESRC	Economic and Social Research Council
EWCA	European Writing Centers Association
FE	Further Education
GCSE	General Certificate of Secondary Education (UK)
HEFCE	Higher Education Funding Council for England
HERDSA	Higher Education Research and Development Society of Australasia
ICT	Information and Communication Technology
ITT	Initial Teacher Training
IWCA	International Writing Centers Association
NCIHE	National Committee of Inquiry into Higher Education
NCTE	National Council of Teachers of English (US)
NGO	Non-Governmental Organisation
NIACE	National Institute of Adult Continuing Education

NLS	National Literacy Strategy
OFSTED	Office for Standards in Education
PEDR	Pedagogical Research
PGCE	Postgraduate Certificate in Education (UK)
QAA	Quality Assurance Agency for Higher Education
RAE	Research Assessment Exercise
RLF	Royal Literary Fund
SAT	Scholastic Aptitude Test (US higher education entry examination)
SEDA	Staff and Educational Development Association (UK)
SFL	Systemic Functional Linguistics
TEFL	Teaching English as a Foreign Language
TESOL	Teaching English to Speakers of Other Languages
WAC	Writing Across the Curriculum
WDHE	Writing Development in Higher Education (UK listserv and conference)
WID	Writing in the Disciplines
WPA	Writing Programme Administrator(s)

List of Culturally Specific Terms

Course In UK higher education the term 'course' tends to refer to the entire 'degree course' on which a student is enrolled. 'Course' is also used as a synonym for 'module' (equivalent to the US term 'class'), a term- or semester-long unit of instruction consisting of lectures and seminars taught by lecturers and tutors.

Faculty In US higher education 'faculty' means a member of college or university teaching staff and is equivalent to the UK term 'academic staff'. In the US, 'faculty' – like 'academic staff' in the UK – can also be used as a collective noun: the phrase 'the Law faculty', for instance, refers not to the School or Department, but to the members of staff who teach/research there. In the UK and Australia, the word 'faculty' refers to a teaching body within a university that teaches one of the major branches of learning: for instance, 'the Faculty of Engineering'.

Graduate and Postgraduate The UK 'postgraduate' and US 'graduate' student are equivalent terms, meaning a person who is undertaking study beyond the undergraduate level.

Tutor In US higher education the term 'tutor' usually refers to the provider of one-to-one tuition, such as a 'writing centre tutor'. In UK higher education, 'tutor' most commonly refers to an academic conducting seminar teaching.

Notes on the Contributors

Alison Ahearn is a Construction lawyer in the Civil and Environmental Engineering Department, Imperial College, London. She teaches Construction Law to Engineers and Academic Writing to Civil Engineering and Medical students. She took a higher degree in Science Communication to enhance her ability to teach writing skills to non-humanities students, and her specialist teaching method, 'experiential learning', has been recognised with a CONSTRUCT Award for best practice and innovation. Alison holds a dual appointment as an Educational Development Lecturer and assists with teaching policy and the training of teaching staff.

Simon Avery is Senior Lecturer in the School of Humanities, University of Hertfordshire, and previously worked as Researcher on the Speak–Write Project at Anglia Ruskin University, Cambridge. He has published articles on teaching and learning in higher education and is co-editor of *Writing with Style* (2001) and *Innovations in English* (2000). He is also the author of *Elizabeth Barrett Browning*, with Rebecca Stott (2003), and editor of *Lives of Victorian Literary Figures: The Brownings* (2004).

Celia Bishop is Study Support Co-ordinator at the London College of Communication, University of the Arts London, where she manages study skills provision including support for students with dyslexia and other disabilities. Her research focuses on writing development with second-language speakers and adult returners.

Margo Blythman is Teaching and Learning Co-ordinator at the London College of Communication, University of the Arts London. She has responsibility for quality enhancement initiatives including study support and student retention. Her research includes the micropolitics of organisations, lecturers' conceptions of their working practices and students' approaches to design and writing.

Robert Catt is a member of the Centre for Language and Communications and the Applied Language and Literacies Group at the Open University. Previously, he taught English in secondary schools and directed the PGCE

English programme at Brunel University. His interests are in language and particularly talk in education, academic literacy and online learning.

Mary Jane Curry is Assistant Professor of Foreign Language/TESOL Education at the Warner Graduate School of Education, University of Rochester. She was formerly a Research Fellow in Academic Literacy in the Centre for Language and Communications, at the Open University. She is co-author of *Teaching Academic Writing: A Toolkit for Higher Education* (2002), and has published articles on second-language pedagogy and immigrant education. One of her current research projects, with Theresa Lillis, investigates writing in academic English by multilingual scholars in eastern and southern Europe. She is also conducting a study of students learning academic literacy through disciplinary content at the Open University.

Bonnie Devet is Associate Professor of English and has been Director of the Writing Lab at the College of Charleston, South Carolina, for sixteen years. She teaches graduate and undergraduate courses in Composition, and has been awarded two distinguished teaching awards. Her research on writing labs, Composition, Technical Writing, Business Writing and grammar has been published in *College Composition and Communication*, *The Writing Center Journal*, *The Writing Lab Newsletter*, *Journal of Teaching Writing*, *Business Communication Quarterly*, *Freshman English News*, *Teaching English in the Two-Year College*, *The International Journal for Teachers of English and Writing Skills* and *College Teaching*.

Alan Evison directs English Language and Study Skills programmes at Queen Mary, University of London. He has taught and managed courses in English for speakers of other languages in Bangladesh, Kuwait, Singapore, Yemen and Japan. His current research focuses on English for Academic Purposes and Writing in the Disciplines.

Aled Ganobcsik-Williams is Lecturer in English at the University of Derby. A specialist in literary Romanticism, he is also a teacher and researcher of Academic Writing. He has taught Academic Writing at the University of Warwick and Composition at two US universities. His publications include an article on Academic Writing and institutional change, and he has presented at conferences on the value of teaching grammar (WDHE), on William Cobbett's *Grammar of the English Language* (CCCC), and on the development of Academic Writing provision in UK universities (EATAW).

Lisa Ganobcsik-Williams is founding Co-ordinator of the Centre for Academic Writing, Coventry University. Formerly Lecturer and Co-ordinator of Academic Writing for the University of Warwick Writing Programme, Lisa has taught writing in a variety of disciplines. She has also taught and tutored writing in US universities. Lisa has published in *Rhetorica*, *The Writing Center Journal* and *Computers and Composition*. Her publications include *A Report on the Teaching of Academic Writing in UK Higher Education* (2004) and articles on designing a corpus of UK student writing and on cross-cultural approaches to teaching writing. In 2005, she was appointed to the board of the European Writing Centers Association (EWCA) and was also nominated for a National Teaching Fellowship.

Gerry Gregory, after National Service in the Royal Air Force, taught English, History and Physical Education in inner-London comprehensive schools for nine years, and in Brazil for three years, before becoming Senior Lecturer in English and Education at Shoreditch College of Education in 1971. He joined Brunel University in 1980, and teaches English on Initial Teacher Training courses, and supervises PhD research. His doctoral research was on working-class writing, community publishing and education, and his current research is on the teaching of grammar and language change.

John Heyda is Associate Professor of English at Miami University, Middletown, Ohio, where he serves as Co-ordinator of English and teaches Writing and Film Studies. He has published in the *Journal of Basic Writing*, the *Writing Instructor*, *College Composition and Communication* and elsewhere. In the mid-1990s he served as Director of the first-year writing programme at Miami University's main campus in Oxford, Ohio.

Roz Ivanič is Senior Lecturer in the Department of Linguistics and Modern English Language at Lancaster University, and an Associate Director of the Lancaster Literacy Research Centre. She researches academic literacy, adult literacy, educational linguistics and discourse analysis, with a special interest in the learning and teaching of writing and the discoursal construction of identity in writing. Her books include *Writing and Identity* (1998) and, with Romy Clark, *The Politics of Writing* (1997).

Mary R. Lea is Senior Lecturer in Teaching and Learning at the Institute of Educational Technology, at the Open University. She has extensive experience of research and practice in student writing in many different university contexts. Her publications include Lea and Nicoll, *Distributed Learning: Social and Cultural Approaches to Practice* (2002), and Lea and Stierer, *Student Writing in Higher Education: New Contexts* (2000). She has also co-authored with Phyllis Crème a successful guide for student writers,

Writing at University: A Guide for Students (2003), now in its second edition. Her recent work has been in the field of academic literacies and new technologies.

Theresa M. Lillis is Senior Lecturer at the Centre for Language and Communications, at the Open University. She has taught in a range of educational contexts including secondary, adult and higher education. Her research interests include academic literacy practices and widening access to higher education, and professional academic writing in multilingual contexts. She is the author of *Student Writing: Access, Regulation, Desire* (2001), and co-author of *Teaching Academic Writing: A Toolkit for Higher Education* (2003).

Sally Mitchell co-ordinates the Thinking Writing initiative at Queen Mary, University of London. Previously, she was a Research Fellow on two projects investigating the nature and role of argument in educational settings. She is co-author with Mike Riddle of *Improving the Quality of Argument in Higher Education: Final Report* (2000) and, with Richard Andrews, of *Essays in Argument* (2000). She has also co-edited *Competing and Consensual Voices*, with Patrick Costello (1995), and *Learning to Argue in Higher Education*, with Richard Andrews (2000).

Joan A. Mullin, Professor in Rhetoric and Composition at the University of Texas, Austin, leads her university's College of Liberal Arts WAC initiative. She founded and directed the University of Toledo Writing Center and WAC programme (1987–2004), and publishes in various writing centre, WAC, and disciplinary journals. Joan is former co-editor of *The Writing Center Journal* and has co-authored, with Ray Wallace, the award-winning *Intersections: Theory–Practice in the Writing Center* (1994). She has also co-authored, with Eric Hobson, *ARTiculating: Teaching Writing in a Visual Culture* (1998). Past president of the International Writing Centers Association (IWCA), Joan researches visual literacy across international curricula and serves on editorial boards and committees nationally and internationally.

Rowena Murray taught Composition while studying for a PhD in English at the Pennsylvania State University. Since 1989 she has worked in the Centre for Academic Practice at the University of Strathclyde, providing staff and educational development. She has published papers on writing development for students and staff, and video packs on *Thesis Writing* and *Writing for Publication*. She has written two books on Academic Writing: *How to Write a Thesis* (2002) and *Writing for Academic Journals* (2005).

Susan Orr was Teaching and Learning Co-ordinator at the London College of Fashion and is now Principal Lecturer for Quality Management and Enhancement in the School of Arts, York St John College. Susan researches higher education pedagogy, focusing on students' approaches to textual and visual assessment, and assessment as a social practice in Art and Design. She has presented at writing conferences in the UK, US and Europe, and has co-authored a range of articles, papers and chapters with Margo Blythman.

Jan Skillen is Senior Lecturer in Learning Development at the University of Wollongong, Australia. She began her career at the University of Newcastle, first in Linguistics and then in the Centre for Learning and Teaching. In 1995 she moved to the University of Sydney's Orange campus to pioneer subject-integrated teaching of generic and discipline-specific writing skills. She takes a similar role in her current position, and works with other academics to put literacy policy into practice at departmental, faculty and institutional level. Jan's unit was shortlisted for a national teaching award in 2000, and she won a personal teaching award from the University of Wollongong in 2003.

Alice Tomic is Professor of English Language and Communications at Richmond, the American International University in London. She is editor of the journal *Language and Intercultural Communication* and a member of the Executive Board of the International Association for Languages and Intercultural Communication. For the last twenty years at Richmond she has developed a structured English Language Development programme and a Writing Across the Curriculum initiative to acculturate students from all over the world to the discourses of the academic community.

Tory Young is Senior Lecturer in English and Co-Director of the Speak–Write Project at Anglia Ruskin University, Cambridge. As Curriculum Consultant she has tailored Speak–Write's materials to improve undergraduates' written and oral communication skills for UK English Departments. In addition to Academic Writing her research interests are in literary Modernism, and she is an organiser of the London Modernism Seminar. Tory is currently writing *The Cambridge Guide to Studying English Literature*, she has edited *Speaking Your Mind: Oral Presentation and Seminar Skills* (2001), and she is co-author, with Katy Price and Vicky Williamson, of *Writing at Work: Advanced Writing Skills for Graduate Professionals* (forthcoming).

General Introduction: Responding to the Call for Academic Writing Theory and Pedagogy

Lisa Ganobcsik-Williams

Academic Writing is emerging as a distinct teaching and research subject in UK higher education. This book provides an overview of theoretical positions in the field of student writing development, and of current practical initiatives in writing support in UK universities. The book is divided into three Parts, each of which takes as its focus one of the keywords – 'Theories', 'Practices', 'Models' – in the book's sub-title. Part I, 'Starting Points for Theory and Pedagogy', describes the context out of which Academic Writing pedagogy has arisen in the UK and evaluates the development of research approaches to Academic Writing. Part II, 'Developing UK Writing Programmes and Initiatives', outlines and assesses a number of Academic Writing projects to show how practitioners of student writing development are exploring a variety of routes for organising the teaching of writing within different institutional contexts. In Part III, 'Responding to Other Models', teachers and scholars from other countries draw lessons for readers from their experience of implementing different national and institutional models of writing support. Taken together, the chapters in this collection demonstrate how a productive discourse about writing in the university has begun to take shape in the UK, and make an important contribution to this discussion.

The movement to develop student writing at university level began in UK higher education in the early 1990s, when the sector as a whole was undergoing an intense period of expansion. Between 1987 and 1992 student participation in higher education nearly doubled. In the mid-1980s the student participation index reached 15 per cent, 'the threshold figure that marks the boundary between élite and mass higher education', and by the mid-1990s, with 32 per cent of the eligible age group enrolled, higher education was already in the process of becoming a 'universal system' (P. Scott, 1995, pp. 2, 5).[1] As a consequence of these increased numbers and the diversification of student backgrounds that accompanied them, both the need for new teaching methods and the need to be more explicit about writing practices began to be recognised.[2] During this period two key groups of writing scholar-practitioners formed: the Academic Literacies research group and the Writing Development in Higher Education (WDHE) network.[3]

The recognition that Academic Writing needs to be taught is now widespread,[4] and the call for teaching writing has come both from outside and from within the university.[5] As government education policy has moved toward the idea of lifelong learning and more open access to higher education, a fear that widening access is resulting in a decline in standards has sparked popular interest in improving student writing.[6] Held accountable to public interest and, more directly, to the requirements of graduate employers, government policy-makers for education are attempting to ensure educational continuity and to clarify graduates' qualifications by establishing targets for key skills – including skills in writing – that students should attain.[7] It is clear that these external pressures on higher education are setting an agenda for developments within institutions, yet student writing development also interests the academic community itself. Findings from an Autumn 2000 survey of academic and student support staff within all universities and higher education colleges in England, Wales, Scotland and Northern Ireland show that 90 per cent of respondents believe it is necessary to teach writing to university students.[8] One explanation for this belief is that many academics and professional staff share public concerns about standards in higher education and recognise that they are in a position to promote pedagogical initiatives for maintaining those standards. Moreover, an increasing number of academics are coming to recognise that explicit instruction in Academic Writing assists the academic and intellectual progression of all students. Indeed, because students today are expected to master an array of written genres,[9] many academics believe that writing instruction and support are essential if students are to realise their academic and intellectual potential.[10]

Scholarly activity is moving rapidly to support the development of Academic Writing programmes and initiatives in UK universities. Hence, although Academic Writing is a young field, it is underpinned by a vibrant research culture that includes discussion networks, conferences and a growing body of scholarship.[11] Specifically, writing pedagogy serves both as the subject and the beneficiary of Pedagogical Research (PedR). While Bennett et al. (2000) cite a representative case of a UK university academic having been 'discouraged from writing about teaching because it was seen as "low-status" research' (p. 47), this traditional value distinction between 'pure' and 'applied' research is undergoing a sea change, at both the national and the institutional level. Classroom-based research whose findings can be applied to further pedagogical development is becoming increasingly valued across the higher education sector, as shown by the revised criteria for the 2008 national Research Assessment Exercise (RAE),[12] which promise that 'due weight will be given to applied research', as well as by the establishment in

2004 of a national Higher Education Academy and national Subject Centres to support and reward university teaching and research-led pedagogy.[13] *Teaching Academic Writing in UK Higher Education: Theories, Practices and Models* demonstrates how practice is being theorised and how research, in turn, is being used to inform practice, with the overall goal of helping students to develop the ability to write effectively in academic genres.

The book has four target audiences: current UK writing practitioners and scholars, UK university staff who are new to writing development, UK higher education policy-makers, and teachers and researchers from other countries. For UK-based writing practitioners and scholars, the collection draws together developments in the field and provides an opportunity to read accounts of the situated practices of other writing teachers and of models employed in foreign higher education systems. The book also introduces advances in Academic Writing pedagogy and research to a wider constituency beyond the scholar-practitioners or 'Writing Developers' who are closely involved in teaching and researching writing. Subject academics who have no experience of teaching writing but who want to assist students because they see that students often under-perform as a result of weak communication skills, will find in this collection an introduction to Academic Writing theories, assessments of various UK approaches to teaching writing in different disciplines, as well as evaluations of models from other cultural contexts. Senior managers, administrators and other higher education policy-makers facing decisions about establishing writing provision in their institutions will also find the book to be highly informative. Part II may be of particular interest to this audience, as its chapters suggest how strategically targeted funding, both at the subject level and at the institutional level, can yield writing provision that addresses governmental and institutional priorities such as lifelong learning, skills development, e-learning, personal development planning and retention and progression. Finally, the perspectives in *Teaching Academic Writing in UK Higher Education: Theories, Practices and Models* will add to the knowledge pool of US scholars and those from other countries whose views on teaching writing may have been informed until now almost exclusively by US Composition pedagogy and scholarship.

As the last point suggests, the study of university writing is becoming increasingly trans-national and comparative in nature. While the field of writing teaching and research has been professionalised in the United States for many decades, for example, the founding of UK and European Academic Writing organisations,[14] the publication of cross-national comparative work on the teaching of writing,[15] and a burgeoning international participation in US, European and UK writing conferences demonstrates that Academic Writing scholarship is becoming unmistakably – and irreversibly – cross-cultural.[16] *Teaching Academic Writing in UK Higher Education: Theories,*

Practices and Models emphasises the importance of comparative research and suggests that although institutional circumstances and national priorities for education may differ, those interested in developing student writing can learn from and contribute to Academic Writing theory and pedagogy developed in other national contexts. A goal of the volume, then, is to provide an exchange of information that makes a useful contribution to trans-national writing scholarship.[17]

Teaching Academic Writing in UK Higher Education: Theories, Practices and Models promotes a lively and growing culture of teaching and research in Academic Writing. It is the intention of all contributors that this book will bring to light a range of possibilities for investigating and supporting students' Academic Writing. Our collective aim is that the theories, practices and models explored here will have both immediate and lasting influence on how university writing programmes and initiatives come to be constituted in the years ahead.

NOTES

1   A mass educational system enrols between 15 and 40 per cent of the eligible age group, and a universal system enrols more than 40 per cent (P. Scott, 1995, p. 2).

2   Research on student writing in UK universities which pre-dates the development of the Academic Writing movement includes work by Dai Hounsell (for example, 1984a, 1984b, 1987, 1988) and James Hartley (for example, 1980).

3   Re-named the Interuniversity Academic Literacies Research Group, the first of these groups was established in 1993 and is convened by Mary Scott at the Institute of Education, University of London. The WDHE, launched by Flo Ali at the University of Northumbria in 1994, operates a discussion listserv and hosts an annual/biennial conference on student writing pedagogy and theory. WDHE conferences have been held at the universities of Middlesex, Luton, Wales (Aberystwyth), Reading, Liverpool, Leicester, Sheffield Hallam and the Open University. A third group, the Literacy in Higher Education research group, is discussed by Alice Tomic in Chapter 4 of this volume.

4   See, for example, Bergstrom (2004) on 'The Status of Writing in the University'.

5   The Royal Literary Fund (RLF) is an organisation that has played a significant role in calling attention to the need for supporting student writing in UK higher education. A registered charity, the RLF launched a Fellowship Scheme in 1999 placing professional writers (including poets, playwrights, novelists, biographers, translators and technical writers) in UK universities and colleges to tutor students in Academic Writing. The RLF has also sponsored a number of reports on student writing in higher education, including Davies (2004), Ganobcsik-Williams (2004), McMahon (2004) and Davies, Swinburne and Williams (2006).

6   A discourse of falling standards in student writing has appeared in newspaper articles since the late 1980s (Street, 1998; Cameron, 1995, pp. 78–115;

Crowley, 2003, p. 249; Clark and Ivanič, 1997, p. 187), and twenty-first-century headlines continue this trend. *See,* for example, McVeigh (2002) and Bright (2004). Journalists assert that 'the current intake of students is the weakest in history' (Owen, 2003), that '[s]tandards of spelling and grammar among an entire generation of English-speaking university students are now so poor that there is "a degree of crisis" in their written use of the language' (Smithers, 2003), and that students 'are in danger of dropping out of university because they cannot string their thoughts together to write an essay' (Garner, 2004). The Queen's English Society has also published reports on standards of student writing; in particular *see* Lamb (1992).

7 *See* Drew (1998) and Dearing (NCIHE, 1997).

8 When asked 'Do you think it is necessary to teach writing to university students?', 90 per cent of respondents (or 111 UK university and higher education college staff members) answered 'yes' while only 10 per cent (13 staff members) answered 'no' (Ganobcsik-Williams, 2004, p. 28).

9 Ganobcsik-Williams's Autumn 2000 survey of university staff generated a list of 64 varieties of writing that are asked of students in higher education (Ganobcsik-Williams, 2004, pp. 13–14).

10 One impact of the university tuition fees introduced in 2006 may be that students come to expect increased student services, including writing support.

11 In addition to the WDHE conferences, an international conference on 'Teaching Writing in Higher Education' was hosted by the University of Warwick Writing Programme in 2001. In a keynote panel discussion between Mary Lea, Roz Ivanič and Andrea Lunsford, the terms 'expository' and 'practical' writing were discussed and 'Academic Writing' emerged as a common term for use in UK higher education. Foundational studies produced by researchers and teachers of Academic Writing include Jones et al.'s (1999) *Students Writing in the University: Cultural and Epistemological Issues*, Lea and Stierer's (2000) *Student Writing in Higher Education: New Contexts*, and Lillis's (2001) *Student Writing: Access, Regulation, Desire.*

12 *See* www.rae.ac.uk/pubs/2004/01/. The national Research Assessment Exercise (RAE), begun in the 1980s, rewards institutions with government funding for the quality and quantity of research they produce.

13 *See* www.heacademy.ac.uk/ for information on the Higher Education Academy and Subject Centres. For Pedagogical Research, see the report 'Building Capacity for Change: Research on the Scholarship of Teaching' produced by the Higher Education Funding Council for England (HEFCE, 2003).

14 There are three main European organisations that study Academic Writing at university level. The European Association for the Teaching of Academic Writing (EATAW) (www.eataw.org/) operates a listserv and has held conferences in Groningen, Netherlands (2001), Budapest, Hungary (2003) and Athens, Greece (2005). The European Writing Centers Association (EWCA), founded in 1998, co-sponsored the first two EATAW conferences and also supports a listserv. EWCA has held international gatherings at the American University in Bulgaria (2000), the American College of Thessaloniki, Greece (2002) and Sabanci

University, Turkey (2006) (see http://ewca.sabanciuniv.edu/). The European Association for Research on Learning and Instruction Special Interest Group on Writing (EARLI-SIG Writing), founded in 1988, includes, but is not limited to, research on university student writing (see www.sig-writing.org/).

15 See, for example, Muchiri et al. (1995), Russell and Foster (2002), McLeod (2002) and Björk et al. (2003).

16 The accelerated growth in international participation in writing conferences raises the issue – which became a subject of debate at the EATAW 2006 conference – about the ability of Academic Writing organisations to retain a regional identity and focus while at the same time welcoming an international membership.

17 The cross-cultural nature of the collection is emphasised by the preservation within chapters of stylistic features such as spelling and comma usage reflecting different UK, US and Australian writing conventions. The 'Oxford' comma, for example, 'so called because it was traditionally used by printers' readers and editors at Oxford University Press', is an optional final comma used before a co-ordinating conjunction (such as 'and') in a list of three or more items (Oxford, 2005). The Oxford comma is also known as the 'serial comma' because it constitutes a 'comma between the last two items in a series' (Hacker, 2005). US grammar books recommend its use 'because omitting the comma can result in ambiguity or misreading' (Hacker, 2005), and therefore in US writing the 'standard usage is to leave it in' (Truss, 2003, p. 84). Although 'British grammarians will concede that sometimes the extra comma prevents confusion', for UK writers 'standard usage is to leave it out' (Truss, 2003, pp. 84–5). In addition to stylistic conventions, terms whose meanings differ between national higher education systems, such as 'Tutor' and 'Faculty', have been retained in the chapters and are explained in a List of Culturally Specific Terms at the front of the book.

Part I

Starting Points for Theory and Pedagogy

Introduction

Lisa Ganobcsik-Williams

This part comprises three chapters, which argue that the most recent theoretical approach to teaching Academic Writing in UK higher education, Academic Literacies, has emerged in response to the limitations of previous non-theoretical – or at least untheorised – approaches to student writing. All of the chapters, but especially Chapters 2 and 3, also draw some implications of Academic Literacies theory for the practice of writing support.

In Chapter 1, Roz Ivanič and Mary Lea outline the historical development of Academic Writing research and practice in the UK. Ivanič and Lea point to the absence of a single research tradition on student writing in UK higher education and explain, too, that writing teachers and scholars originate in a variety of professional and disciplinary backgrounds. While the range of areas from within which UK writing pedagogy has emerged has been fruitful in generating diverse research approaches, this diversity suggests important questions, addressed in a variety of ways in subsequent chapters, about who is responsible for student writing and of where Academic Writing initiatives and programmes can best be located within institutions.

Like the majority of the authors in this book, Ivanič and Lea propose that interest in Academic Writing pedagogy is concurrent with the shift in the UK from an élite to a mass system of higher education. As this process of expansion in the higher education sector accelerated and previously excluded student populations entered the university, the search by practitioners for viable models of writing support within a UK context revealed two default models for teaching Academic Writing. The first, perhaps most often associated with former polytechnics and further education institutions, is a skills approach, which views student writing as a problem to be remedied by separate study skills instruction that attempts to teach writing as a set of discrete techniques without relation to curricular content. The second model, more prevalent in traditional universities, is socialisation or acculturation, which views Academic Writing proficiency as something that students absorb through their immersion in disciplinary practices and exposure to disciplinary modes of knowledge: with varying degrees of directness students are inducted into disciplinary habits of thought, including knowledge of how to write. Both models of student writing support are inadequate, Ivanič and Lea suggest, for the new institutional contexts that are evolving as a result of the expansion of higher education. In response to the insufficiency of these models, Ivanič and Lea, as well as the authors of the two remaining chapters in this section, advocate a more recent theoretical approach, called 'Academic Literacies'.[1]

This division of approaches into 'skills', 'academic socialisation' and 'academic literacies' is derived from Lea and Street (1998), whose seminal work is cited in Chapters 2 and 3 and elsewhere throughout the volume.[2] As an approach to student writing, Lea and Street argue that Academic Literacies draws upon but also moves beyond the two previous models. Academic Literacies is emerging as the dominant way of theorising student writing in the UK and several of the contributors to this book make use of its insights. Perhaps the key contribution of the Academic Literacies approach, and what potentially makes it radically different, is that it challenges the assumption – implicit in the skills and socialisation approaches – that it is the students who are in deficit and need to learn to adapt to the university. For proponents of Academic Literacies, the institution itself with all its taken-for-granted practices and values and roles should also adapt to a new higher education context which is, as Theresa Lillis notes in Chapter 3, 'premised upon notions of diversity and inclusion'.

Academic Literacies has been extremely productive as a method for critical analysis, and words such as 'change', 'challenge' and 'critique' reverberate throughout the discussion in Part I and elsewhere in the book. The spirit in which this critical method is intended is as a way of encouraging reflection on traditional professional practice. Academic Literacies theorists make the case that writing is not a student problem only, but a challenge for all members of the university as they attempt to adjust to new forms and technologies of writing and studying, as well as a variety of student backgrounds and experiences. As Robert Catt and Gerry Gregory observe in Chapter 2, '[t]o place writing more centrally within the learning process would, undoubtedly, demand institutional change and innovation'. However, as Lillis argues in Chapter 3, while Academic Literacies has primarily been invoked in order to assess and critique existing approaches to student writing, the challenge now is to explore how this new theoretical framework might inform practice.

Both Chapters 2 and 3 draw on data involving student-participants, and in doing so add primary research findings to bolster theoretical positions. These chapters also begin the work of considering the implications of the Academic Literacies approach for practice; Catt and Gregory from the perspective of subject academics and Lillis from the perspective of a writing development tutor and researcher. Both explore the idea, for example, that the genres or assignment types through which students are assessed need to be made more flexible, and both emphasise the importance of the nature, scope and timing of tutors' responses. Catt and Gregory, in particular, suggest a variety of practical strategies for teachers. Both chapters also make reference to the need for a re-allocation of time and resources in order to enable teaching staff to work effectively with students on their writing. Academic Literacies argues that student writing should be a priority on the institutional agenda, and as to the question of who is responsible for student writing in the university, proponents of Academic Literacies would answer 'all members of the institution are'.

NOTES

1   'The notion of academic literacy has been developed from the area of "new literacy studies" in which literacy is seen as a social practice rather than a set of cognitive skills to be learnt and assimilated. This approach takes account of the cultural and contextual component of writing and reading practices' (Lea and Street, 1996, p. 2).

2   This critical framework was generated as a result of the 'Perspectives on Academic Literacies: An Institutional Approach' project, conducted in 1995–6 by Mary Lea and Brian Street and funded by the Economic and Social Research Council (ESRC).

1 New Contexts, New Challenges: the Teaching of Writing in UK Higher Education

Roz Ivanič and Mary R. Lea

▶ Introduction

This chapter examines how political, social and cultural beliefs about the function of higher education – and the educational practices generated by those beliefs – have resulted in particular approaches to the teaching of writing in UK higher education. Traditionally in the UK undergraduate education has been viewed as training in an academic discipline, with students specialising in well-established disciplinary areas and studying in order to become, for example, 'an historian' or 'a chemist'. As a result, the majority of university courses used to be 'single majors', with students specialising and only able to take a limited number of courses, if any, outside the department of study into which they were admitted. The education system leading up to entry into higher education was progressively more and more specialised in order to prepare students for this type of regime at university, with few students taking more than three subjects after the age of 16. Thus, writing in higher education was limited to its role in subject-specific learning and demonstrating of learning, and has not, up until now, had a place in the curriculum in its own right.

Further, it was not considered necessary to teach writing in the disciplines. It was an unspoken assumption that students already knew how to write before going to university, since a prerequisite for university entrance is a good pass in the compulsory subject 'English Language', which includes 'essay writing'. In addition, the advanced or 'A Level' courses which students normally take between the ages of 16 and 18 to qualify for university entrance were expected to provide discipline-specific preparation for the subjects in which students would specialise at university. So a student entering a university course in, say, Law, will have already specialised for two years, taking A Level courses and exams in subjects such as History, English Literature and German, including the writing requirements of these subjects. Such a student will have written many essays, which are assumed to be broadly comparable to those which will be required on the Law degree. By contrast, a student entering a university course in, say, Geology, might have taken A Levels in Chemistry, Geography and Maths – subjects in which writing is not emphasised. Traditionally this lack of practice in writing would not have been considered a disadvantage, nor would any compensatory measures be taken, since Geology as a degree subject would not have been seen to require much writing.

Because higher education in the UK is undergoing a period of transition, we found it hard to decide whether to use the past or the present tense in this account. Whilst the state of affairs we have presented here applies to the vast majority of university education in the UK in the past, from the mid-1980s onwards there have been changes, and these are what we are referring to as 'new contexts, new challenges' for the teaching of writing in higher education.

▶ The new context in the UK

To understand the context within which the teaching of writing in UK universities has begun to take place, developments need to be set against some important changes in higher education policy. From the mid-1980s there was an unprecedented expansion in higher education, and by 1995, 32 per cent of the population under the age of 30 had entered the sector (P. Scott, 1995, p. 2). This expansion was aided by the 1992 Education Act, which abolished the established binary divide between polytechnics and universities, bringing them together for administrative and funding purposes under one body, the Higher Education Funding Council for England (HEFCE). Furthermore, in 2003 the Labour government set itself a target of 50 per cent of 18–30-year-olds in higher education by 2010 (Department for Education and Skills, 2003, pp. 57, 59). This development of mass higher education has not come without its costs. As a result of the unprecedented rise in student numbers, academic members of staff are teaching larger and larger classes, and are spending less and less time with individual students and more and more time on administrative tasks. At the same time, material resources for students – such as library facilities – are poor in many of today's universities. The issue of the lived experience of teaching and learning – from both student and tutor perspectives – is central to understanding student writing in a system which now precludes most students from receiving the individual, discipline-based tuition that was available when higher education was an élite rather than a mass system.

The expansion of higher education has also been accompanied by other fundamental changes with important implications for teaching and learning. The first of these is the modularisation of degree programmes, a move led in the sector by what have been termed the 'new universities', that is institutions which were previously polytechnics and had university status conferred upon them in 1992. Modular degree programmes allow students to follow their own pathways to degree completion (Davidson and Lea, 1994). Rather than following a strict linear progression in a specific discipline or subject area, students are offered the opportunity to follow 'Combined Studies' degrees and thus to combine courses from different fields of study. This means that teaching staff can no longer make any assumptions about the bodies of knowledge that students might be bringing to any particular course, as they could when students followed more traditional routes of disciplinary study. Accompanying this move to modular course delivery has been a growth in interdisciplinary courses of study, such as Environmental Sciences, Health Studies, European Studies and Childhood Studies. These courses draw on many different disciplinary knowledge bases, requiring students to negotiate a range of different discourses and genres rather than introducing them to the specific discourses of a defined discipline.

The moves towards mass higher education have led, too, to greater expansion in the development of vocational and professional courses than in the more traditional academic subject areas. This is having profound consequences for what counts as knowledge in the university. Traditionally, universities have been seen as the bastions of academic knowledge, but the increased emphasis on vocational courses – often coupled with work-based placements – is raising questions about the very status of universities as both knowledge-holders and knowledge-providers in the twenty-first century. Questions about the status of knowledge are integrally linked to a further aspect of today's higher education, the increasing use of information and communication technology (ICT) in teaching and learning. The use of ICT challenges many of the long-held assumptions about the construction of knowledge in the university. Arguably, the reliance on the authority of the published book or journal article is being called into question as both academics and students draw more eclectically on web-based resources in their work. In addition, moves towards more collaborative models of teaching and learning – based on students working together in online environments – challenge some deeply held assumptions about the ways in which knowledge is constructed and who has the right to claim ownership of that knowledge.

At the same time as these profound changes have been taking place in both the curriculum and its delivery, universities have come under pressure to show themselves to be widening access to groups who have not traditionally participated in higher education, such as UK students whose home language is not English, older students and students from a variety of ethnic backgrounds (Department for Education and Skills, 2003). In addition, the increasingly global nature of higher education has led to steadily growing initiatives to attract 'international students' to higher education in the UK.

Institutions have responded to these factors by providing support in 'study skills' and 'English for Academic Purposes' in an effort to ensure that these new groups of students succeed in their courses.

Accompanying these changes has been a bureaucratisation of higher education, with government-led quality assurance initiatives and teaching quality assessments, as well as league tables quantifying the 'quality' of provision for students in different subjects at different universities.[1] Academic literacy support for students with 'difficulties', and increasingly, for all students, is beginning to be seen as a marker of good provision. As a result, something which in the 1980s would only have been found in polytechnics for 'less academic' students, or in universities taking in large numbers of students for whom English is a foreign language, is now becoming more or less a requirement for every university in the country. In building structures to support student writing and in the 'competition' to impress assessors with the quality of support for student writing, the 'new universities' are leading the field.

▶ The teaching of writing in this new context

The roots of today's attention to student writing in UK higher education can be found in the early days of language support in post-compulsory education. This first began to emerge in the 1970s in technical colleges, which offered 'communication courses' to post-secondary 16-year-olds who were following vocational day-release classes. In the 1980s Access courses began to be provided either in Further Education (FE) colleges or within universities themselves.[2] These courses focus on intensive preparation for university study, including specific attention to essay writing. With the expansion of higher education in the 1990s, increasing numbers of institutions – in particular the post-1992 universities – began to offer fairly comprehensive programmes of study skills, which usually paid some attention to writing.

Prior to the 1990s, provision of writing support in the UK tertiary sector had been fairly idiosyncratic, depending upon the circumstances of each individual institution and its particular student body. This can be contrasted with the situation in US universities, where dedicated writing support has existed since the late nineteenth century in the form of first-year or 'freshman' writing courses. In addition, as Grabe and Kaplan indicate, alongside the compulsory first-year writing course, the expansion of US higher education in the 1960s led to the setting up of remedial or basic writing courses for those students who were not deemed ready for the freshman courses. In tandem with the compulsory requirement for all US university students to follow a freshman writing course came the development of the College Composition movement, which was well established from the 1960s in the

US, as practitioners who were responsible for teaching writing courses began to theorise their work in publications concerned with teaching writing.[3] Until the 1990s there was no such comparable organisation of practitioners working in the field of writing support in the UK.

▶ The nature of provision

Because of the history of the teaching of writing outlined above, it has developed as a form of support provision rather than as a subject in the main curriculum in UK universities. The common pattern has been for the teaching of 'study skills', 'academic literacy' and writing to be provided by separate units such as 'study skills centres' or 'learning support units', or as part of Counselling, Student Services or the Library. A consequence of the separation of the teaching of writing from academic departments is that it has been treated as a low-status area of work in the university, and therefore has been minimally resourced, and marginalised in the hierarchy of activities of the university – except, of course, when the quality assurance inspectors are visiting. Writing staff are often on 'teaching-only' or 'academic-related' contracts even in research universities, are usually less well paid than their lecturer colleagues and are often part-time. Because of the origins of provision in special units serving speakers of English as a second or foreign language, teachers of writing often have backgrounds in Linguistics, Applied Linguistics and teaching English as a foreign language (TEFL). Others have come into the teaching of writing through student support services, often with a background in Social Sciences, Anthropology or Social Linguistics. Increasingly, writing teachers interested in staff development are entering the field from the area of Higher Education Development. In contrast to the US, teachers of writing in the UK are rarely English Literature graduates, and there is no tradition of Composition and Rhetoric studies in the UK.

For the reasons outlined above, provision usually has been devoted not just to writing but to academic support more broadly, covering many aspects of learning and communication for academic purposes. In many instances, writing and other aspects of academic literacy have been taught as a free-standing syllabus with no direct connection to the content of the curriculum being followed by students, either for interdisciplinary groups or for subject-specific groups of students. Writing and other aspects of academic literacy may be more directly linked to the curriculum content in seminars or courses which are provided for specific groups – often postgraduates. Other contexts in which academic literacy is taught in conjunction with content are 'foundation courses': first-year, introductory courses designed to prepare students for an area of study (for example, 'The Humanities'). Until recently, these classes would have been optional, and recommended only for students who 'need' them. However, it is now becoming more common for writing to be a compulsory element within, for example, foundation courses.

As a consequence of the *ad hoc* way in which such courses have evolved, there is currently a wide diversity of approaches to the teaching of writing. Most are inspired by a desire to give students access to the academy, but how this aim is translated into practice varies a great deal. Practice is underpinned by widely differing views of the nature of literacy, of what is involved in writing and learning to write (Lea and Street, 1998), and particularly there is a divide between courses designed mainly to acculturate students into the norms of academic literacy, and those designed also to raise critical awareness of those norms and to encourage contestation.

The resulting context for the teaching of writing in the UK is characterised by a number of tensions that have to be resolved by those who want to offer provision, such as:

- Is the teaching of writing only for struggling students or for all?
- Is it for 'academic support' or does it offer something broader?
- Does it focus on 'acculturation' into the academic community, or on critique?

And in recent times another question has come to the fore:

- Is technology taking centre-stage, and overshadowing more fundamental issues of literacies in higher education?

▶ Research approaches to student writing in the UK

The tensions between these different practice-based approaches to teaching Academic Writing are informed in part by different traditions of research on student learning. During the 1980s a body of literature emerged in northern Europe which was concerned more generally with student learning. This research, in what was termed the 'phenomenographic tradition' (Marton et al., 1997), concentrated upon variations in the student experience of learning. In the UK the work of the Oxford Centre for Staff Development dominated the field of research into student learning in this tradition. Gibbs's (1992) work on the contrasts between 'deep' and 'surface' learning was particularly influential with learning support practitioners.[4] Also within the phenomenographic framework and strongly influenced by psychological approaches to learning, Hounsell's (1988) research on student writing in a UK context was both seminal and unique in exploring students' acculturation into academic discourse. Hounsell continues to work in this field as one of the directors of the Teaching and Learning Research Programme project 'Enhancing teaching–learning environments in undergraduate courses'.[5] This project takes a whole teaching–learning environment approach to investigating what enables and constrains quality learning across a wide variety of disciplines. Its work has included identifying discipline-specific ways of thinking, and the effects of different forms of feedback, and the lack of it, on student development (Hounsell, 2003).

However, what has been missing from the broader literature of the field has been attention to the importance of language in the student experience of learning. In the 1990s, as UK higher education institutions began to focus more upon the explicit development of skills in the curriculum – for example, notions of 'transferable skills', 'graduateness', 'competencies' and 'outcomes-based education' – a group of researchers began to see that there was little attempt to incorporate attention to issues of language and learning into these curriculum initiatives. It is this gap which 'Academic Literacies' research has sought to address since the mid-1990s. This research offers a different way of understanding not just student writing but learning and teaching in higher education more broadly. In contrast to approaches that concentrated on the acquisition of decontextualised skills, Academic Literacies research points to the complexity of the codes and conventions that students need to negotiate to become accomplished players in the academy; in so doing it encourages exploration of the ways in which issues of meaning-making and identity are implicated, not just in student writing, but in teaching and learning more generally.

This approach provides an alternative to a 'deficit model' of student learning. A deficit model positions the student as lacking in basic skills; the task of support staff, academic staff or curriculum design is to enable students to acquire the skills they are deemed to lack in order to complete their studies successfully. Such skills are conceptualised as decontextualised; that is, once learnt they can be easily transferred from one context to another both within and outside the university. In relation to student writing, a deficit model suggests that students lack basic writing skills, for example, those concerned with grammar, spelling and punctuation; it does not take account of the ways in which writing is related to much deeper questions of epistemology and what counts as knowledge in the university. Academic Literacies research contrasts both with the focus on acculturating students into academic discourse and with the concerns of work in the phenomenographic tradition and the student experience of learning. It considers issues of student writing within a broader and contested institutional perspective.

For example, Lea (1994) argues that in order to understand more about student writing it is necessary to move away from a framework which conceptualises writing in terms of study skills, and to consider the institutional, disciplinary and social contexts within which students' written texts are produced. Drawing on critical Linguistics, she suggests that there is a gap between staff and student expectations of appropriate writing practices and that, therefore, academic staff need to examine the ways in which knowledge is constructed in their own fields. Similarly, Lillis (1997) and Ivanič (1998) examine the experiences of mature students entering the academy, using a Linguistics and language-based framing for exploring student writing. Lillis (1997) argues that dominant academic linguistic practices and conventions serve to constrain mature adult students' full participation in higher education and limit their possibilities for making meaning through their writing. She suggests that universities need to find ways of providing different spaces for 'meaning-making' which would include rather than exclude groups of students who are new to academic study. The work of all three authors is informed by a practitioner perspective, supporting adult students working on their own writing. Ivanič is concerned with the social struggles in which the self is implicated through the act of writing. She explores how what she terms the 'discoursal self' is constructed through the discourse characteristics of the text, which are imbued with the values, beliefs and power relations that contextualise the act of writing. Both Lillis and Ivanič draw on critical language awareness and critical discourse analysis in foregrounding ideology in their explorations of power and authority in student writing. This particular orientation by all three writers (Lea, 1994; Lillis, 1997; Ivanič, 1998) laid the foundation for the more contested approach to student writing, which has become the hallmark of Academic Literacies research during the last decade.

What characterises this emerging body of work on student writing is its specific focus on writing as social practice and a recognition of the multiplicity of practices, whether conceptualised as discourses or literacies. As discussed in more detail in a number of chapters in this volume, Lea and Street (1998) developed the field further in outlining three models of student writing in higher education: 'study skills', 'academic socialisation' and 'academic literacies'. They explicitly privileged the Academic Literacies perspective, concentrating on issues of meaning-making and identity, the contested nature of academic knowledge and the implications of this approach for understanding student writing.

At that point, developments in the area of student writing research and practice were twofold. On the one hand, Applied Linguists and Literacy Theorists who were interested in literacy more broadly were beginning to see 'higher education' as a location for studying writing and literacy/ies; on the other hand, a wider body of academics and support staff wanting to enhance their practice as teachers of writing were beginning to ask questions and seek answers through theory and research. As a result there is now a shared understanding that academic literacy involves a great deal more than technical skills, and that the object of study should be pluralised: not 'literacy' but 'literacies'. Much Academic Literacies research has been small-scale, qualitative, using case-study and ethnographic approaches. Since many of the researchers are Applied Linguists, studies often use textual analysis, including the identification of generic and discoursal characteristics of particular types of writing. Research questions and topics that studies have addressed include cultural and contextual diversity in writing, issues of identity and epistemology, student–teacher dialogue around writing, and differing perceptions and interpretations of disciplinary expectations. More recently researchers' interests have expanded to include literacy practices not just of learners, but of all academics; differences between literacy practices in higher education and other settings; and the impact of technology on academic literacies.

Publications in the field of Academic Literacies have been influential in challenging the dominant models of student writing in higher education (Jones et al., 1999; Lea and Stierer, 2000). This work has been carried out in different university settings with diverse groups of students (Baynham, 2000; Ivanič, 1998; Lillis, 1997). Research has included students studying at a distance (Lea, 1998; Stierer, 1997), non-native speakers of English (Pardoe, 1994) and postgraduate trainee teachers (M. Scott, 2000). Read et al. (2001) focus on power relationships in essay writing and Francis et al. (2001) add the dimension of gender and writing style to the field. Despite the variety of contexts being studied, the findings concerning students' struggles with writing and the gaps between tutors' and students' expectations and understandings are remarkably constant.

▶ Conclusion

In focusing on the UK context, we have outlined the particular development of writing support against a broader backdrop of educational, social and political change. Evidence of a specific response to a changing context is, of course, as pertinent in other situations; for example, see Thesen (1994, 2001) for discussion of the South African higher education context and Vardi (2000), Clerehan (2003) and Skillen's chapter in this volume for Australia. Writing support is an institutional issue and a response to specific concerns at a particular time; thus it is always a political act (Clark and Ivanič, 1997) but it is frequently not recognised as such by those responsible for developing learning support programmes. As this chapter has outlined, higher education in the UK is expanding rapidly, and this expansion has been accompanied by profound changes. All of these changes raise fundamental questions about the changing nature of what counts as knowledge in today's academy, and we believe that issues of language and literacy will continue to be central to debates about the status of the university in the twenty-first century (Delanty, 2001).

NOTES

1 The government's Department for Education and Skills (DfES) has produced school and college performance tables since 1992. University league tables are compiled by the media (Gibson, 2005).
2 A high level of skills support in FE colleges continues today.
3 See Bartholomae (1986), Bizzell (1982) and Bazerman et al. (2005, p. 20). Also see Part III of this volume for details of the history of the first-year writing course and of the development of Composition as a professional field in US higher education.
4 The concepts of 'deep' and 'surface' learning originated in the work of Marton and Säljö (1976) and have been explored by many researchers, including Gibbs (1992).
5 See www.ed.ac.uk/etl/

2 The Point of Writing: Is Student Writing in Higher Education Developed or Merely Assessed?

Robert Catt and Gerry Gregory

▶ Introduction

> If . . . the art of writing cannot be taught, the teacher can nevertheless offer students situations in which it can be learned. (Young, 1980, p. 344)

Writing – in the sense of producing texts composed of written words – seems to be difficult for most of us (Wason, 1980, p. 357). Our reluctance to start writing and our strategies to interrupt the process once started can be illustrated through a host of anecdotes and examples. Even when the task is completed, there is a commonly reported dissatisfaction with the final draft as compared with what had been envisioned at the outset. Vygotsky's characterisation of writing as high on abstraction and like 'speech without an interlocutor, addressed to absent or imaginary persons or to no one in particular' (1986, p. 181) goes some way to explaining writing's near-universal difficulties.

In particular, Academic Writing is difficult (Torrance et al., 1994, p. 379), and it is unsurprising that students in higher education find it so. Many students have difficulty achieving *text level* organisation: structural weaknesses are evident, with some failure to sustain ideas logically and effectively. Composition is sometimes faulty at *sentence level*, with a common lack of effective sentence marking – including punctuation. At *word level*, spelling miscues are common, constituting a distraction from writers' meaning and argument.

Piolat and Roussey (1996, p. 113) distinguish the characteristic practices of 'novice' writers from those of 'more experienced' counterparts; and Hoadley-Maidment (1997, p. 57), referring to the work of Ballard (1984) and Ballard and Clanchy (1988), uses the notion of 'cultural shift' to explain the process that novice writers undergo in learning to write appropriately. Lea and Street (1998), however, caution against conceptualising Academic Writing as monolithic, preferring to think in terms of a plurality of 'academic literacies'. One implication of this notion is that '[t]he patterns of reasoning that we expect in Academic Writing are not inherent in our thinking; they are conventional, learnable forms of argumentation and rhetoric' (Glaser, 1999, p. 94). Nightingale (1991), too, is unhappy to 'let students flounder along and gradually pick up the expectations of academia in general and [particular] section[s] of it in particular' (p. 7). We share this unease and this is our starting point for what follows.

The *intrinsic* and *extrinsic* importance of writing

Writing is a powerful means of communication – transcending time and space – and can be transformative. The act of writing carries intrinsic importance because learning can take place in and through the writing process: in addition to knowledge being transferred through the writing process it may also be mediated or constructed through writing practices (Lea and Street, 1998, p. 170). However, Scardamalia and Bereiter (1994) warn against assuming – especially in respect of 'novice writers', in whose ranks they want to include many higher education students – that just to write is to experience such a transformation.

Writing ability also has extrinsic importance, and is viewed as a characteristic of 'graduateness'. The 'ability to write clearly and fluently is undoubtedly one of the more important skills required of graduates' (Torrance et al., 1999, p. 189), and effective writing is fundamental to success in higher education. Graduates need to be able to develop and sustain complex ideas with a clear sense of purpose and awareness of readership. Clearly, writing competence is foregrounded more in some degree studies than in others. However, recent work on the notion of 'graduateness' has reminded us of an 'old saw': namely, that every teacher is a teacher of language, and in this case, of writing. Accordingly, recent Quality Assurance Agency for Higher Education (QAA) 'subject benchmark statements' for computing, law and chemistry – to take three random examples – include explicit references to writing competence.[1] Further, following the continuing emphasis upon improved educational standards, undergraduates and postgraduates involved in Initial Teacher Training (ITT) courses in the UK are now given literacy skills tests which demand accuracy of written expression.

▶ Student experiences and perceptions

Our interest in literacy practice within higher education prompted us to ask approximately 150 Postgraduate Certificate in Education (PGCE)[2] students from the 2000–1 cohort about their undergraduate writing experiences. We made use of questionnaires and group discussion. Students varied in age, and while some were recent university graduates, others had completed degree courses years previously. The cohort questioned had undertaken 72 different degree programmes representing a range of disciplines, and had earned their degrees from approximately 50 different higher education institutions. The key experiences and practices they reported were as follows.

Amount of writing

The average number of pieces of writing each student had submitted for tutors to read was 42. There was remarkable variation in this number: from 200 to 9. Clearly, 'pieces of writing' is a crude category label – ranging from brief Maths or Computer Science reports to 5000-word Humanities essays. Future work is required to refine this classification and to develop a typology of writing tasks.

Writing for assessment

Seventy-one respondents reported that all of their submitted written work had been assessed. In fact, there are two reasons for thinking that the true percentage might be higher in respect of degree programmes offered recently and currently. First, some respondents took 'for assessment purposes' to mean 'counting towards final degree classification', hence excluding early work that had been assessed but counted only for course progression. Secondly, a handful of students referred to undergraduate studies undertaken as long ago as the 1970s, which was before in-course assessment became common.[3] If such respondents interpreted 'for assessment purposes' as above, then their responses would have given the (false) impression that none of their written work (excepting unseen examination answers) had been assessed.

Help at the draft stage

Students were asked if any writing had been seen by a course tutor or lecturer at the draft stage. Excluding undergraduate dissertations, long studies and final-year projects, well over two-thirds of students said that tutors had read none of their writing at all at the draft stage; 16 per cent reported that tutors had read perhaps 10 per cent or more of their pieces of writing at this formative stage. Some respondents recalled tutorial help, before final submission, that fell short of attention to drafts:

- 'Some help after a plan had been devised. Feedback on plan and other possibilities suggested early on in process'.

Where drafts were welcome there were marked variations in tutors' responses:

- 'If he/she was shown a rough draft, it was only read on the surface and I was given either a positive or negative response.'
- 'Feedback sheets on how it would have been marked if handed in like that, received before final copy was due.'
- 'I was not confident with poetry and sought guidance about an essay based on T. S. Eliot's *The Waste Land*. I was directed to *York Notes* and other critical works.'

(compare Carey, 1995, p. 131)

There was also some variation as to who responded to drafts. One student referred to help from a personal tutor who had no direct involvement in the course being studied, rather than the teaching tutor responsible for marking the assignment. There was also variation in the medium of guidance:

- 'Any tutorial guidance was by telephone: academic adviser liked to work from home.'

Feedback

Unsurprisingly, 'feedback' was offered by tutors almost exclusively at the point when written work was returned after assessment. While for the great majority of respondents there was written feedback only, about a quarter of students made reference to oral feedback: 6 per cent of students reported that their tutors were available at any time, and 3 per cent that optional one-to-one sessions to discuss students' work were on offer. Two per cent made reference to *group* oral feedback; and just one student to 'peer assessment' arrangements.

The feedback itself was various. Some tutors concentrated chiefly on form:

- 'Use of similes, metaphors, commas, capital letters, use of short paragraphs, correct spelling'.
- '[I was] told to put in quotes. Comments on marked work, such as: "called person by forename rather than surname", "vague", "most illuminating", "interesting point of view" – nothing helpful'.

Other tutors focused only on content:

- 'No feedback on writing, but . . . some guidance on use of statistics'.

Some reported negatively on the feedback received:

- 'My . . . tutor . . . made suggestions how I could improve my work. I didn't find it helpful but over-critical so I didn't ask for any further assistance.'

However, more reported positively:

- 'Assignments were returned promptly with annotated script, plus A4 page of comments on style and content of assignment. Tutors always available at the end of the telephone.'
- 'Detailed tutorials after writing of each essay'.
- 'After an essay was handed back there would be the tutor's written commentary and often the week's supervision on that piece.'
- 'Relaxed feedback sessions arranged amicably between tutor and student'.

One respondent reported a tutor intervention that had really helped – though lamented that it had not come earlier:

- 'It wasn't until I got to the second year . . . that a tutor took the time to teach me how to write an essay . . . . She literally took me to pieces. I can remember coming out feeling so distressed but I thought here I am, second year at university and my writing is being taken to pieces and she's telling me no you can't do it that way you've got to do it this way. But at the end of the day I thanked her for it. But that's crazy that you can get to that point and have to be taught that.'

Another was less fortunate:

- 'I've never been told, ever. All my education . . . I've been told how *not* to do it, but I've never been sat down and shown *how* to do it. So I've had my work pulled apart but never put back together again – or been shown how to put it back together again.'

Timing of 'feedback'

Typically in UK universities, assignments are submitted at or near the end of modules, terms or semesters. In some institutions or departments, students are given a provisional grade fairly quickly, subject to 'second-marking' by a colleague within the same department, and to external examining and examination board approval. For the overwhelming majority, however, assignment return and feedback are considerably delayed.

Task-setting: criteria for success

Students were asked about the task-setting process for writing assignments and whether they had been supplied with detailed criteria for successful performance. It emerged that while provision of *general* criteria, such as descriptors for assessment grades, was pretty well universal, it was much rarer for tutors to supply detailed success criteria for *particular* writing tasks.[4] A little over a quarter reported the publication of detailed criteria for some writing tasks – of whom about a third had worked to such criteria for virtually all such tasks.

▶ Discussion

These findings from our survey, and some possibilities for developing practice, will now be discussed. In considering some features of the undergraduate writing experience which might be improved, we suggest that literacy initiatives in primary and secondary schools are of interest.

It is also worth noting that apparent to higher education colleagues, but less visible in our data, are the affective aspects of students' academic literacy practices. Tutorial discussion with a 'failing' student can be difficult and emotional. Although abrasive denial can be an impediment to improvement, it is often more welcome than tearful despair. Often, too, there is the disclosure of personal difficulties. Writing counts: success and failure are consequential in students' lives. Tutorial intervention, therefore, demands time, sensitivity and stamina.

Amount of writing

As acknowledged, what 'pieces of writing' signifies across a range of degree programmes needs to be unpacked. The nature and scale of 'pieces of writing' will vary hugely between, say, Maths and History. However, while our finding confirms that writing tasks loom large across a wide range of undergraduate programmes, it also suggests that some afford vastly more practice in writing than others.

In our view, literacy *practices* are significant. We began by reflecting upon the difficulty of writing. This difficulty is eased through habitual practice. A student upon whom few writing demands are made is likely to move more slowly towards the achievement of an 'instinctive' expertise (Glaser, 1999) than one habitually immersed in the writing process. In our conclusion we refer to students' literacy practices as an intrinsic feature of a learning culture. It is important to insist, however, that while practice is necessary, it is not a sufficient condition for what Wason (1980, p. 357) calls 'happy writing': 'a kind of writing, familiar to experienced writers, in which the output is associated with a sense of elation and commitment [or engagement]'.

Proportion of writing assessed

Responses to our study indicate that the overwhelming bulk of writing produced by students is for assessment purposes. This 'taken-for-granted' feature of academic practice needs examination. There could, for example, be some consequent marginalisation of writing for oneself, or writing for learning, or to transform ideas. Many courses encourage the use of a reflective journal, in which thinking can be made explicit and in which ideas can be tried out (Seshachari,1994). Such writing is probably accorded less value by students to whom the sole presented purpose of writing is the acquisition of marks. Again, Lea and Street (1998) discuss a range of academic literacies and raise concerns regarding the unquestioned and monolithic status of a preferred genre. However, the writing practices in which students participate are likely to be constrained where purposes are narrowed in the cause of assessment.

Tutorial help at the draft stage

An exception to the reported lack of tutorial intervention at the drafting stage related to the writing of dissertations, long studies and major projects. Although our study discounted explicit references to extended, traditionally supervised projects, it seems likely that some student reports of tutors responding to drafts did refer, implicitly, to such contexts of work. Hence, even the 16 per cent finding of at least some formative intervention by tutors may be higher than the true figure. The amount – and especially the nature – of tutorial response to written drafts invites further research. Our findings at this stage indicate a remarkable variety of practice. Given the effort of drafting – and the tedium of reading unpolished drafts – a merely 'positive or negative' response to work in progress would seem to be unproductive, if not discouraging.

In our experience, a considerable investment of time is required if weak writing (with fundamental weaknesses of structure, syntax and spelling) is to be improved. This experience will qualify some of the possibilities for drafting explored below. Further, our experience of effective practice is that it is discursive, preferably face-to-face and with the draft to hand. Telephone (and email) discussion can certainly be productive, but both tutor and student need a copy of a well presented and line-numbered draft. Only the more capable student is likely to benefit from mere direction to critical sources.

Feedback

Our findings relate to both the *timing* and the *nature* of feedback. In discussion with students it was clear that not all were familiar with such procedures – fairly standard in the UK – as 'blind' marking, sampling and standardisation of student writing submitted for assessment. The majority experienced what they considered to be a considerable delay between the submission of assignments and the return of grades and feedback. This is a concern. Vacations may have intervened and students' thinking moved on, especially given the 'course switching' patterns associated with multidisciplinary and modular programme structures (Lea and Street, 1998, p. 61; Hoadley-Maidment, 1997, pp. 63–4). Few students have opportunities for discussion with the tutors who marked their work. In taking new modules, many will be taught by tutors who are at square one in respect of their specific skills and needs as writers: 'Academic staff reported that they were unable to make best use of standard feedback sheets because these were received by students after module completion . . . . Effectively, there is no feedback' (Lea and Street, 1998, pp. 169–70).

While a feature of our data is the variety of student experience, equally palpable is an associated strength of feeling that feedback is 'over-critical' and, arguably, short of a reasonable learning entitlement: 'I've had my work pulled apart but never put back together again.' Positive responses point to 'guidance', routine ('the week's supervision on that piece'), tenor ('relaxed feedback sessions arranged amicably'), and the availability of the tutor. As we saw above, for some students tutor intervention can be something of a critical incident – 'She literally took me to pieces. I can remember coming out feeling so distressed' – albeit with a positive outcome: 'But at the end of the day I thanked her for it.' No doubt like most tutors, we believe that through the writing process ideas can be transformed and learning can take place. As indicated above, however, such transformative possibilities seem unavailable to many, usually reluctant, writers. Insufficiently investigated, in our view, is what would seem to be effective practice: intervention at the drafting stage, detailed and discursive feedback and collaboration and peer review between student writers.

Task-setting: criteria for success

The publication of departmental handbooks of *general* success criteria and assignment guidance would seem a standard feature of academic practice – perhaps in response to the quality assurance procedures discussed by Ivanič and Lea, and others in this volume. Our findings, however, suggest that students found such general criteria less helpful than specific guidance. There seems, too, an absence of appropriate exemplars and, consequently, some students have difficulty in meeting success markers framed as seemingly remote objectives. A paraphrase, drawn from handbooks of assignment guidance, offers a general criterion for a high-grade assignment as: one which uses a wide range of literature and draws upon ideas of a general educational nature as applied to the subject-specific situation, integrates reading, and analyses ideas and critical approaches used in evaluating those ideas.

Comparison can be made here with secondary school practice. Teachers preparing school students for the General Certificate of Secondary Education (GCSE) examinations, generally undertaken at the age of 16 and at the end of compulsory schooling, are given detailed criteria and involved in standardising meetings, where sample scripts are marked and discussed. It is common practice for these criteria and exemplars to be shared with students, who are given specific pointers for achievement.

The exemplification of criteria is also often a feature of university work at Master's level, where the *general* – 'critical analysis and engagement', for example – is related to the demands of a *particular* assignment. A workshop task for postgraduate Education students might, for example, ask them to grade mock essays and to justify their decisions against the criteria. Interestingly, the same approach appears in secondary school classrooms where students gain value from playing the role of teacher-examiner.

Although our literature search reveals surprisingly little on the specific application of criteria, there are some valuable exceptions. Lillis (1997), for example, discusses the need for practice and criteria to be explored critically in discussion with students. Below we air a possibility: a systematic exploration of this kind as a 'frame' for writing. In our experience, although students have some awareness of criteria, the ways in which these are applied to actual scripts are often opaque. But then, the problematic nature of criterion assessment, particularly within the hurried context of much assessment practice, will be familiar to most colleagues.

Branthwaite et al. (1980) point interestingly to a mismatch between criteria applied to their essays by students themselves and those which tutors actually deploy when assessing. This strengthens further the case for addressing these issues.

▶ Possibilities

We now air some possibilities for improving student writing although we are as aware as others working in higher education that present and foreseeable working conditions constrain what is practicable. However, if only to promote discussion, shared practice and small-scale innovation, we attempt to elaborate in an incremental form some features of our own findings and discussion. We will make reference to current literacy initiatives in schools and we are keen to frame possibilities for improved practice within the context of a learning culture. Rather than identifying weaknesses in writing as a matter of individual deficit, we think it important to locate particular difficulties within a broader set of literacy practices. A crude example might be the sometimes 'macho' neglect of the assignment task by some groups of students. Individual difficulties may be obscured by a group approach which privileges a hurried, last-gasp, early-hours preparation of the assignment. Systematic drafting, evaluation, re-writing, proofing and professional presentation are, in our experience, by no means typical features of many UK students' literacy practices (Hayes and Flower, 1980, p. 392). Many students, complaining that writing is difficult, seem to regard this as an unusual and personal failing – relating to what Wason (1980, p. 357) calls the 'affective dimension' and the ways in which academic achievement is caught up with emotion and a sense of self-esteem. We would argue that the difficulties and demands of the academic genre need explicit acknowledgement and strategic discussion. Institutional literacy practices and expectations also need to be examined and promoted.

Applying general guidance for successful writing

As noted, it would seem to be standard practice to provide general guidance (including word length and referencing conventions) for writing within overall programmes of study. Our concern is that students may be unaware how best to exploit the general guidance published in course programmes: 'No doubt students become accustomed to inferring the type of document and the nature of the guidelines in each case – *but this developing skill remains hidden from institutional view and is seldom part of the teaching and learning process*' (Lea and Street, 1999, p. 67; emphasis added). The practice we are proposing would involve course tutors ensuring (perhaps through 'workshop' activities) that guidance is read and understood and that students have an awareness of its application to specific assignment demands.

Providing detailed task briefs and criteria for successful performance

It is unlikely that course tutors deliberately set obscure or cryptically worded writing tasks. Yet the task itself might be complex and there is then obviously much to be gained from setting out clearly what components and characteristics a satisfactory response will need. As we have indicated above, such guidelines may be a feature of many students' relatively recent GCSE experience.

However, is this merely what some colleagues denigrate as 'spoonfeeding'? It could well be a tutor's intention that students should wrestle with a question, perhaps to unpack and react to a quotation full of ambiguities, where the open-endedness and an original form of response – 'the intolerable wrestle with words and meaning' (Eliot, 1963, p. 198) – are precisely the point.

There is still much work to be done on task-setting and negotiating in higher education (Nightingale, 1988) and any steps to develop the use of detailed task criteria must avoid the malign aspects of externally imposed criteria mechanically and rigidly applied. As a study by O'Brien (1995) reveals: 'the most successful essays in the data set came from a sub-group of students . . . who had been told by their tutor that he was looking for evidence of understanding the source texts and having struggled intellectually with some of the difficulties that their authors were struggling with' (pp. 475–6). But this needs saying. The value and purpose of intellectual struggle need to be conveyed, and there is an important distinction between productive struggle and hopeless floundering. A well phrased and carefully explained assignment brief should promote intellectual engagement. Inexplicit guidance and obscurity of expression are more likely to exacerbate students' frustrations. Points from the work of Scardamalia and Bereiter (1994, p. 307) could be explored with students here. These authors point to the productive tension between substantive ideas – 'I know what I want to say' – and the rhetorical demands of the genre – 'I find it difficult to get it down on paper.'

We suggest the possibility of developing practice following Lillis (1997, p. 186) on the application of criteria. Experience in schools suggests that pupils learn to improve their writing by examining and discussing texts: for example, by *finding patterns* for spelling, punctuation, organisation and cohesion, rather than by starting from given 'rules'. Similarly, higher education students might find value in commenting on sample scripts and discussing qualities against agreed criteria. While the danger in using exemplars of slavish imitation of an apparently preferred model is inherent, the advantages in making criteria explicit *through application* are overwhelming.

Providing early feedback after assessment

'What did I get?' is an understandable response from students chasing optimal degree classifications. However, a good deal of work has been undertaken in schools with regard to teachers' response to writing and the ways in which formative comments are intrinsic to improved performance. This is not to gainsay the importance of an awarded grade, but clearly early intervention is necessary if students' development is to be shaped. For this to happen, something more sophisticated than the instrument of a grade award is necessary.

Lea and Street's (1998, p. 170) research provides food for thought. If effectively there is no feedback, then we must question the purpose of writing in the first place. Not only should feedback be swift, it must purposefully inform students' learning. Where there are modular gaps and fences, as students change courses, some strategic collaboration between teams of tutors is demanded (Hoadley-Maidment, 1997, p. 63).

Early and purposeful feedback is certainly a feature of study valued by students. There is an important protocol best understood through the experience of students who, at least, find it discourteous that work over which they have laboured should disappear into the maw of an impersonal assessment machinery. At worst they can feel discouraged and disinclined to invest future effort. However, we have been struck by the remarkably energetic efforts of colleagues, reported in the data, who often under very difficult circumstances rapidly 'turn round' large numbers of students' scripts and provide detailed formative guidance and encouragement.

Providing opportunities for unassessed writing

Although high on the scale of possibilities for improving writing, a strategy of allowing students to undertake unassessed writing or allowing sufficient writing tasks that some may be discarded for assessment purposes has obvious practical disadvantages as it is likely to add to students' and tutors' workloads (Candlin and Plum, 1999, p. 197; Green and Klug, 1990, p. 462). Our research found considerable variation in students' experiences of writing. Frequent written tasks – in some cases a number each week – and subsequent tutorials were a feature of some degree programmes. This suggests the existence of tutorial systems and staff/student ratios of which many of us can but dream. Yet writing is an important feature of learning. The writer must externalise thoughts and make ideas explicit for the scrutiny of others. In writing, the contextual strategic detours and deviations of speech are not available and in this there is much advantage for learning. Perhaps, consequently, written tasks should be more centrally placed in degree programmes. Perhaps we need also to accept that developing students' writing (including subject-specific writing), and promoting their learning through writing, are as important as any other higher education teaching tasks. Academic Writing has the potential to generate learning. To write is to give material form to thought, to render it inspectable. Viewed thus, writing is coterminous with many other learning aims that courses proclaim. To write about prescribed subject matter is both to learn it and to produce evidence of learning it (Nightingale, 1991, p. 6).

Providing tutorial support at the point of writing – especially early in courses

Given the status of writing and its value in the learning process, it would seem odd that, at present, many students are offered writing 'coaching' only at the post-writing, post-assessment stage. Paradoxically, the most intensive tutorial support seems to be provided at the final stages of degree courses, typically when students are preparing theses, dissertations and other types of long studies.

There is a parallel here with pupils' experience in schools. The National Literacy Strategy (NLS) points out that whereas the National Curriculum English Order provides a model of the writing process which stresses that children should learn to plan, draft, revise, edit, present and evaluate their writing – and that 'effective teaching will often focus on particular aspects of this process, e.g. planning or revising' – the implicit sequence to much *actual* teaching, by contrast, has the teacher stimulating pupils' ideas for writing; the children writing independently; and then the teacher responding, discussing marks and criticisms. The NLS then notes that this analysis shows how 'the teaching of writing can easily be reduced to teaching by correction – teaching after the event – instead of teaching *at the point of writing*'. Finally, it suggests that 'repeated experiences of this kind are likely to reinforce, rather than overcome, children's problems, making them increasingly reluctant writers', and asserts 'teaching *at the point of writing*, in contrast, focuses on demonstrating and exploring the decisions that writers make in the process of composition' (Department for Education and Employment, 2000, pp. 11–12; emphases added).

A discussion paper by Her Majesty's Inspectors (HMI) on the teaching of writing in primary schools begins with the 'headline': 'There is still insufficient teaching of writing; where writing is taught, there are significant weaknesses in too many lessons' (Ofsted, 2000, p.6). Criticism in this report is, however, mitigated by attention to and examples of 'good practice', including 'intervention at the point of composition to teach writing skills, rather than reliance on marking or correction after the event' (p. 6).

▶ Conclusion

We have aired some possibilities, tentatively, from a starting point of some preliminary and small-scale research, but perhaps more securely from the foundation of our experience in higher education. Our observations of school practice, particularly in the light of recent literacy strategies, suggest that some potentially productive comparisons can be made and that post-compulsory students, too, would benefit from more intervention *at the point of writing*.

Increased attention to writing in higher education, particularly at the drafting stage, would have significant implications. Allowing for reading and commenting on draft material entails transparency of process. Guidelines would need to be published explaining the nature of the coaching to be provided ('offered' is clearly not enough if equal opportunities criteria are to be met). There would also be some challenge to much current assessment practice if explicit account were taken of the possibly collaborative processes which have shaped students' work. Collaboration was once more popularly known as 'cheating' and much assessment continues to be predicated upon assumptions about *individual* effort and production, narrowly defined.

To place writing more centrally within the learning process would, undoubtedly, demand institutional change and innovation. It is our belief that this would, nevertheless, be worthwhile. Such a move would require the investigation of literacy practices and, to follow Lea and Street (1998), a critical examination of academic genres. As we have indicated, a corollary of the move to problematise academic literacy would be the acceptance of a wider range of permissible genre. Although the implications of developing pedagogy and institutional structures for placing writing more centrally will need to be teased out elsewhere in this volume, it is our hope that here we have, at least, given emphasis to the need for a more explicit awareness of students' writing practices in higher education and the importance of tutorial intervention.

NOTES

1 See Computing (p. 5, paragraph 2.2), Law (p. 7, paragraph 19), and Chemistry (p. 4, paragraph 'c') (Quality, 2000).
2 The PGCE, a one-year postgraduate course in teacher training, is a popular route to attaining Qualified Teacher Status in the UK.
3 In UK universities, assessment has traditionally rested on final written examinations rather than on coursework.
4 Provision of general criteria is often in the form of 'handbooks': compare Lea and Street (1999); Candlin and Plum (1999, p. 197).

3 Moving towards an 'Academic Literacies' Pedagogy: Dialogues of Participation

Theresa M. Lillis

▶ Introduction

The UK is in the process of shifting from an élite to a mass higher education system, where there is greater cultural, linguistic and social diversity than in the past. The number of people taking part in higher education has increased dramatically since the mid-1980s and has come to include significantly higher numbers of 'non-traditional' students, that is, students from social and ethnic groups who historically have not participated in higher education in the UK. Today's students therefore bring a wide range of experiences and interests, as well as complex patterns of participation, and different reasons for wanting to participate in higher education. The changing nature of the student body within the context of official support for widening access and lifelong learning raises fundamental questions about what, and how, we should teach in higher education. These questions are particularly to the fore in debates about student writing, not least because students' written texts continue to constitute the main form of assessment in UK universities.

In this chapter I set out to do the following:

- To offer an overview of the different approaches to student Academic Writing in UK higher education, the conceptualisations of language implicit in them and their relationship to the broader institutional goals of higher education.
- To summarise a recent theoretical approach to Academic Writing in the UK, referred to as Academic Literacies, which to date has served as a critical research frame rather than explicitly informing writing pedagogy.
- To contribute to the development of a pedagogy which draws on critical insights from Academic Literacies, by calling for **dialogue** to be placed at the centre of such pedagogy. In developing this last point, I illustrate four different kinds of dialogic interaction around written texts, which I suggest are necessary to facilitate student-writers' participation in existing practices, whilst offering opportunities for exploring alternative ways of meaning.

The extracts from dialogues and the ideas on which this chapter is based are drawn from a longitudinal study I conducted with ten 'non-traditional' student-writers from across a number of academic disciplines and institutions (Lillis, 2001, 2003).

▶ Current approaches to student writing

In Table 3.1[1] I outline the main approaches to student Academic Writing currently visible in the UK.[2] The categories in bold type in the third column, student writing pedagogy, are drawn from Lea and Street (1998) and Ivanič (1999). Lea and Street offered a three-levelled model for theorising approaches to student writing in higher education, now widely referred to within the UK context. The three levels are defined as 'skills', 'socialisation' and 'academic literacies' (1998). These levels are marked as a, b and e in the table. Ivanič (1999) provided categories which correspond in some ways to those of Lea and Street, as well as introducing others not explicitly included; these are what I refer to in the table as 'creative self-expression' and 'socialisation (2)'. The differences between these approaches are indicated in Table 3.1 in terms of their pedagogic focus, the 'theories of language they embody' (Ivanič, 1999), and their relative status within higher education.[3]

Table 3.1 Approaches to student writing in higher education (UK)

Status within UK higher education	Theory of language	Student writing pedagogy
Dominant	Language as a transparent and autonomous system made up of discrete elements	(a) **Skills** – explicit teaching of discrete elements of language
	Language as discourse practices appropriate to different contexts	(b) **Socialisation (1)** – teaching as (implicit) induction into established discourse practices
	Language/meaning as the product of individual mind	(c) **Creative self-expression** – teaching as facilitating individual expression
	Language as genres which are characterised by specific clusters of linguistic features	(d) **Socialisation (2)** – explicit teaching of features of academic genres
Oppositional	Language as socially-situated discourse practices which are ideologically inscribed	(e) **Academic literacies** – *What are the design implications for pedagogy?*

Table 3.1 is clearly a simplified representation of actual practice. However, it helps to identify and situate the dominant approach to writing pedagogy in many UK universities; this can be summarised as a combination of two intersecting models, what I refer to as 'socialisation (1)' and 'skills'. Briefly, socialisation (1) functions as the institutional default model: students will 'pick up' writing as part of their studies without any specific teaching or practice. When this implicit induction approach seems to fail – for example, when students are not writing according to expected conventions – the skills model often comes into play,[4] most evident in the type of guidance offered on writing and in feedback comments on students' written texts submitted for assessment. The focus tends to be on the more visible 'common sense' notions of what Academic Writing is or should be, such as surface language features (including spelling and a cluster of features referred to as grammar), simplified notions of structure (for example, 'introductions', 'conclusions'), and the mechanics of citation conventions.

This skills approach to writing and writing pedagogy is often considered to be a welcome improvement over implicit induction approaches (socialisation (1)) but two fundamental criticisms can be made: the skills model assumes **transparency** in relation to language, and **transmission** in relation to pedagogy. Emphasis tends to be on language as a transparent medium, as a reflector of meanings – the idea that we put meaning into words – rather than on language as discourses which constitute whole areas of meaning. Telling students about the most visible aspects of writing, briefly outlined above, is often viewed as the obvious and relatively straightforward way of teaching students how to produce written academic texts. Problematising these notions of transparency and transmission has been central to an Academic Literacies critique of current approaches to student writing.[5]

▶ Academic Literacies: a critical approach

The Academic Literacies approach, category (e) in Table 3.1, has proved to be a useful theoretical framework for researching student writing, raising fundamental questions such as: What is the nature of Academic Writing? What does it mean to 'do' Academic Writing? What is involved for different participants in different disciplinary and institutional contexts?

Thus, whilst categories (a)–(d) in the table describe current approaches to student writing pedagogy in higher education, the last category, (e), works as critique by serving as an oppositional frame to conventional approaches to student writing. Academic Literacies work raises questions about dominant practices and foregrounds many dimensions to student writing which had previously remained invisible or had been ignored. For example, a key contribution is to emphasise that students are expected to engage in a very specific type of writing – 'essayist literacy', most obviously in the form of the essay – which involves a particular kind of language and sets of relationships between writers and readers and which is a historically and culturally specific practice, rather than being intrinsically the 'best' (Scollon and Scollon, 1981). Studies from an Academic Literacies approach have explored the nature of this essayist literacy and linked it to other dimensions such as the impact of power relations on student writing, the centrality of identity in Academic Writing, Academic Writing as ideologically inscribed knowledge construction, and the nature of generic academic, as well as disciplinary-specific, writing practices.[6]

Academic Literacies has proved to be highly generative as a critical research frame, challenging many common-sense assumptions about what is involved in student writing and foregrounding the limitations in much current writing pedagogy. However, as a design frame it has yet to be developed. I am using 'design' here in the broad sense of the application of research findings and understandings to pedagogy. But I also want to bear in mind Kress's use of design (Kress, 1998, 2000), which involves taking account of critique – such as the issues raised, above, about power and identity in Academic Writing – when planning writing pedagogy. How can teachers draw on the critique evident in Academic Literacies research? Buried in this is a further question, often raised in writing pedagogy discussions in the UK: How can we as teachers ensure that student-writers can participate in existing dominant practices in higher education, such as essayist writing, whilst allowing space for challenging conventions in a changing higher education context which is premised upon notions of diversity and inclusion?[7]

One significant way I suggest this pedagogical goal can be achieved is through a combination of different types of dialogue between student-writer and tutor-reader. Such dialogues can enable participation in dominant academic literacy practices as well as provide opportunities for challenging aspects of such practices.

▶ Dialogues of participation

Mary: *I've never experienced talking to anyone about my essays before, so I find it very interesting and I appreciate. Nobody's ever sat down and talked to me about my essays. They've just said, oh, 'hard to fathom at times'* [laughs].

Siria: *It's like going through a narrow corridor, when somebody else looks at it* [written text], *they probably open a door or window, or turn left, turn right. That's what I think happens* [in talk].

The comments by Mary and Siria illustrate a recurrent theme expressed by student-writers in a study I carried out to explore the Academic Writing experiences of ten 'non-traditional' students in higher education over a period of 2–6 years (Lillis, 2001): the desire for more dialogue with their tutors/lecturers around their writing. This desire was repeatedly expressed and seemed to hold out for the student-writers the opportunity for learning essayist conventions, as a key part of their participation in higher education, while at the same time providing a way of stepping out of these conventions.

In the rest of this chapter I illustrate four particular types of dialogue which I suggest might go some way towards meeting these different demands and desires:

- tutor-directive dialogue aimed at talking the student-writer into essayist literacy practice;
- tutor-directive dialogue aimed at making language visible;
- collaborative dialogue aimed at populating the student-writer's text with her own intentions (after Bakhtin, 1981, pp. 293–4);
- talkback dialogue aimed at allowing the student-writer to say what she feels about the conventions she is writing within and to explore alternative ways of expressing meaning.

You, the reader, may protest: we don't have time for such dialogue in our institution, or, I have too many students, or I teach online and don't even see my students . . . so why even think about such dialogues? In response I would say two things. First, with regard to mode or medium – whilst the examples I discuss here come from face-to-face interaction, there are ways of constructing possibilities for such encounters via other modes, such as online conferencing or written commentary (Coffin et al., 2003). Secondly, and in response to the more pressing concern about time constraints and large student numbers, I agree that it often seems impossible to consider giving more time to individual students. However, the limitations and shortcomings evident in our current contexts shouldn't prevent us as teachers from discussing what might be desirable for teaching and learning . . . and as educationalists, managers and curriculum developers, from pushing for institutional transformation which would enable more creative and inclusive teaching and learning practices . . .

Dialogue 1: Talking writers into essayist literacy

Mary: *To me, essay writing is a bit like implicit knowledge.*
Theresa: *In what way?*
Mary: *Not all explicit, is it?*

Theresa: *What do you mean?*
Mary: *It's like common sense, not common sense, it's like implicit knowledge. You know it's intuitive in a sense. Like, you* feel *that you should mention his name* [discussing particular section of her text]. *The problem is, some people might not feel it.*
Theresa: *The problem is, how do you get to feel it?*
Mary: *Yes. Because I <u>do</u> know what you're talking about when you do make your criticisms because I recognise them myself, but I just don't know how to put my finger on it. I wish I could get a bell in my head which says 'Hey, something's wrong here. I don't know what it is but I'm not quite sure but, you know, if I show it to Theresa, she'll point it out' and I'll, oh yes.*

Mary's comments indicate that it is difficult to learn the conventions of essayist literacy, but also that a way of learning them is to be with someone who already *feels* what the conventions are; she thus echoes the work of those who foreground the notion of learning as a relationship of apprenticeship between newcomers and experts in a particular community of practice. Heath, for example, argues that 'outsiders' need to be apprenticed to 'insiders' in order to learn culturally specific ways of meaning-making (Heath, 1983).[8]

All the student-writers expressed the desire to spend more time talking with tutors to learn the 'rules of the game' for writing in higher education. I will look in detail here at one extract from tutor-directive dialogue to illustrate how student-writers can be talked into what is for many an unfamiliar practice. Such dialogue can be considered a form of implicit induction, similar to 'socialisation (1)' in Table 3.1 but with a significant difference, which I will outline below.

Table 3.2 shows an extract from a draft text written by Sara, alongside an extract from our talk about the text. The essay question she was addressing was from a first year undergraduate course in Language Studies.

Essay question

Discuss the ways in which different linguistic environments affect the development of bilingualism in pre-school (under 5 years) children.

In this extract, my aim as Sara's tutor is to talk her into a specific way of meaning-making. How does the dialogue achieve this?

In the talk episode, the institutionally sanctioned roles of teacher and student are prominent. I, as tutor-assessor, control the opening and closing of the sequence. In general, I control the talk by assuming my institutional right to ask questions and make evaluations of the student-writer's

Table 3.2   Sara's draft text and our talk about the text[9]

Extract from Sara's text	Talk about text
I hope that by the end of this assignment I may have come to some sort of conclusion, as to why some children are proficient in some languages and not others.	1 T: *That doesn't seem to me to be really* 2 *what you're doing.* (Re-reads section) 3 S: *What about linguistically capable?* 4 T: *But you're talking about a specific* 5 *group of children aren't you?* 6 S: *Bilingual children.* 7 T: *Right, so I think you need to be* 8 *specific here as to why some* 9 S: *[bilingual* 10 *children,would that be better?* 11 T: *Well let's try and follow that through.* 12 *Some bilingual children are* 13 S: *[well, yes.* 14 *I mean some bilingual children are* 15 *proficient in some languages and not* 16 *others.* 17 T: *But if you've already called them* 18 *bilingual, you've got a problem there.* 19 S: *Yes, well but the business about* 20 *what is bilingual though.* 21 *I mean, who is considered* 22 *a bilingual, when <u>are</u> you* 23 *bilingual?* 24 T: *Right okay, let's take it like that.* 25 (T re-reads Sara's extract) 26 T: *Have you come to any conclusion* 27 *about what might be the best* 28 *environment?* 29 S: *Yes. I mean, there were some things in* 30 *there* (source text) *that I thought* 31 *that's a good idea, I could use that* 32 *myself.* 33 T: *Well, don't you think then that what* 34 *you're saying is I may have come to* 35 *some sort of conclusion as to why* 36 *certain environments help children to* 37 *become bilingual more than others.* 38 *Isn't that what you're doing?. . .* 39 S: *I think that's probably what I'm trying* 40 *to say but I haven't written it down* 41 *properly.* 42 T: *It's just that, what you've written here* 43 *is too vague.* (T re-reads Sara's extract) *The* 44 *second reason given here should be* 45 *the key.* 46 S: *Yes* (sounds unsure). *So if I said erm* 47 *that by the end of the assignment I may* 48 *have some idea* 49 T: *[as to why some children . . .* 50 S: *erm . . .*
What effects different environments have on their development.	51 T: *develop bilingual skills and what* 52 *effect that has on their development.* 53 *I mean that's what you're talking about,* 54 *aren't you?* 55 S: *How they develop bilingual skills.* 56 T: *Yes* 57 S: *Can I write that down or I'll forget.* 58 S: (Writes) *As to why, no . . . how some* 59 *children develop bilingual skills.* 60 T: *I think that's much more what you're* 61 *saying . . . and then what effects.* 62 S: *Yes.* (Writes)

comments: there are obvious, although extended, initiation–response–feedback patterns (IRF), for example at lines 1–7, 26–45, where I act as questioner and evaluator of her work; I engage in what Edwards and Mercer (1987) have called, in their analysis of classroom talk, *cued elicitation* at lines 12–14, where I guide the student-writer's contribution by seeking to elicit specific responses; I also engage in cued elicitation as part of modelling written text (lines 49–52) and joint modelling with the student-writer. I use *modelling* here to mean instances in talk where we rehearse sections of written text orally.[10]

There is evidence of me attempting to persuade Sara to take up my directives, whilst minimising my directive role through different types of hedging: for example, *That doesn't seem to me to be really what you're doing* (lines 1–2); *don't you think* (line 33), *isn't that* (line 38), *I mean* (line 53). Whilst some of these exchanges take on a particular significance for the teaching and learning of essayist literacy, they are also politeness strategies; such hedging allows me the possibility of re-directing Sara's construction of text without directly rejecting her current text and views, and thus potentially jeopardising our talking relationship.[11]

All of my contributions are directed at pushing Sara towards constructing the unifying central focus demanded in essayist literacy (Gee, 1996, p. xvii; Newkirk, 1995). I do this by introducing wordings from the essay question in my talk and then attempting to elicit them in her talk: at lines 4–6 I direct Sara towards the group of people intended to be the focus of the question, *bilingual children*; at lines 26–8 I direct her towards the particular dimension of their experience to be explored, that is, their *environment*. I ignore Sara's comments at lines 29–32 on the usefulness of a particular academic text she has been reading, in order to steer her towards a central focus on the effect of the environment on the development of bilingualism. Having established the focus in terms of the 'who' and 'what' of the essay question, I work with Sara to model written text, at lines 34–50, which she might include in her essay.

Sara actively works with me in the talk, by responding to my direct questions (lines 6 and 29), by offering suggestions (lines 3 and 9), by introducing her own questions about a term (line 19), by introducing her own opinion on a source text (lines 29–32), by echoing my comment that there are problems with the way she is using the word *bilingual* (line 22) and by working with me to model text (lines 34–50).

A significant feature of our talk, and a prominent way in which I talk Sara into the essayist way of constructing unity in her text, is my insistence that I know what she is saying, as compared with what she actually says – either orally or in her written text. This connects with what Edwards and Mercer, in their analysis of schoolteacher talk, have called *reconstructive paraphrasing*

(Edwards and Mercer, 1987, pp. 128–59). Such a practice is evident throughout the episode above: I open and close by suggesting that I know what Sara is trying to say, as compared with what she has written; at line 1, *That doesn't seem to me to be really what you're doing*; at line 33, *don't you think then that what you're saying is*; at line 53, *I mean that's what you're talking about, aren't you?*; at line 60, *I think that's much more what you're saying*. In closing, I suggest that all of our talk has been about making Sara's intended meanings textually explicit. Sara's comment at line 39, *I think that's probably what I'm trying to say but I haven't written it down properly* indicates that she is willing to accept my interpretation of what I think she's trying to do, although *probably* indicates her doubts as to whether I, and perhaps she, know her intended meanings. Her comment also suggests that she is willing to go along with my reconstruction of her meanings in order to engage in a practice which is new to her.

Such talk can to a certain extent be considered a form of implicit induction – socialisation (1) in Table 3.1. However, there is an important difference. Meaning-making in writing is a specific focus here: rather than assuming the student will 'pick it up' as part of her general study, opportunities are made for focusing in detail on her writing (and establishing a relationship which makes such discussion possible). The tutor is thus actively working to scaffold the student-writer into essayist literacy practice.

Dialogue 2: Talking to make language visible

It may seem banal to say that language is important for writing. Perhaps it is less so to say that tutors', students' and institutions' (implicit and explicit) theories of language – and thus how language is treated – are important in shaping writing pedagogy. In contrast to the 'common sense' notion of language as a transparent medium, evident in the skills model, for example, Academic Literacies argues that language is neither transparent nor autonomous – that is, separate or distinct from the contexts and histories of language use. The words, phrases and discourses that we use are, rather, embedded in, and have the 'taste' of, the contexts from which they have emerged. This is one if the reasons why, for example, telling a student to 'write in your own words' is far from easy. Bakhtin states that language should be viewed as a *living utterance*, which, 'having taken meaning and shape at a particular historical moment in a socially specific environment, cannot fail to brush up against thousands of living dialogic threads, woven by socio-ideological consciousness around the given object of an utterance; it cannot fail to become an active participant in social dialogue' (1981, p. 276).

Taking control over such an *active participant* is not easy. Helping student-writers to make language visible as a resource requiring considerable

Table 3.3   Extract from Sara's text

Extract from text	Talk about text
Children from minority groups can have many distractions towards the second language, in a foreign country.	T: *Why 'foreign' country?* S: *Well, like me, for instance. I'm living here and everything but everybody else considers me as a foreign person because it's not my country, really is it?* T: *Well, you tell me.* S: *Well, I don't feel that it is. Because if you don't get treated as if you belong somewhere, you don't <u>feel</u> as if you belong. Even though, you probably will because you've been born and bred here and you know, this is the only place you really know but . . . other people don't make you feel as if you belong. I think you still feel like a foreigner, you know.* T: *So this, when you say a foreign country, is that how, like the children view it, or how the people in society view it, or both?* S: *Both.*

care is essential as a first step to taking control over writing. In Table 3.3 I problematise Sara's use of the term *foreign* in a section of her text. In her oral explanation Sara points to the more complex meanings surrounding her use of a particular wording – here *foreign* – which are buried in her written text. In the written text she echoes, or *ventriloquates* (Bakhtin, 1981, p. 293), and hence appears to agree with, the dominant discourse on speakers of minority languages in the UK as being *foreign*, rather than British. Yet her talk indicates the meaning is complex; that she is using 'foreign' because that is how others refer to British-born Pakistani women (and children); that she agrees that she is *foreign* in the sense that she doesn't feel she belongs and others don't make her feel that she belongs; that she does belong – and hence is not *foreign* – because she was born in England. However, her use of 'foreign' in the text at this stage does not constitute the complexity of meanings that she expresses orally. Dialogue around specific words and phrases can help to make the resource necessary for writing – language – visible and something to be carefully crafted.

It is also important to make visible not only the more obvious 'content' words, as in 'foreign' above, but also more grammatical words. In the extract of talk in Table 3.4, Mary and I are discussing her use of 'however', which I am saying is incorrect. What becomes clear through the talk is that while

Table 3.4   Extract from Mary's text

Extract from text	Talk around text
In fact all types of West Indian Creoles should be viewed along a continuum. However, there is a large number of Creole speakers, but no one speaker uses a creolised speech to the same extent.	M: *I thought 'however' meant another change of thought.* T: *It does, but it means a change of direction of thought.* M: *I thought it meant the same direction. Oh, a completely different idea?* T: *It's like, say. I like shopping however I'm not going today.* M: *Whereas I've been saying, I like going shopping however I'm going to buy some. (Laughs)* T: *Exactly.* M: *It's serious. And I just used it casually like it was nothing, but it's very serious.* *I'm glad you've shown me that anyway.*

Mary was usefully viewing 'however' as a linking device, but she was treating it as if it were empty of any particular meaning. Through language-focused discussion around a particular section of her text, using analogies from everyday life, Mary seems to grasp the meaning of this linking device and more generally the need to treat this word (and others?) with greater care.[12]

Dialogue 3: Talking to populate with intention

Making language visible as an object of explicit discussion is a step towards taking control over the resources of language for meaning-making. Taking control, however, is not easy: 'Language is not a neutral medium that passes freely and easily into the private property of the speaker's intentions; it is populated – overpopulated – with the intentions of others. Expropriating it, forcing it to submit to one's own intention and accents, is a difficult and complicated process' (Bakhtin, 1981, p. 294). To help the student-writer to *populate her texts with intention* (p. 293) we need to acknowledge that texts are always meaning in the making, involving struggles around taking control over language which, in turn, are bound up with the writer's sense of authority as a writer (Ivanič, 1998; Lillis, 2001). Tutor/student dialogue can make visible such struggles and thus facilitate the construction of a student-writer's preferred meanings by encouraging her to take greater control over the voices in her text. Dialogue aimed at identifying the diverse voices in the student-writer's text, as illustrated in the extracts of talk below with Nadia, is a step towards establishing which voices the student-writer wishes to

Table 3.5   Extract from Nadia's text

Text	Talk about text
1 The education authorities 2 are under a great deal of 3 stress due to the vast 4 increase of ethnic minority 5 children entering British 6 schools.	1 T: *Is that something that you* 2 *would say, that you think?* 3 N: *Well it is true, isn't it?* 4 (T re-reads section) 5 T: *Is this what you think?* 6 N: *Well, it is true. Well, it's not true* 7 *but . . . they're not under a lot of* 8 *stress. I don't believe in that.* 9 T: *So, this sounds as if it's your idea.* 10 N: *No.* 11 T: *So how do you make sure that it* 12 *looks as if it's not your idea?* 13 N: *Just say, oh!, reference.*

own/disown. As such, this exemplifies a key aspect of student writing pedagogy built on the call of Academic Literacies for greater writer involvement and control over meaning-making.

Based on what I understood Nadia's feelings to be, from comments on her personal experience as a bilingual learner and a worker in schools, my surprise at the content of the draft extract in Table 3.5 led me to query whether the text represented her views (lines 1–2). Her text seemed to be simply echoing the dominant discourse on immigration in the UK, emphasising the way in which immigration is problematised in terms of numbers, as signalled in the reference to a *vast increase*, and in the emphasis on immigration causing problems for the 'host' community, as signalled in the reference to education authorities being under a *great deal of stress*. Following further discussion, I discovered, and Nadia realised, that her text was indeed simply *ventriloquating* (Bakhtin, 1981, p. 293) an official document dated 1963.

After our talk, where I questioned whether the text represented her view, Nadia made two specific changes to her final draft which distinguish her voice from that of the source text referred to above: in these she clearly separates her voice from that of the source text by inserting 'according to' and citing the source reference; she claims some authority over the subject matter by including insider accounts as a bilingual pupil and teacher.

Dialogue 4: Talking back

The three types of dialogue above can be used to get on with the *business-as-usual* of academia (Ellsworth, 1989). Here I want to turn to the potential of 'talkback', where the tutor allows the control over the text to shift away from her and towards the student-writer (hooks, 1988). 'Feedback' typically has the following features: a focus on the student's written text as a product, and a tendency towards closed commentary, including evaluative language such as 'good' or 'weak'. Talkback, in contrast, involves focusing on the student's text in process, an acknowledgement of the partial nature of any text and hence the range of potential meanings, an attempt to open up space where the student-writer can say what she likes and doesn't like about the conventions she is expected to make meaning within. Opportunities for talkback are rare and constitute an additional element to the usual cycle of writing and response to student writing. But providing such opportunities is an obvious way of more actively involving student-writers not only in the project of their immediate writing task but in the project of higher education itself. Here Mary is talking about her views on the use of the first person, 'I' – she can't see why it shouldn't be used – and on the prohibition on the use of contractions – such as 'can't'. She sees these prohibitions as creating unnecessary barriers between writers and readers:

> Mary: *I do still feel the same about that. I do still think 'why separate people'? Why does there have to be a distance, aren't we all bloody humans?*
>
> Theresa: *But which people are being separated from what, do you think? Everybody?*
>
> Mary: *No, the person who's writing the idea is separating himself from what he's actually . . . obviously it's all that stuff about being objective and even if you're writing to somebody official, you never put 'I'. Why? Why? Isn't it you? Isn't it you that's writing the letter? Isn't it you you're talking about? Why not be direct and say 'I'?*
>
> Theresa: *So what's the effect of separating people? Why would the institution want to do that?*
>
> Mary: *It's like a standing off, like I'm not interested in the person, I'm just interested in what they've written. Which I think is a bit . . . it's like, I just want your ideas, I don't want to know you.*

Talkback spaces enable student-writers to discuss what they would like to do as well as what they do not like doing. Thus Kate, who enjoyed learning how to produce the kind of rational argument required in essayist texts, at the same time likes to find ways of undercutting or challenging the value of rational argument. She would like to include extracts of poetry in her social science undergraduate essays as *a little protest against the convention of rational argument* (Lillis, 2001, p. 126). Kate showed me an example of where she had done this in a pre-university Access course (Table 3.6).

The student-writers who took part in my research project expressed the desire to use language for meaning-making in writing in ways which both

Table 3.6 Kate's text-poem and talkback

Text-poem included in essay	Talk about text

'The Mother'
By Anne Stephenson
 	
Of course I love them, they are my
  Children.
That is my daughter and this is my son.
And this is the life I give them to
  Please them.
It has never been used. Keep it safe,
Pass it on.
	K: *It sums up . . . and this poem, to me says what happens to women who have families erm like my mum. Her whole life has been the family. She will argue, but I think she could have done an awful lot with her life. And so, and that poem says, 'this is my life that I give to my children to please them'. In other words I do everything for them, and they're precious . . .*

draw on conventional essayist practices and include other ways of conveying meaning: thus they pointed to enjoying argument and theory, whilst at the same time wanting to include more emotion. They wanted to use new words, such as discipline-specific and formal expressions, but also wanted to use informal language, such as colloquial vocabulary and contracted forms used in speech.

However, what has also been clear from the student-writers' comments is that, in most instances, they do not feel they are in a position to do anything other than write within what they understand to be the dominant conventions (even though these are often a mystery to them). Challenges, whilst confidently asserted in the talkback space, are muted in the actual construction of texts. Representative is the position adopted by Mary, who restricts her oppositional stance to imagining what she might do one day:

What I'm going to do, I'm going to hand in an assignment, give it in, and put in a little note, a little note at the top, saying 'I've used a lot of informal language. And I hope you don't consider it to be inappropriate'. [Laughs]

► Conclusion

In this chapter I have argued that dialogue needs to be placed at the centre of an Academic Literacies pedagogy. I have illustrated four different types of student-writer/tutor dialogue: tutor-directive dialogue aimed at talking the student-writer into essayist literacy practice; tutor-directive dialogue aimed at making language visible; collaborative dialogue aimed at populating the student-writer's text with her own intentions; and dialogue which facilitates student 'talkback'. I suggest that all four types of dialogue need to be placed at the centre of an Academic Literacies approach to pedagogy, in order that students' participation in current dominant practices in higher education is ensured and that students are provided with opportunities for challenging such practices.

The illustrations of different types of dialogue in this chapter are from face-to-face talk. Indeed, the students who took part in my study repeatedly expressed the desire for more talk, more face-to-face contact, with tutors. However, the principles governing the types of dialogue discussed here can be applied to other modes of communication, albeit in varying ways, and can be summarised as follows. As tutors, we need to:

- acknowledge that different types of dialogue – interaction around texts – are important for facilitating learning how to write and take control over writing in higher education;
- use our 'insider' knowledge to direct student-writers' construction of texts and thus to give them an opportunity to practise writing within the conventions even before they know what these conventions are;
- direct student-writers' approaches to language itself in ways which allow them to see language as a powerful yet problematic resource;
- make space to hear student-writers' own views and desires for writing;
- explore ways in which alternative meaning-making practices in writing can be institutionally validated.

NOTES

1 For fuller discussion of this table see Lillis (2001, 2003).
2 I have not included 'process' as a writing approach as I am signalling different epistemological positions on student writing. A process approach is often linked to the notion of writing as creative self-expression, as in 'c' in Table 3.1. However, 'process' as a pedagogy, with an emphasis on drafting, planning and revising, can be connected with any of the approaches in the table.
3 For fuller discussion, see Lillis (2003).
4 See Chapter 10 of this volume, in which Jan Skillen details the move from skills-based teaching approaches to the teaching of writing as a component of teaching content in Australian universities.
5 See Lea and Street (1998), Lillis and Turner (2001) and Turner (2004).
6 For examples, see Ivanič (1998), Lea and Street (1998), Jones et al. (1999) and Lea and Stierer (2000).
7 For discussions relating to writing, see R. Clark (1992), Clark and Ivanič (1999) and Lillis (2003); for critical literacy more broadly, see McKinney (2003).

8   For a detailed exploration of writing as apprenticeship, see Prior (1998).
9   The transcripted interviews in this chapter use the following key: '[' indicates overlaps/interruptions; . . . indicates a pause lasting longer than two seconds; and *underlining* indicates a word that is being stressed.
10 For IRF patterns in school-based talk, see Sinclair and Coulthard (1975) and Mehan (1979); for cued elicitation as one element in their analytical framework, see Edwards and Mercer (1987, pp. 128–59) and Mercer (1995, pp. 26–7).
11 See Baynham (1996) for discussion of significant use of hedges in the context of adult teaching of literacy.
12 For debates around what kind of language description is most useful with students, see English (1999) and Coffin et al. (2003).

Part II

Developing UK Writing Programmes and Initiatives

Introduction

Lisa Ganobcsik-Williams

While Part I has reviewed current theory underpinning the teaching of writing in UK universities, Part II takes a sustained look at a number of practical projects for supporting student writing development. This section provides examples of good – and often innovative – practice at a range of levels and within a variety of institutional contexts. The breadth of Academic Writing programmes and initiatives covered and the depth of analysis offered should be of interest to UK readers and to those in other countries in which the field of Academic Writing is emerging. It will also be of use to US readers who are seeking alternative ways of teaching writing and of managing institutional structures for writing provision.

For most teachers of Academic Writing, scholarship grows out of practice. Many of the chapters in this section are representative of the way Academic Writing teachers generally work: moving from the practicalities of designing and trialling pedagogies to fit the needs of particular students, courses, academic departments and institutions, to formulating the theoretical implications of such pedagogies. Writing teachers at whose institutions Academic Writing instruction is developing will certainly identify with this process, but US Compositionists will also recognise it as part of the nature of writing research.[1] The chapters in this section also demonstrate that Academic Writing teachers may share practices but theorise them differently. For example, both Rowena Murray in Chapter 9 and Sally Mitchell and Alan Evison in Chapter 5 assess the higher education context but respond in different ways: Murray theorises an individualised approach to helping academics undertake writing development, while Mitchell and Evison argue for the need to engage in setting up university-wide writing programmes to involve academics in valuing and teaching writing.

While the rapidly increasing need for Academic Writing teaching dictates that many of those who teach writing must work from practice to theory, Part II also includes examples of those who have had opportunities to start from theoretical ideals to create practical models to service those ideals. The first chapter in this section, in which Alice Tomic provides a description of writing programme administration within a London university conversant with US Composition theories and course structures, exemplifies this movement. Tomic chronicles the development of one of the UK's earliest Academic Writing programmes, at Richmond, the American International

University in London, in the mid-1980s. She explains that long before the recruitment of international students became a priority for most UK universities, Richmond established a policy for recruiting students from all over the world. Tomic and her colleagues therefore faced, earlier than most of their UK counterparts, an issue now high on the UK educational agenda: how to introduce 'non-traditional' students to the academic discourses of the university. This chapter chronicles 'sites of negotiation' in the development of a university writing programme, and demonstrates how combining US writing research and methodologies with European and UK theory and practice has stimulated pedagogical innovation and ongoing reflection.

Tomic's chapter makes reference to 'Writing Across the Curriculum' (WAC), an organisational model which is discussed further in many of the chapters in Parts II and III. As a movement encouraging the use of writing to engage students in the learning process, WAC takes as its 'central working assumption' the concept that '[s]tudents should not only learn to write but write to learn' (Bazerman and Russell, 1994, p. xiv).[2] Tomic's example of helping academic colleagues to explore 'how they were using writing assignments in their courses to help students to learn' exemplifies the WAC focus on 'Writing to Learn' pedagogies.

Chapter 5 introduces 'Writing in the Disciplines' (WID), a more specialised subcomponent of WAC that 'refers to both a research movement to understand what writing actually occurs in the different disciplinary areas and a curricular reform movement to offer disciplinary-related writing instruction' (Bazerman et al., 2005, pp. 9–10).[3] The chapter's co-authors, Sally Mitchell and Alan Evison, acknowledge the importance of both WAC and WID for building institution-wide writing programmes.[4] This chapter describes a WID initiative inaugurated in 2001 at Queen Mary, University of London, and charts its attempts to move the teaching of writing into mainstream subject curricula. Though inspired by a US university writing programme, the Queen Mary initiative has had to develop within a set of very different organisational, financial and cultural constraints. Mitchell and Evison show that progress has been dependent on a number of factors, including the ability to reshape the discourse surrounding writing within the institution; the ability to link writing with thinking, learning and disciplinary expertise; and opportunities for sharing and developing practice. The chapter evaluates the initiative's attempts to change disciplinary and institutional perceptions of student writing pedagogy and provides examples of what has been accomplished in a number of disciplines. Mitchell and Evison argue that the key to achieving change in the way student writing is conceptualised is to promote an understanding of writing as integral to processes of learning and thinking, and therefore as a central concern and responsibility of disciplines and the institution.

Chapters 6, 7 and 8 exemplify how approaches 'to offer[ing] disciplinary-related writing instruction' (Bazerman et al., 2005, p. 10) are not necessarily dependent on cross-institutional initiatives but can emerge from within disciplines themselves. Chapter 6 examines the Speak–Write Project, established in the English Department of Anglia Ruskin University in 1997 to improve English degree students' speaking and writing abilities. Tory Young and Simon Avery explain how the Speak–Write team have formulated a model that embeds the teaching of writing within disciplinary study and that is designed to reach all students, not just those who seek help or are deemed to be failing. The chapter discusses the development of the Speak–Write Project from its inception in the Key Skills agenda to a re-evaluation of the Project in light of WID scholarship, and emphasises the need to tailor writing instruction to disciplinary content.

Chapter 7 also explores the development of student writing provision within an English Department. Influenced by the Speak–Write model, Aled Ganobcsik-Williams and his colleagues at the University of Derby have designed a sequence or 'vertical pathway' of writing modules and tutorial support to meet the needs of their degree students. In this chapter, Ganobcsik-Williams stresses the importance of academic staff taking responsibility for developing their knowledge of Academic Writing theory. The chapter shows, too, how staff can work within institutional constraints and connect with institutional priorities and funding sources in order to establish departmental writing provision.

Chapter 8 further demonstrates how academics in the disciplines can develop the ability to teach and support student writing. Focusing on the Civil Engineering classroom, Alison Ahearn argues that 'motivating students to want to write' is a key factor in students' writing development. As the co-ordinator of writing courses for the first-year Civil Engineering programme at Imperial College London, Ahearn outlines the function of a writing imperative in her students' experience of university studies in the first year and beyond.

The final chapter in this section, by Rowena Murray, describes the types of support for teaching writing that can be offered to academics by Writing Developers, or Learning and Teaching Lecturers, working in the area of staff development. While the range of Academic Writing practices detailed by Murray does not on its own constitute a university writing programme, the chapter signals that if universities move toward requiring more systematic writing instruction for students, then academic staff will also require more systematic guidance on how to teach writing. Murray, referring to higher education's increasing emphasis on staff development in teaching, concludes Part II by predicting that WAC and WID ideals and practices are most likely to take root in UK universities once 'a new generation of academics comes through, having experienced more in the way of training in teaching in higher education'.

The use of WAC and WID in this collection is a key example of the cultural cross-over inherent in the field of Academic Writing. Although the WAC movement started in the 1970s in the United States, WAC's 'intellectual roots [are] largely in the British classroom research and theorising of James Britton and his colleagues at the London School of Education from 1966 to 1976' (Bazerman and Russell, 1994, p. xiii).[5] The work of Britton and other educational reformers influenced UK school curricula from the mid-1970s but was not applied to writing at university. Conversely, in the US, WAC theory and pedagogy were developed initially at the higher education level and later began to be extended to primary and secondary education (Bazerman et al., 2005). Because UK university students specialise within disciplines very early in their degree programmes,[6] many of those now teaching and theorising Academic Writing in UK higher education are drawing upon WAC and WID concepts and strategies, rather than looking to the model of the general first-year writing course which features so prominently in US higher education.[7] 'Writing in the Disciplines' has particular resonance in the UK because of higher education's early focus on discipline-specific learning, and this is perhaps why WID rather than WAC has become the operative term for UK writing programmes.[8]

Finally, it is important to note that while the authors in Part II of *Teaching Academic Writing in UK Higher Education: Theories, Practices and Models* outline efforts to build writing provision within existing institutional timetables, course delivery mechanisms and assessment structures, the essential vision to which they subscribe is to update departmental and institutional frameworks to enhance student opportunities for learning how better to accomplish Academic Writing.

NOTES

1 This practice-based relationship between writing pedagogy and scholarship was articulated by Stephen North (1987), who used the term 'lore' to describe knowledge acquired through practice, application and experience, which develops into 'the accumulated body of traditions, practices, and beliefs in terms of which [teachers] understand how writing is done, learned, and taught' (p. 22). While the field of Composition Studies is based on a research model, North's description of learning from implementing innovations into everyday teaching practice remains relevant.

2 Janet Emig's 1977 essay 'Writing as a Mode of Learning' argued for the idea of writing to learn, and laid the basis for WAC theory in the US (Bazerman and Russell, 1994, p. xiv).

3 See the WAC Clearinghouse (http://wac.colostate.edu/) for detailed definitions of WAC and WID. The WAC Clearinghouse 'brings together five journals, four

book series, and resources for teachers who use writing in their courses' (WAC Clearinghouse, 2005). It functions as 'a gateway to learning more about how to implement discipline-specific practices for Writing Across the Curriculum. In addition to the resources at the site, there are well-maintained links to bibliographies, teaching resources, research, programs, [and] organisations' (Bazerman et al., 2005, p. 130).

4   In practice, WID and WAC overlap, as demonstrated in this volume and elsewhere. In the edited collection *WAC for the New Millennium: Strategies for Continuing Writing-Across-the-Curriculum Programs* (McLeod et al., 2001), for example, David Russell finds it more useful to conflate rather than to separate the two terms (Russell, 2001, pp. 259, 283, 290–1).

5   The phrase 'writing across the curriculum' originated with the British Schools Council project (Britton et al., 1975) and the chapter 'Language Across the Curriculum', to which Britton was the main contributor, in the National Education Commission report of 1975 (the Bullock Report) (see Russell, 1994, p. 14, and Bazerman et al., 2005, pp. 20–2). J. Harris (1997) provides an account of the landmark 1966 Dartmouth Seminar which brought UK educational theorists in contact with US educators and introduced the work of Britton and others to a US audience.

6   Early subject specialisation and three-year undergraduate degree courses in UK universities make the undergraduate experience very different from that of US universities, where degree courses traditionally span four years and follow a general education curriculum in the first two years.

7   See Chapters 11 and 12 for more information on the US university first-year writing course. Also see Ganobcsik-Williams (2003), ' "Is this Freshman Composition?": Teaching General Studies Writing in Europe', for a consideration of the generalist writing course in European higher education. In her keynote address at the first conference of the European Association for the Teaching of Academic Writing (EATAW) and European Writing Centers Association (EWCA) in 2001, Olga Dysthe emphasised the importance of teaching writing within disciplines and questioned the relevance of generalist writing courses to European and UK higher education (Dysthe, 2001, p. 9).

8   In addition to the WID programme at Queen Mary, University of London, described in Chapter 5, Coventry University founded a university-wide WID programme in 2004 (www.coventry.ac.uk/caw). The Writing and Learning Mentor Project at University College, London, also describes itself as being modelled on a WID approach (www.ucl.ac.uk/calt/acp/wlm.htm).

4 A Critical Narrative of the Evolution of a UK/US University Writing Programme

Alice Tomic

▶ Introduction

> [S]ites of construction, tension, divergence, and conflict. They happen at the intersection of diverse goals, values and assumptions, where social roles interact with personal images of one's self and one's situation . . . [They] are often sites of negotiation, where the meaning that emerges may reflect resolution, abiding contradiction, or perhaps just a temporary stay against uncertainty.   (Flower, 1994, p. 19)

Flower's description of literate acts could be a description of the academic world in its current state of flux. Writing in the university can be seen as a catalyst of shifts and re-alignments in the wider sphere and perhaps even as a metaphor for them. In this first part of my chapter I want to suggest the extent to which world events are shaking up the identity of the university and academics' role in it. The impact of globalisation, with many people 'on the move' (Bauman, 1998, p. 77), the internationalisation of higher education with growing overseas recruitment, the widening access to higher education – all these factors lead me to ask how far we academics are taking such changes into account in our theory and practice. This chapter is a critical narrative about one particular 'site of negotiation' in the midst of this setting of widespread change.

Is subjective experience relevant to discussing the topic of writing in the university? I am reminded of the student who asked, 'How much "I" can I put in this essay?' This question, associated in my mind with Roz Ivanič's work on student identity and its relationship to Academic Writing, may be familiar to many. I believe that theoretical and practical conclusions *can* be drawn from the case study of one particular institution of higher education as it has striven for over two decades to address the question of teaching Academic Writing. This chapter describes the cultural identity of this institution, and the influences that have worked upon those of us teaching there to enhance our approaches to teaching Academic Writing by remaining open to influences from both sides of the Atlantic.

'We are all reluctant to make changes in our work practices unless we can find "meaning" in the changes' (Fullan, quoted in Lea and Stierer, 2000, p. 63). Where did the 'meaning' reside for my colleagues and myself to consider adopting changed practices and new strategies? The answer to that question is, *in our students*. Our students, coming from a range of cultures and educational backgrounds, dictated the need for constant reflection, innovative practices, re-appraisal and mediation between individual students and our institution's intercultural mission. As Diane Belcher and George Braine (1995) have said, 'If contact with the academic discourse community transforms the self in some way, it is also true that the community itself is changed by those who join it' (p. xxi).

Changes in the role of the university: the academic world in flux

A changing student body that includes greater numbers of non-native speakers of English and 'non-traditional' students has caused some ripples on the academic horizon. Most readers would acknowledge that such students are leading us into more reflection on the role of the university and our place within it. In his 1999 Reith Lectures, Giddens described the impact of globalisation as affecting not only what is 'out there' but also what is 'in here', the way we see ourselves in relationship to fellow humans. Ron Barnett (2000) has also written about the 'supercomplexity' of the world into which we launch our students and the impact this has (or should have) on our pedagogical approaches (p. 6).

Bourdieu's concept of *habitus* – connoting the individual as configured by a nexus of cultural predispositions, of symbolic orderings and of value positions – is relevant here (Barnett, 2000). If the university is finding a new *habitus*, as Barnett suggests, looking for 'a new location in society, a new ordering of its perceived value, and a new register of meaning and understanding' (p. 13), then perhaps those of us interested in writing in the university are also seeking a new *habitus*. In a climate of upheaval and re-positioning, we can either respond by coming from a different direction, or we can suffer personal and professional insecurities as traditional approaches we are familiar with come under threat from new imperatives and preoccupations. Those of us involved with writing in the university are, *force majeure*, revisiting what precisely the discourse of the academic community is.

Added to the preparation of native English-speaking students for the rigours of undergraduate writing, there are the specific needs of those for whom English is not their mother tongue. English for Academic Purposes (EAP) and Academic Writing are no longer discrete entities but are closely linked. Tensions exist between the need for positivistic assessment and the idealistic goal of having diverse 'voices' heard in the academic community.

Absolute standards of 'correctness' seem a preoccupation of the past as we strive to enable students struggling in a second, third or even fourth language to engage with academic debate. Many people are asking how much flawed English teachers can accommodate (Barber, 1992). Even if we do not make the Anglocentric assumption that everyone in the world 'needs' English, it is often hard to see the intelligence of our students under the linguistic imperfections. Shaughnessy (1977) rightly reminds us of 'the intelligence of [students'] mistakes' (p. 11). '[E]ven the most error-ridden prose arises from the confrontation of inexperienced student writers with the complex linguistic and rhetorical expectations of the academy' (Zamel and Spack, 1998, p. 28).

Despite the growing number of non-native English speakers in our universities, Academic Writing should play a critical rather than a remedial role (Turner, 1999). This term 'critical' (as in 'critical thinking'), however, is a predominantly Western concept – a cultural norm for teachers in UK universities but not necessarily for our students. Equally, assumptions about what constitutes 'knowledge' are problematic. So, whereas at my institution our student body is predominantly non-native English speaking and many students need support in grappling with English language skills, my colleagues and I have tried to focus on critical aspects of teaching writing, while never under-estimating the problems this can create.

The institution's cultural identity

Richmond, the American International University in London, where I work, is a truly hybrid institution. It is an American liberal arts university based in London, offering around eighteen undergraduate degrees and a postgraduate degree. The thousand or so students represent over a hundred nationalities and the teaching faculty also come from a range of cultural backgrounds. Since its founding in 1972 the institution has followed a global recruitment strategy, long before this became an imperative for most UK universities. The undergraduate degree is a four-year programme in which students take a range of courses across the disciplines in their first and second years (equivalent to the UK concept of 'Combined Studies') and specialise in their third and fourth years in the discipline of their chosen degree. Post-Dearing Report models of modularisation and the semester system, and the current focus on 'critical thinking' and 'transferable skills', will be familiar to UK colleagues.[1] The Dearing Report (NCIHE, 1997) built bridges between the US and UK higher education systems by focusing on skills perceived by both systems as significant. Access to higher education has widened in the UK, making its ethos more similar to the US model. Indeed many differences between US and UK degree structures have been eroded in recent years and Richmond's degrees have joint validation – from a US accrediting body and from the UK's Open University Validation Services. We were the first university in the world to hold this joint validation.

The institution, therefore, has a complex cultural identity. It also offers a particularly fruitful environment in which to experiment with different approaches to teaching writing. First, Richmond's students have already made a cognitive and affective leap by choosing to study at an 'international' institution and by travelling many thousands of miles to do so. We find that international students are often more engaged with the challenge of joining the discourse community of the university than many US and UK students, who assume that their grasp of the language equips them *per se*.

Secondly, the General Education model (Combined Studies) ensures that in their first and second years students are exposed to a variety of disciplinary discourses. Thus, students have practical experience, at the same time as taking their required writing courses, of being confronted with a bewildering array of discourses, and this exposure can be foregrounded in their writing courses.

Thirdly, for dual validation purposes we have developed a structure of research and writing courses at each point of the degree: in the first year, third year and fourth year when students complete a 5000-word Senior Seminar paper. This writing sequence gives us strategic points at which to reflect on the effectiveness of our teaching approaches and the response of individual students to that process.

The institution fifteen years ago

When I joined the university to run the English Language Development Programme (ELDP) in 1986 I brought with me a first degree in English Language and Literature from Bristol University, and experience in working for the British Council, in secondary school teaching, language school teaching and in teaching European managers one-to-one on a management development programme. I had also taught communication skills in the commercial sector, and was a part-time faculty member at Richmond for four years before my appointment as Director of ELDP. I later took a postgraduate degree in Film and Television in Education before designing a degree in Communications for the university. I came to the task of running courses in English for Academic Purposes and a university writing programme, therefore, as something of a generalist, which may account for the level of openness to new approaches I encouraged in myself and my colleagues. To be blunt, to some extent I was learning 'on the job'.

As a 'Brit', new to the US system of liberal arts universities, I found that all undergraduates, whether native speakers of English or not, took a two-semester course in writing, widely known as freshman composition, at my university, called 'Principles of Writing'. In the mid-1980s these courses were taught at Richmond by a mixture of English Literature faculty and part-time staff who were either practising writers themselves or out-of-work journalists.[2] Most were British or American.

As a product of the British system of higher education I was surprised to find that students were being given guidance in Academic Writing. Beyond comments in the margins of my A Level essays, no one had ever offered me guidance as an academic writer. Admittedly, for many students whose first language was not English, the exercise was remedial, at the level of requiring 'correctness' in grammar and paragraph structure.

The goals of Richmond's writing courses in the mid-1980s rested upon widespread assumptions of what it meant to write in appropriate academic discourse (although few of us at the time were familiar with that term). Those delivering the courses taught often in isolation with no attempt at parity of expectation or assessment across multi-sectioned courses. I recall widespread use of a sinister acronym – NCM – Not College Material, which really meant that the student had failed to grasp what was required of him or her in terms of Academic Writing. The acronym suggested to those that used it that there was one way and one way only to assess the fitness of someone for an undergraduate degree, namely that individual's willingness to adopt academic discourse without question and without being helped to explore what it meant.

What followed from the mid to late 1980s was a microcosm of much that has happened in the wider sphere of Academic Writing theory and practice, as I strove to lead my department to keep up with what was happening in both Europe and the United States by applying everything I learnt. Looking back, I can see that I was lurching from one theory to another, pursuing what was probably, with hindsight, very much, in Flower's phrase, 'a temporary stay against uncertainty' (1994, p. 19). Echoing in my mind was the familiar phrase of David Bartholomae, 'Everytime a student sits down to write for us, he has to invent the university for the occasion' (1986, p. 4). The resonance of this sentence remains telling.

▶ The emerging discipline of Academic Writing

Through my work in my other area of responsibility, the university's EAP programme for non-native speakers of English, I began to connect with some of the major issues at stake in the task of helping undergraduates to write in a way which they found 'authentic' and which met the demands of the university. I explored issues of Language and Intercultural Communication. I researched the complexity of cultural identities, the concept of the fluidity of cultural identity and of multiple subjectivities (Tomic, 1996). I explored issues of power and authority and began to understand the ideological implications of the university education we were offering to students who came to us from all over the world.[3]

Above all, I started to reject the notion that students could be passed through some kind of laundry system in the form of EAP preparation and the two required writing courses and emerge, lily white as it were, to continue their degrees, writing flawless and persuasive prose. It became clear to me that the issue was much more complex and involved their evolving identity as writers *throughout their four-year degree*. The responsibility for nurturing student writing needed to be shared beyond the second year by faculty colleagues using writing assignments *in all degree programmes* to help their students to learn. In a small institution, it was relatively easy to collaborate with colleagues in all disciplines on setting writing tasks which encouraged the development of student-writers. Workshops produced interesting discussions about how we graded written work, what we were looking for and how far a grade should reflect grammatical errors if the writing communicated meaning clearly. It became clearer that the issue of student writing had a direct connection with the interest the faculty members had in *whether their students were learning*. In other words, we had the beginnings of a Writing Across the Curriculum (WAC) initiative.[4]

I followed the work of Toby Fulwiler (1980, 1984, 1987) and Anne Herrington (1981) and others in the forefront of WAC in the United States and sought to apply their ideas. The need for this work was highlighted at Richmond by the diverse nature of our student body and the nature of the liberal arts degree, requiring all undergraduates to follow courses in a wide range of subjects rather than the then specialised degrees in the UK system. With hindsight, I suppose we were enacting an early engagement with the issue that later came to be called 'Academic Literacies'. We found the very idea that the term 'literacy' could be altered epistemologically by making it plural – 'literacies' – to be significant.

Transatlantic influences

It was at this point in the early 1990s that I appointed a US academic who had studied for a postgraduate degree in Professional Writing at the University of Southern California. As part of her apprenticeship in that programme, Catherine Davidson had taught in the equivalent courses to our own, the writing courses for first-year undergraduates known as freshman composition. Her arrival brought to the institution and to our work the latest US writing theory and practice. Because Composition had been established there for several decades as a discrete academic discipline with doctoral programmes and a strong sense of professional identity, a major spin-off from her influence was that those of us at Richmond felt a renewed commitment and stronger sense of identity as professional teachers of writing.[5]

Our new colleague introduced us to a range of new texts for students in writing classes. In approaching the writing-development needs of our disparate group of international students at Richmond, however, we found US texts to be helpful but not appropriate in their entirety. We tried out several, but none proved definitive for our particular learning environment.[6] Although progressive in addressing, for instance, issues of gender, studies of difference tended to focus on racial and ethnic populations specific to the US context. There was almost no reference to the educational backgrounds and learning needs of students from Japan, the Gulf States, Turkey and elsewhere in the world from whence our students were drawn. Nevertheless, the work of people like Irene Clark (1993, 1997), and in particular her 'Three Pass Reading Approach', brought us new strategies which we were ready to try out.

Injected into our work were approaches which are now familiar but were then very new to us: *writing as a process versus product debates*; *the importance of draft-writing and feedback*; *the difference between local and global revision*; *writing as a collaborative rather than a lone occupation*; *the use of ethnographic practice to explore oneself and others as writers*; *the exploration of issues of power and authority in writing tasks: questions of gender and class, of privilege and marginalisation*; *holistic versus composite grading*; and *the use of journals and portfolios*.

My colleagues and I were beginning to have the confidence to adopt US theories and practices or to mould them to our particular academic community. With Swales's book on genre (1990) we felt a particular affiliation; his work on EAP and writing matters reflected the fact that he was a 'Brit' who had gone to work at the University of Michigan and who seemed to have the same transatlantic approach that we felt we had. Not many other writers and theorists in the early 1990s seemed to enjoy this distinction of being aware of what was going on 'both sides of the pond'.

The immediate task in applying US ideas was to give greater leadership and coherence to Richmond's multi-sectioned Academic Writing courses for first-year students (Davidson, 2000). Regular meetings of those teaching this course critiqued the theory and practice to see what was relevant to our institution's cultural identity, and today these debates continue on a fortnightly basis and are an important part of our professional development.

We developed a Writing Workshop for students at all stages in their degree and made a point of publicising that the Workshop was not 'remedial' but for ambitious students who wanted to excel. This Workshop still runs for six hours a week, providing a safe environment for one-to-one support from one of the teachers of the required first-year writing courses. It is attended by self-referring students and by those referred for help by lecturers in all disciplines. Work includes the understanding of an assignment, brainstorming for a thesis statement, critiquing resources, global and local revision, and above all helping the individual student gain confidence in acquiring a voice in the academic community. Later we developed a Language Workshop for those struggling with syntax. Both workshops offer a steady flow of guidance to students and are now complemented by offerings online from universities around the world.

We also researched how new technology could be harnessed to motivate students to revise their writing and have a stronger sense of their identity as writers through collaborative learning and peer review.[7] The American identity of the institution meant that technology was regarded as a high priority so we were fortunate to enjoy well equipped computer labs, ahead of some of our UK counterparts. The use of online course management systems, like First Class and, more recently, Blackboard, has been encouraged and is used increasingly but without replacing the one-to-one help provided through individual tutorials and the Writing Workshop. We followed the work of US Compositionists Gail Hawisher and Cynthia Selfe and attended European conferences where the impact of computers on writing was being explored, and we learned how the Internet was altering the whole concept of 'writing'.

As the 1990s progressed, my colleagues and I worked with library staff to design a Research Skills component in these writing courses which taught students not only how to use search engines and online sources but also to evaluate the usefulness and authenticity of websites and to critique their value for research projects (Thurlow et al., 2004). Also during the 1990s, we started appointing teaching staff who had themselves in some way crossed cultural borders, whether across disciplines or across geographical space, because it seemed to us that the cognitive and affective leaps made during such 'journeys' fed into their teaching of such a diverse student body.

Graff (1990) encouraged academics to 'teach the conflicts', and one of the results of adopting this strategy and exploring the range of pedagogies already mentioned was the introduction into classroom debate and into reading and writing assignments of precisely those issues which make one student 'different' from another. It was exciting to be able to integrate Freire's (1970, 1974) ideals of the enormous potential of liberatory education and Giroux's (1993) concept of a critical pedagogy into our work with students from such diverse backgrounds.

The impact of these discoveries was profound, on both institutional and personal levels. The profile of writing in the institution was highlighted; those hired to teach it were increasingly highly qualified (several doctorates and doctoral candidates), which raised our esteem from colleagues in other disciplines; and management began to acknowledge that in an international institution such as ours, the issue of academic literacies formed a spine or armature to the university's academic activities. In 1990 I wrote a proposal for a WAC initiative and we secured funding for the new permanent post of University Writing Co-ordinator, to enable these theoretical and practical ideas to be enacted beyond the limits of the first-year writing courses and in all the disciplines at all stages of the degree programmes. Any WAC programme comes up against difficulties (Fulwiler, 1984) and ours was no exception, but the professionalism and enthusiasm of the appointed Co-ordinator, Catherine Davidson, were contagious and many colleagues warmed to the task of exploring how they were using writing assignments in their courses to help students to learn. This is, however, very much a work in progress; we continue to look into ways of inducting faculty into the complex issue of writing across the curriculum at Richmond.

These new ideas also had an impact on me personally. I found, in our Writing Co-ordinator, a mentor for my own writing. I was able to share with my students the discoveries that I was making about my own writing processes – what worked, what didn't – and thus the power structure of the writing classroom changed radically for me as well as for some of my colleagues.

Perhaps one of the most innovative results of the influence of our new University Writing Co-ordinator was the discovery that Creative Writing, far from being a hothouse plant to be kept in another room entirely, was yet another dimension to the issue of student writing. The opportunity now provided to take a first-year or fourth-year Creative Writing class has spelt out for students the concept of 'genre' and of their own multiple subjectivities and complex cultural identities (Davidson, 1999). For some years one of the most thriving student societies has been the Creative Writing Club. Mike Sharples's *How We Write: Writing as Creative Design* (1999) also appealed to the students (and to colleagues) as they started seeing the potential for creativity in their own writing. Students began to see writing as an art in which they had their own potential to fulfil, rather than a science governed by rules. I have heard Roz Ivanič say, on more than one occasion, 'the creative is at the heart of the academic', and I am convinced that this is an approach which will burgeon.[8]

UK influences

In terms of pedagogical hybridity, what was the influence of UK colleagues on our work at Richmond? Feeding into our work in equal measure to the US influences have been our collaborations with UK colleagues in the field, notably the Literacy in Higher Education research group at King's College,

University of London, and the Academic Literacies research group at the Institute of Education, University of London.[9] Discussion at these groups has provided open-minded debate about the differences between cultural and epistemological aspects of UK and US higher education and their relationship with the teaching of writing in the university.[10]

In the mid-1990s we also followed the work of Sally Mitchell (1994) on teaching argument,[11] and Roz Ivanič's *Writing and Identity* (1998) gave a new political urgency and intellectual stringency to the theoretical underpinning of work on Academic Writing. Ivanič's innate humanity was matched by the sophisticated theoretical explorations she made in her study, and this book remains a seminal work. Perhaps most pervasively, however, the work of Mary Lea and Brian Street (1998), in categorising three approaches to student writing in higher education, has served us well and reflects to some extent the historical progression of our approaches at Richmond. As outlined in previous chapters, Lea and Street describe three models: the first, 'study skills', treats writing as something which can be 'fixed' by attention to surface, language, grammar and spelling, and it approaches the subject of student writing as a question of student deficit. In the second model, 'academic socialisation', the student is acculturated into academic discourse but student writing is seen as a transparent medium of representation. The third model, 'academic literacies', serves to help students negotiate conflicting literary practices and sees student writing as constitutive and contested. It views literacies as social practices played out against a background of discourses and power with issues of identity and of how knowledge is validated playing a significant role. The third model makes even more resonant Bartholomae's sentence about students 'inventing the university' every time they write. This model is also particularly appropriate when teaching students from different cultural backgrounds.

▶ **Teaching the theory**

Reflecting on what a university is and the place that writing holds in the academic community has provided us with new ways of teaching at Richmond. While this chapter describes the *habitus* of one particular university, claiming to be 'international', and the place of Academic Writing in that institution, Lea and Street's (1998) Academic Literacies approach has provided fertile ground for our writing courses which may prove useful for others. Writing as social practice is now integrated into the curriculum of the required writing courses: students are asked to explore where they are coming from, their past literacy histories and their reactions to being invited to join the academic discourse community, to articulate the struggles they undergo, and to 'theorise' them. The strategy of 'teaching the theory' has been effective in enabling students to objectify the adjustments they go through and to find an authoritative voice in which to express their arguments and views (Davidson, 2000). Working in this area has brought us close to UK colleagues, notably those focusing on distance learning at the Open University, and to those who are exploring writing as social practice in many different university settings.

In the relationship between US and UK theory and practice in higher education, we are faced with a classical model of Intercultural Communications. There are similarities and there are differences, which are often masked, as the clichéd maxim reminds us, by our use of the same language. It seems to us at Richmond that there is now a real ground swell of interest from UK educators and administrators in what can be learnt, adapted or rejected from US writing theory and practice. From our point of view, this interest has been a relatively long time in coming.

▶ 'A temporary stay against uncertainty'

Lest you find this chapter in danger of lapsing into self-congratulation rather than the 'critical narrative' promised in my title, I will mention the problematics still hovering over us in our work, particularly as I suspect they are shared with a wide constituency of readers. These problematics form a creative tension to make us constantly re-appraise our theories and practice. In our case, the tension resides:

- between the ideology of the institution and the range of cultural backgrounds from which our students come;
- between the cultural and educational backgrounds of those teaching within the writing programme;
- between student expectations of being taught a body of knowledge (along the lines of Freire's (1970) concept of 'banking knowledge') and our emphasis on encouraging students to become autonomous learners;
- between the institutional need for assessment and our preoccupations with process and self-discovery through writing;
- between the personal voice – the 'I' – and each student's new identity as a member of an academic community;
- between the need for an acceptable level of content in written assignments (as a mark of 'knowledge' acquired) and for presentation (in terms of accuracy of language, clarity of argument and overall communicative effectiveness);
- between colleagues who mark work in a composite way and those who mark holistically;[12]

- between our view of writing as a responsibility shared with all colleagues in the university and the insistence of some that those of us in the Writing Programme should 'prepare' students for a repertoire of written assignments in their degrees;
- between the need for one-to-one and small-group work, which we find important, and the relatively low level of importance such academic 'housekeeping' is given;
- between the need to set 'enough' assignments and to leave enough 'space' and time around assignments for students to reflect on draft-writing and to learn from extensive individual feedback.

▶ Hybridity as a fruitful strategy

Discourse 'is often a matter of negotiation, contestation and hybridity' (Gee, 1996, p. 149). When I use the term 'hybridity' in the context of this chapter, I mean the blending of two or more components. But I could also be using the more specific meaning ascribed to the word by post-modernist literary critics in describing authors from colonised states who use the language of the coloniser in which to write.[13] Many of the students we teach are from former British colonies and those from other parts of the world often have mixed feelings about the global domination of the English language and its use as the channel of communication in their university studies. This, too, can provide introspective material for debate in the teaching of writing in higher education.

Whereas 'Hybrids between species are usually sterile' (*Collins Dictionary*, 1979, p. 749), I hope to have demonstrated that a hybrid approach to teaching writing in the university, including a range of strategies from US and UK theory and practice, is anything but sterile. This case study shows historical parallels between a specific institution, with a hybrid cultural identity, and the development over a period of years of approaches to teaching writing in the university. An openness to influences from both sides of the Atlantic, even if it has entailed periods of 'lurching' between what Flower called 'sites of construction, tension, divergence and conflict', provides fruitful 'sites for negotiation', reflection and critical analysis of the advantages and drawbacks of each approach.

▶ Conclusion: still travelling hopefully

In *Realising the University* (2000), Barnett focuses on six strategies for moving higher education forward. Those of us involved in teaching writing at university could usefully adopt these: *critical interdisciplinarity, collective self-scrutiny, purposive renewal, moving borders, engagement* and *communicative tolerance.* As educators we should be practising openmindedness and resisting the pressures brought to bear on us to defend academic 'territories'. At Richmond, my colleagues and I have come some way in learning that it is not a question of 'either/or' in exploring ways to teach writing but of listening to each other's ideas and building on them. Perhaps if we adopt Barnett's suggested approaches in our work, the 'negotiation, contestation and hybridity' to which Gee refers will produce a pool of research and scholarship leading to teaching practices which reflect more closely the needs of the times we live in and the culturally diverse students we teach.

NOTES

1　I thank Roberto di Napoli for referring me to Assiter (1995) on transferable skills.

2　Today much of the teaching of these multi-sectioned courses at US universities is undertaken by postgraduate students. See Davidson and Tomic (1999), and Heyda's and Mullin's chapters in this volume.

3　This work blossomed into the launch of the International Association of Languages and Intercultural Communication, and its journal, *Language and Intercultural Communication.* See www.ialic.org

4　See the WAC Clearinghouse at http://wac.colostate.edu/intro/pop3a.cfm for an outline of the basic principles of WAC.

5　For more about the 'professionalising' of writing teachers in the US, see Davidson and Tomic (1999).

6　Over the years these included *The Norton Reader* (Peterson, 1992), *The Holt Reader* (Scarry and Scarry, 2003), Donald McQuade and Robert Atwan's *Thinking in Writing* (1997), Jeanne Gunner and Ed Frankel's *The Course of Ideas* (1997), Robert E. Miller's *The Informed Argument* (1997), Joseph Trimmer's *Writing with a Purpose* (2003), and Irene L. Clark's *Writing About Diversity* (1997).

7　See Davidson and Tomic (1994), Hartley (1998) and Scott (2001).

8　Ivanič stressed this point at Academic Literacies seminars at the Open University in 2000 and at Richmond in 2001. The connection between Creative and Academic Writing was also one focus of the 'Teaching Writing in Higher Education' conference held by the University of Warwick Writing Programme in 2001.

9　See the general Introduction to this volume for more details on the latter group, which has been re-named the Interuniversity Academic Literacies Research Group. A subsequent publication bears witness to the collaboration between members of these two groups (Jones et al., 1999).

10　This has been the case, too, of one-day seminars on Academic Literacies held at the Open University (2000), at Richmond (2001), at the School of Oriental and African Studies, University of London (2002), at King's College, London (2004) and at the Institute of Education, London (2005).

11   Also see Andrews (1995), Mitchell and Andrews (2000) and Mitchell and Riddle (2000).

12   Our experience shows that colleagues who mark in this disparate fashion very often reach the same conclusion when giving marks in range-finding exercises.

13   Zamel and Spack (1998, p. 62) quote the African writer Chinue Achebe: 'I feel that the English language will be able to carry the weight of my African experience. . . . But it will have to be a new English, still in communion with its ancestral home but altered to suit its new African surroundings.'

5 Exploiting the Potential of Writing for Educational Change at Queen Mary, University of London

Sally Mitchell and Alan Evison

▶ Introduction

> Unless writing is fully integrated into the intellectually stimulating work that is articulated in higher education through the disciplines, students will not do their best writing, and instructors will not be reading and responding to writing they understand to be an integral part of their higher educational mission. (Monroe, 2003a, p. 7)

It is characteristic of UK universities – Queen Mary is no exception – that they do not have well developed ways of talking or thinking about writing, what its possibilities are and what role it might play in the learning of their students. When writing is talked about it tends to be as an idealised form – often the argumentative essay – representing a kind of pinnacle in under-graduate achievement (Giltrow, 2000). Or, more frequently, as a counter-point to this, writing is talked about as something that students cannot do – and that seemingly every year they do worse and worse. Referred to thus as a deficit, writing has the tendency to be reduced to little more than a technical activity involving rules of punctuation and grammar, with no connection to knowledge, thinking or activity within the discipline.[1] Seeing writing this way, as divorced from thinking, enables subject teachers to shunt away conceptual difficulties that manifest themselves in writing, where in fact research suggests increasingly that 'students' writing problems reflect semantic and epistemic uncertainties, not simply lack of language proficiency' (Warren, 2002, p. 91).[2] The divorce between language and thinking is also seemingly contradicted by an opposite tendency to elide the surface features of language with higher-level thinking – for example, the conventional features of written argument with the *process* of arguing (Groom, 2000; Mitchell and Riddle, 2000) – so that teaching emphasises the mastery of conventional form rather than the encouragement of critical thought.

Questions of how students learn, and of how they show that they have learnt, tend to be similarly confused or under-articulated. In course directories, content dominates: content is what courses are about, content is what students learn and also what they learn that learning is about (Donald, 1992).

When students do not do well, the refrain is that they 'can't write', not that they are struggling with learning. When students write well, on the other hand, their writing becomes a transparent conduit to the meanings they have grasped. So subjects and writing are intimately bound up on one level (most obviously where writing is the primary vehicle for assessment); and divorced on another. Again, writing, as an object of discussion, tends either to appear – when it is bad – or to disappear – when it is good. In each case, the result is to enable subject specialists to disconnect the 'problems' of students' writing from their responsibilities as disciplinary teachers and to maintain both what Lillis (1999, 2001) has called 'the institutional practice of mystery' and what Rose (quoted in Russell, 2002, p. 7) has called 'the myth of transience' – the idea that once the problem of writing is solved, the academy can get back to its proper work. If any action is to be taken to help students with their writing, it is by someone else, generally a language or study skills specialist, who rarely has a matching disciplinary background. Bourdieu and Passeron (1990) provide an eloquent summary of the logic underpinning this situation:

> The whole logic of an academic institution based on pedagogic work of the traditional type and ultimately guaranteeing the 'infallibility' of the 'master', finds expression in the professorial ideology of student incapacity, a mixture of tyrannical stringency and disillusioned indulgence which inclines the teacher to regard all communication failures, however unforeseen, as integral to a relationship which inherently implies poor reception of the best messages by the worst receivers.   (p. 111)

The well-known *Times Higher Education Supplement*[3] columnist Gary Day (2004a) captures the kind of situation which results from such communicative relations and from the often unexpressed connections between writing, thinking, learning and content. We quote here at length from Day's article:

> 'To every thing there is a season, and a time to every purpose under heaven. A time to be born and a time to die' – a time to write essays and a time to mark them. For it's round these times of year that your courses return to you shredded through your students' brains. Your pigeon-hole overflows with essays . . . . Where had all these scripts come from? There were never this many students at the 9am lecture on Monday mornings. And the seminars were equally sparsely populated, except by the hard core who persisted in showing up despite never having read the books. They would sit there waiting grimly for me to do something useful such as summarise the plot of Kafka's *The Castle*. I would say there isn't a plot

as such. 'What happens, then?' 'Nothing really.' 'What's the point of writing a book about nothing?' 'Well, it's not really about nothing.' 'You just said it was.' 'I meant that nothing much happens.' 'Why are we studying it then?' 'Because Kafka is an important writer.' 'But he doesn't write about anything.' 'He does, but he does it symbolically.' 'What's the castle a symbol of, then?' 'Lots of things.' 'Such as?' 'Er, well, the pointlessness of human endeavour.' We all stop, feeling the truth of that at this moment. Essays are the students' revenge. They follow the inexorable logic of a Greek tragedy. You bore them and they bore you. En masse. You recognise the words as English but not the language. Page upon page, riddled with solecisms, spelling mistakes and *non sequiturs*. 'The sisters agree that they do not wish to marry themselves'. Is this why forests were felled? And then there's the logic: 'People need to be removed from reality to survive existence' – this is probably best appreciated if you're high on something. Still the first few essays, though cumbersome, are bearable, even affording a bit of light relief: 'Mrs Ramsey reads allowed'. But after the 15th, you wonder if you're in the wrong job. After the 25th, you laugh at the stipulation that assessment should measure outcomes. After the 35th, even Alan Titchmarsh begins to look interesting; after the 45th you're just bored. After the 55th, you become obsessive: is this a 42 or 43? After the 64th, you start to hallucinate: surely they're all the same piece of work? And after the 75th, the cat decides it might be best to leave home. And then, just when the universe starts to crack and you're wondering whether to book a one-way ticket to a Swiss clinic, you come across a line such as this: 'Love is the real thing, it gives purpose, is experienced and endured.' Yes indeed. You are reconciled to the world.   (p. 15)

We think this extract is worth taking seriously as a piece of popular higher education discourse about the business of education; its humour derives from the reader acknowledging at least some elements of the situation as recognisable. Day characterises students' writing as an inevitable, perennial problem, but in our reading the problem lies elsewhere, with the overall context, the teaching and assessment: the students' poor writing is simply symptomatic. The act of writing essays for assessment is portrayed by Day as the sole means by which students make an active investment in a course of study – they may not turn up to lectures or prepare for seminars but when the time comes to write, they write. They write not because they enjoy it, are good at it, have anything to say, but because writing constitutes assessment: it counts. Commonly, as here, writing also equates with 'essays'; so writing equates with essays which equate with assessment. But writing conceived this way does not necessarily equate with learning, with engagement with the curriculum or even, as Day's piece indicates, with attendance on the course.

In reality, we are sure that Day engages with students more than he suggests in his article, but the cause-and-effect relationship between poor teaching and poor writing ('you bore them, they bore you'), although used to raise a laugh at his students' expense, is actually no joke. At some level his students want to do well; they do the work that has been signalled to them as counting, but they do it badly, mechanically, rarely showing insight or writing to transformative effect. Day also likes it when they do well; it makes his efforts worthwhile. But as he caricatures it, Day's teaching is devoid of strategies, inventiveness or resources that might address the palpable alienation of teacher from students and students from their learning.

▶ Starting a conversation about writing, thinking and learning

Since 1999 at Queen Mary, University of London, we have been working to address some of the issues raised here and to create more informed, sophisticated and productive thinking about writing, disciplinarity, and teaching and learning than may be typically the case in UK higher education. The prime vehicle for this work has been a 'Writing in the Disciplines' project, funded through HEFCE's Teaching Quality Enhancement strand from 2001 to 2004. Now internally funded by Queen Mary, the project – re-named 'Thinking Writing' – is based in the Learning Development Unit and Sally Mitchell is appointed to it on a part-time basis as Co-ordinator.

The thinking behind this project was germinated in 1999 in a conversation between Alan Evison and Leonard Olschner, Professor of German. As Director of English Language and Study Skills (ELSS) in Queen Mary's Learning Development Unit, Alan had for a long time felt a sense of frustration with the status quo. Since 1997 ELSS had provided a fairly typical programme of 'add-on' short courses, drop-in classes and individual tutorials on a variety of 'study skills', including writing. Student take-up of these opportunities was poor, though an in-sessional EAP programme for international students was – and continues to be – very popular. Efforts to build partnerships with teachers to embed writing development within disciplinary curricula led to *ad hoc* arrangements – a lecture here, a workshop there: again a typical pattern in UK higher education. These arrangements had in common the assumption that whatever space was created for writing within students' programmes of study would be filled by input from the writing and study skills 'specialist', the role and responsibilities of the subject teacher remaining largely unchanged.

Alan's conversation with Leonard marked a turning point, however. It drew attention to an alternative way of thinking about the teaching of writing and the role of writing in relation to disciplinary learning, and provided concrete examples that would enable academics to connect that alternative thinking with different practices. Leonard had taught at Cornell University in the United States, a prestigious institution with a well established, highly-prized programme of 'writing-intensive' courses located within and taught by the academic disciplines themselves at both introductory and senior levels of the undergraduate degree (Monroe, 2002, 2003b).[4] Coming to Queen Mary, Leonard had been puzzled at the lack of attention within the curriculum to the development of student writing; he found instead a culture of complaint[5] and a relative blank in terms of constructive ideas, models and practices.

The discussion with Alan prompted him to contact the director of Cornell's writing programme, Professor Jonathan Monroe, who invited representatives from Queen Mary to attend Cornell's Summer Consortium for Writing in the Disciplines, an annual event attended by a select number of universities seeking to develop their writing programmes. Queen Mary was the first non-American university to participate in the consortium, and it did so in 1999, 2000 and 2001.

Writing in the Disciplines (WID), as it has developed in US higher education, is guided by the argument that since writing is part and parcel of disciplinary activity, teaching writing should be not a remedial or add-on activity, but an integral, ongoing part of disciplinary learning for all students. Teaching writing should, therefore, be part of the responsibility of disciplinary academics and should occur within the discipline's curriculum. This argument, and its successful manifestation at Cornell and other US institutions, gave us a clear and categorical starting place for making changes at Queen Mary. What was needed was direct engagement with disciplinary teachers and mainstream curricula. Though both our present and historical contexts differ (Monroe, 2002), we were able to draw directly on several decades of pedagogical research and practical experience from US Writing across the Curriculum (WAC) and Writing in the Disciplines (WID) programmes.[6] We could use this work, as well as significant insights drawn from UK research and practice, to equip academics to recognise writing as a valuable learning process and to support writing effectively in their courses.

At Queen Mary, our approach to changing the culture of how writing is talked about and valued is via dialogue and collaboration rather than through edict. The Thinking Writing initiative hosts an annual series of workshops and seminars including an 'exchange of practice' forum where staff are invited to discuss their work on writing with colleagues from a mixture of disciplines. A considerable effort is put into promoting these events to staff – the message is that a worthwhile community of interest is developing across the institution. Accordingly the events change from year to year in response to the perceived needs and interests of staff and to developments in the wider field. All, however, are guided by a framework of ideas which tends to be challenging, rather than confirmatory, of the dominant discourse around writing. What we hope to achieve is a transformation of unexamined assumptions and a changed awareness of where the 'problem' of student writing may be located and how it is constituted. For example, whilst students are often seen to fail in their assessments, it takes a shift in consciousness – and in the 'logic' that Bourdieu and Passeron describe – to see the writing students do as a kind of feedback on the teaching they have received, or to say that it is lecturers who often fail in the assessments they set. It is this kind of – often uncomfortable – shift that we hope to achieve.

We also want to offer a real sense of the practical possibilities for the teaching of writing and for teaching involving writing. So at a more specific level an important part of Sally Mitchell's role is to collaborate directly with departments and individual staff to develop, initiate and evaluate new courses and approaches to writing. In the last two years this partnership work has been considerably helped by 'secondments' for academic staff that enable them to invest the time needed to develop new understandings and ideas and to make curricular changes.[7] As a resource for these collaborations, we have developed a website (www.thinkingwriting.qmul.ac.uk) to take staff through the first steps in rethinking the role that writing might play in their teaching and which offers resources to view and download.[8]

We are cautiously optimistic that our strategies are having effects at the departmental level. Recently Leonard Olschner, now Dean of the Arts Faculty, reflected in an email:

> I have noticed that in the professorial interviews in Arts and even more in the review of promotions applicants more and more people are recognising the place of a culture of writing in the academy and are foregrounding writing in their course amendments/proposals, etc. This is beginning to feel like a ground swell. . . .   (Olschner, 2004)

▶ An expanded view of writing possibilities

When we introduce staff to the possibilities offered by a WID approach we often use a simple hand-drawn slide (Figure 5.1) showing a continuum from private process to public product and suggesting how writing can function, and be interpreted, differently at each end. We also suggest that instead of the process–product line being uni-directional it might be possible, by

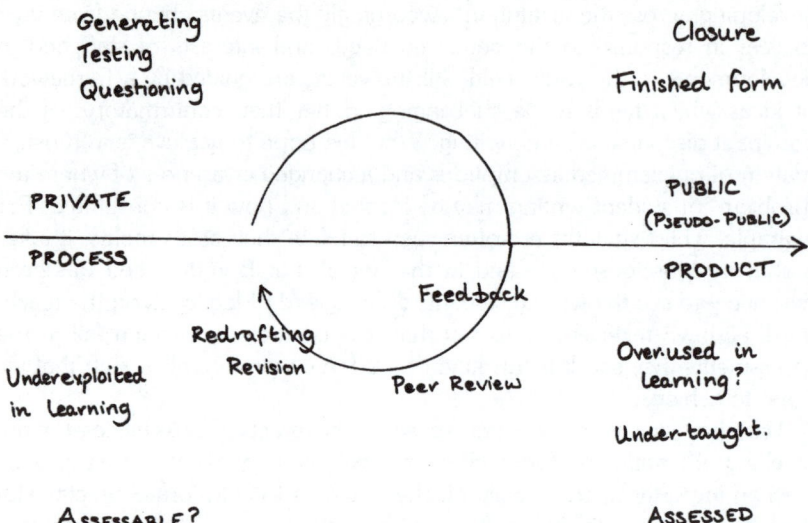

Figure 5.1 Hand-drawn slide of writing process/product continuum

adopting practices such as feedback, peer review and revision, to see the relationship as circular – a bad essay may, after all, be a good first draft.[9] Equally we comment that reflecting on the kinds of writing students might do as part of a learning process can lead to an expanded view of what constitutes a product, and so to diversified assessment.

An important vehicle for these ideas about writing is the notion of the 'writing-intensive' discipline-based course. Such a course employs writing right along, or right around, the continuum/circle we have described, so the aim is both 'writing to learn and learning to write' (Britton, 1982, p. 94). Writing is valued both as an epistemic *process* in which thinking and reflection develop – what Britton calls 'shaping at the point of utterance' (p. 98); and as a communicative *product*, structured in particular ways by particular conventions and forming particular, recognisable social functions. Different forms or genres of writing thus tend to be characterised by different functions and purposes, more personal and expressive on the one hand (journal or freewriting) and more publicly accountable – also slower to craft and develop – on the other (report or article). For the student, moving between personal and public disciplinary discourse may not be a straightforward transition. Art Young (2002) points out that the student needs to:

figure out how to write like an academic, or like a physicist or a political scientist, before actually becoming an academic or a physicist, that is, before knowing what a physicist knows and before acquiring the habits of mind and discourse conventions of physics that come with knowledge and experience in that discipline. Such a rhetorical situation sometimes leads students to 'fake' writing like an academic . . . . (p. 58)

The writing-intensive course provides what Young calls the 'middle ground' (p. 57) between personal and public discourses. This middle ground is the classroom environment, whether actual (face-to-face) or virtual (electronic). Here writing, perhaps in the form of notes, questions and emails, has a conversational function, which helps to build the classroom community as a place where active learning can occur. In the UK and particularly in higher education, classroom/seminar situations tend to be given over to the medium of talk, often teacher-directed and teacher-dominated (Mitchell, 1994, p. 194), and the idea of using writing to generate social and cognitive engagement has been greatly under-exploited. Mason and Washington (1992) comment that practical exercises in writing and reading can be 'far more valuable than the somewhat aimless discussions which often pass for work in seminar and group tutorials' (p. 73).

The change that developing 'middle ground pedagogy' (Young, 2002, p. 59) in writing can make is radical. Below is how a Queen Mary lecturer, Josep-Anton Fernandez, described the writing-intensive course he developed after attending the Cornell Consortium. His starting point is recognisably similar to the situation Gary Day describes, but whilst Day caricatures the problem and implies that as a subject lecturer he does not know how to address it, Fernandez concentrates on developing Young's 'middle ground pedagogy' and, as shown in the following interview extract, this gives a quite different orientation to the project of teaching:

My involvement in Writing in the Disciplines began from my frustration, which matched that of my students. My course on Catalan Culture covered interesting material in a structured way, but the students didn't seem to be learning what I was teaching. At least, their essays didn't show this. . . . I made a first attempt last year, adding a writing component to the course, but the results weren't so successful. A much better approach was to redesign the course with writing as an essential part. The writing and the content go together, they move along together. *What does this mean in practice?* A lot of different things! It means writing in the class – from warm-up exercises ('what do you want to find out today?') to analytical summaries – one sentence, one paragraph, one page. It means short homework assignments – say, a

300-word account of the seminar, to be shared in the next session. It means a writing journal. More formally, it means two 1000-word assignments, which count towards the final assessment – but here the crucial thing is that these will be discussed, self-assessed and peer reviewed and then re-written. . . . *And it must mean more marking?* Mmm, that's what you might expect. But the writing assignments do not all attract formal marks, and most are anyway very short. The aim is to get the students where they want as regards essays, and in the end I believe the process makes marking less onerous, because the graded course essays will be more focused, better presented, more clearly argued. . . . *And finally?* It's more fun for me and more fun for the students. You know they come thinking that it's a great chore to write an essay. It's certainly no fun to mark essays like that! . . . [w]e want [students] to enjoy intellectual activity, and do as well as they can. And I am certainly having an easier time – much less frustration! (Fernandez and Marsh, 2002, pp. 3–4)

Fernandez's comment about planning the course is significant. He began by adding more writing to an existing course but found that this did not allow him to exploit the potential of writing fully as a vehicle for learning. So the following year he redesigned his course from scratch, starting by inventing and sequencing short tasks that would engage the students in the kinds of flexible, creative and critical thinking and research he hoped for as learning outcomes. Figures 5.2 and 5.3 show two iterations of his planning process (each figure represents the first two weeks of a 12-week course). Figure 5.2 shows how Fernandez started with a relatively blank framework. Although he had a sense of what topics he wanted to cover and the order in which they might fall, he mainly made notes about what writing activities he might devise. Once he was clearer about how he wished to stage the students' learning – both in class and between classes – he selected texts he felt would work well with the writing tasks (Figure 5.3).

This method of teacher planning can represent a considerable challenge to what Bourdieu and Passeron describe as the 'duty' of higher education teachers and students 'to over-estimate the quantity of information that really circulates in pedagogic communication' (1990, p. 113). It is thus a challenge to conventional ways in which curricula are defined in terms of content to be covered and in many, though not all, disciplines, by the construction of 'the reading list'. But by orientating his thinking towards the quality of his students' learning – taking on board our adopted maxim that 'coverage is the greatest enemy of understanding' (Gardner, quoted in Biggs, 1999, p. 47) – Fernandez allowed this not to be a problem:

with in-built writing assignments, the course doesn't have time to cover the same amount of content. But this doesn't mean they learn less. In fact they learn more. They absorb more from the materials, and they respond better, raising questions with the texts, thinking critically. Eventually they will become independent learners.   (Fernandez and Marsh, 2002, pp. 3–4)

Catalan Culture: History, Language, Art

Week		Topic	Activity & task for next session	Deadlines
1	a	Introduction	Explain course objectives, assessment, and ground rules.	
			Reading: 'Culture', 'Nation' and 'Regional' from Raymond Williams, *Keywords*, and a short piece on Catalonia (perhaps from Sobré, *Catalonia: A Self-Portrait*). Task? *Porcel's autobiographical text?*	
	b	Seminar		
			Reading: . *'Remove what is not relevant'*	
2	a	Language politics		Give out essay title for Essay 1
			Reading: *H.W.: Summarise article*	
	b	Seminar	*Students in pairs compare their summaries then write together a shorter one.* Reading:	

© Josep-Anton Fernandez (2002)

Figure 5.2   Fernandez's first notes on planning a writing-intensive course

Week		Topic	Activity & Task for next session	Deadlines
1	a	Introduction	Explain course objectives, assessment, and ground rules.	
			Warm-up: define 'culture', 'region' and 'nation'. This is discussed with whole group. Then: rewrite these definitions as if conceived by a Scottish person.	
			Some basic facts about the Catalan Countries.	
			Reading: 'Culture', 'Nation' and 'Regional' from Raymond Williams, *Keywords*; Joan Estruch, 'The Social Construction of National Identities: The Case of Catalonia as a Nation in the Spanish State', in *State and Nation in Multi-Ethnic Societies*, ed. Uri Ra'anan, pp. 135–42.	
			HW1: Writing before reading: 'When is a culture a "minority culture"?' (300–400 words to be handed in – I want to see their level).	
			HW2: Read the articles provided. Make the first entry in your journal: Does the reading confirm your views? Has it challenged them in any way? Go back to the reading and mark any specific passages that have had such effect.	
	b	Seminar	Students write as many questions as they want (min. 2) about anything they wish to know regarding Catalonia – but their questions must be related in one way or another to the marked passages in the readings. Each question is written on the board and answered (wherever possible!) by JAF. Then students get in pairs and try to rewrite their original questions – from the point of view of the Catalan article's author (Joan Estruch).	
			Reading: Clare Mar-Molinero in Labanyi & Graham; John England, 'The Debate on the Languages of Spain: A *Diàlogo de sordos*?', *JHR*, 2 (1993–94), 289–96; Marc Leprêtre, *The Catalan Language Today*.	
			HW: 'Remove what is not relevant' in Mar-Molinero's article (summary as negative image). Journal: What did you learn in today's seminar? What do you think the point of this seminar was?	
2	a	Language politics	Start discussing exercise. Then: what would I most want to find out in this lecture?	Give out essay title for Essay 1
			Lecture: basic facts about Catalan sociolinguistics, legal framework, etc.; Spanish and French official policies re: peripheral languages; language and identity.	

© Josep-Anton Fernandez (2002)

Figure 5.3 Second iteration of Fernandez's plan for a writing-intensive course

▶ Going alternative in the mainstream

We believe that the kinds of thinking and practices we are developing at Queen Mary start to occupy the 'design' space for Academic Literacies work that Theresa Lillis talks about in Chapter 3 of this book. We begin working with subject staff by thinking about the 'socialisation' (Lea and Street, 1998) of students into writing and thinking practices valued by their disciplines, and ask questions about writing, written forms, writers and readers which suggest challenges and open up alternative possibilities. Writing comes to be seen not as a problem so much as usefully problematic.

Figure 5.4 contains questions addressed to staff which suggest how this movement from blueprinting to questioning and change might be encouraged.

---

1 What do you want students to learn about kinds of thinking in the discipline? What kinds of thinker would you like them to become?

- processes of enquiry, experimentation, observation, reading, analysis, argument . . .
- rigorous, logical, divergent, self-critical . . .

2 What do you want students to learn about the disciplinary ways in which thinking is expressed?

- individually, collaboratively
- aspects of genre, style, structure, references to authority, integration of quotations . . .

3 What do you want students to know about the written conventions of your discipline/department?

- presentation, referencing . . .

4 What kinds of writing would it be possible/desirable for your students to do?

- convergent with disciplinary norms
- challenging of/alternative to disciplinary norms

5 What kinds of writers would you like the students to be? People who:

- effectively communicate information/a point of view
- carefully structure an argument/analysis
- are recognisable members of the discipline
- can respond flexibly to different rhetorical demands
- enjoy writing; learn from it
- use writing to explore the possibilities in an idea
- make connections between different areas of their learning, including personal experience
- generate questions . . .

Figure 5.4   Questions for staff about student writing

The questions develop from a focus on existing conceptualisations of how writing relates to thinking in the disciplines.

The first three questions address values and expectations. Explicitness in these areas is rarely straightforward or fully realisable. Staff may agree, for example, that 'argument' is an objective but what they mean by this term may not lend itself to further clarification or may turn out to be quite different from a colleague's definition.[10] Nonetheless, the process of scrutiny is valuable. 'Essay' is another such term. In some disciplinary areas it is a catch-all term for any text written as prose; in others, it connotes argument and the making of a case. Perhaps most pervasively, the term 'essay' refers simply to an assessed outcome, a shapeless empty vessel that will catch the student's learning whatever and however he or she has been taught. The essay, as Peter Womack suggests, assumes a kind of naturalness in an educational setting, 'as if intellectual activity produced essays the way a tree produces leaves' (Womack, 1993, pp. 42–3). Ask what an essay is, and the answer is often none too clear, though the question, we have discovered, can be a productive one.

Around question 4, further questions arise: 'What is the relation between the way you have always asked students to write and the disciplinary thinking you value? Is the connection a necessary one?' Asking these questions can again begin to expose the peculiarly 'schooled' nature of a form like the essay – not written to persuade, but to persuade that you can persuade (Womack, 1993) – or the 'experimental lab report' written on an experiment or demonstration for which the results are already known. They can also reveal more diversity in existing practices – and therefore more potential for further increasing diversity – than short-hand use of terms like 'Academic Writing', 'reports' and 'essays' suggest.

An Engineering colleague, Julia Shelton, frustrated at students' switching between active and passive constructions in their writing, and prompted by our questions, began to explore issues of equivalence and non-equivalence between disciplinary writing (such as academics might do themselves) and 'school' writing (which masquerades as disciplinary writing but is written for the purpose of monitoring and assessment). She recognised confusion between her department's desire to monitor students' educational process (in an active narrative mode) and its ambition to equip them to produce effective technical writing for a 'professional academic audience'. The students' writing problems stemmed in part, she realised, from the 'fallibility' (to invert Bourdieu and Passeron's term) of the department's pedagogic understanding; her first move was to change the assessment task, replacing an existing hybrid 'report' with two writing goals, each more clearly defined in terms of audience and purpose.

Tackling the kinds of questions suggested here can focus staff interest on further options for writing, beyond the binaries of expert and novice and of 'real' disciplinary writing versus 'unreal' 'school' versions of such writing. It can open up the area of 'writing for learning'; writing, that is, which seeks to engage the student in the curriculum rather than to reproduce an already blueprinted written form. So, for example, when Fernandez wanted his students to argue between two distinct but related courses of action he set a dialogue rather than an essay – a challenging task which was then extended by collaborative work to turn the dialogic text into a monologic one, whilst retaining the argument (Mitchell, 1994, pp. 167–79; Andrews, 1995, 2003). Other writing developed in this category includes the short write-to-learn tasks in Professor Wilfrid Hodges' Mathematical Logic course:

> Your local newspaper runs a column answering readers' questions. A reader has written in with the following question: 'When we look at ourselves in a mirror, why do we see ourselves with right and left reversed but not upside down?' The newspaper invites you to write the answer for them. Use at most 200 words.   (Hodges, 2004)

Also, on Catherine Maxwell's Nineteenth-Century Aesthetic Prose course, an 'intellectually-based writing journal' is supplemented by short creative exercises imitative of the prose writers' styles (Maxwell, 2004). Because these forms of writing have been chosen with learning as a primary objective, they are diverse and inventive, even where an eventual goal may be, as in Fernandez's case, for the students to produce an essay text. Staff are generally happy to allow these forms of writing to count for assessment purposes, with some drawing on the notion of the 'patchwork text'[11] as a way of pulling the learning experience together.

Diverse forms of writing may also – see question 5 – allow for, and value, greater expression and development of the student as a person and a writer. Thus Maxwell found that the journal form allowed students to experiment with register and voice and to make more connections across sections of the course than they may have done working within the stranglehold of the conventional essay. As a result, she discovered more about her students as thinkers and writers – and took pleasure in doing so.

The experience of pleasure is interesting. What both the diversification of writing practices and the closer attention to students' writing appear to do is to change the communicative relation between teacher and student. The teacher who consciously sets up opportunities for writing and pays attention to its purpose and value moves into a closer engagement with the learner. Work in writing-intensive courses on revision and redrafting further develops this differently-attentive relationship – the teaching imperative shifts from the transmission of subject expertise to encouragement and crafting of students' active response to the subject: their construction of knowledge. Students as a result, it seems, become more capable of positively surprising their teachers, and bringing about disruption to the established pattern of communication (evident in Gary Day's piece) in which, as Bourdieu and Passeron again find a way of putting it, 'all the wit and wisdom go from teachers to students and all the dullness and crudity from students to teachers' (p. 112).

▶ Conclusion: aiming for recognition

Jonathan Monroe (2003a) at Cornell University insists that if Writing in the Disciplines work is to be sustained and embedded within an institution, then high-level support is essential:

> Where the most profound institutional changes have occurred, the involvement of higher-level administrators (associate dean and above) in redesigning and restructuring the role of writing in undergraduate education has been crucial. As the most effective of these administrators have understood, implementation of a WID-based approach depends first and foremost on ongoing campus-wide faculty commitment and dialogue. (p. 5)

Although our WID initiative at Queen Mary has had good, and increasing, take-up at a 'grass roots' level, we have until recently been unsure of top–down support. Exchanges with senior management suggested that the initiative was thought of as a narrowly focused, time-limited project whose concerns were peripheral and whose success at the departmental level, though pleasing, was surprising. The situation is shifting all the time, however, and the post of Thinking Writing Co-ordinator was recently made permanent. This feels like a considerable boost. It enables us to plan further ahead, to embrace new opportunities and ideas, to assure participating departments of continued support, and to encourage others to find out about the growing body of practice across the university.

Whether the permanent post signals the kind of senior management commitment that Monroe describes remains to be seen, however. Queen Mary is fairly typical of 'old' universities in the UK,[12] as it places highest value on academic scholarship and research as visible measures of its identity and status. Questions and policies relating to its role as a teaching establishment tend to be less owned and less integral to the institution's sense of itself. Like other similar institutions, Queen Mary responds strategically to government requirements relating to its educational mission – promoting, for example, e-learning, personal development profiling, key and employability skills to its academic departments – but is reluctant, as Rowland (2004) puts it, 'to lead [its] own development' in matters educational. So it is one thing to maintain a single part-time post but would be quite another for senior managers to advocate actively the use and support of writing to its academic departments and to set up policies and structures by which this aim could be promoted. It is this level of commitment that we will continue to work for. We need to argue that the work we are undertaking on writing, by going to the heart of disciplinary thinking, has the potential to bridge the gap between the research institution's principal self-image as a creator of new thinking and knowledge and its reluctance to invest seriously in questions of pedagogy. By drawing attention to the role of writing in developing, representing and communicating disciplinary thinking, we need to show how the 'problem' of writing in fact represents one of the highest intellectual challenges for both teachers and students. The measure of success will be not only improved student experiences of learning to write in the disciplines, but the greater visibility of writing in the university's representation of itself as an educational institution.

In addition to this work on our home territory, we need to disseminate our thinking and practice on the national higher education scene. The same is true for much of the excellent work on writing that is developing in the UK; it is time to move beyond the margins to which 'writing' as a topic is traditionally confined and to inform and engage those who make the policies to which the universities must respond.

NOTES

1   This view of writing corresponds to the 'study skills' model described by Lea and Street (1998).

2   Also see Lea and Street (1998), Jones et al. (1999), Lea and Stierer (2000) and Lillis (2001).

3   The *Times Higher Education Supplement* is the UK's leading higher education weekly newspaper.

4   See www.arts.cornell.edu/knight_institute/ for more information on the John S. Knight Institute for Writing in the Disciplines at Cornell University.

5   See Russell (2002, p. 6), on the culture of complaint about student writing.

6   We made use, in particular, of the following WAC and WID resources: Bazerman and Russell (1994), Bean (2001), Gottschalk and Hjortshoj (2004) and http://wac.colostate.edu/index.cfm

7   The idea of secondments came from a scheme run by Education and Professional Development at University College, London. We applied to the Westfield Trust, a source of funding internal to Queen Mary, which supports enhancements to the learning environment, and were awarded £16,000 in 2003–4 and a further £12,000 in 2004–5. We invited departments and individuals to bid for funds of

up to £4000 primarily to buy staff out of teaching and administrative commitments, but also to buy-in development assistance, though not teaching, from postgraduate students and to fund visits to conferences. Before funds are released, a short contract is drawn up between the department and the Thinking Writing project that specifies objectives, timescale, expected support from Sally Mitchell and a commitment to dissemination of some kind.

8 The 'Thinking Writing' website received a subsidy from the Learning and Teaching Subject Network (LTSN) Generic Centre (www.ltsn.ac.uk/) and was developed in partnership with Queen Mary's department of Education and Staff Development.

9 This pithy comment was made by John Bean at the first European Association of Teachers of Academic Writing (EATAW) conference in 2001.

10 See Giltrow and Valiquette (1994), Giltrow (2000), Freedman (1993) and Gonzalez Arnal and Burwood (2003).

11 Richard Winter, Professor of Education at Anglia Ruskin University, developed the notion of the 'Patchwork Text' to improve student-writers' engagement, ownership and learning. Winter et al. (2003) is a special issue of the journal *Innovations in Education and Teaching International* containing accounts of the patchwork text in practice.

12 See Chapters 1 and 7 of this volume for a discussion of 'old' and 'new' universities.

6 Teaching Writing within a Discipline: the Speak–Write Project

Tory Young and Simon Avery

▶ Introduction

In 1997 the English Department of Anglia Ruskin University, Cambridge,[1] established the Speak–Write Project, an educational research and development project designed to improve the written and oral communication skills of first-year undergraduates studying on degree programmes in the discipline of English. The Project has been highly commended by other academics working within the subject area[2] and has resulted in the publication of five books[3] based on its progressive approaches to the teaching of advanced skills in writing and speaking.

This chapter details the history and work of the Speak–Write Project through its two main phases: the first, three-year, phase from 1997 to 2000, which resulted in the development of the undergraduate modules that are the Project's main focus as well as the publication of the first four books; and the second phase, from 2000 to the present, which has resulted in a curriculum consultancy and continued research into the teaching of writing, both within the disciplines and as a degree subject in itself. This chapter explores the educational and political contexts for the Project, assesses the Project's impact, and explains how the Project Team's views on 'embedding' writing instruction have evolved in response to Writing in the Disciplines research and to theoretical developments in writing pedagogy in the UK.

▶ Contexts for the Speak–Write Project

The Speak–Write Project originally developed from an increasing perception among members of staff in Anglia Ruskin's English Department and across the higher education sector generally that the written and oral communication skills of undergraduates needed strengthening. Indeed, these were views which were also being frequently rehearsed in the press and by employers with reports that many graduates' understanding of grammar and punctuation was not as strong as it once was, that graduates were not always able to construct a coherent and logical argument, and that they were often unable to give an effective oral presentation.[4]

Believing that it could go some way to finding creative solutions to these perceived deficiencies, Anglia Ruskin's English Department bid for and won funding from the Higher Education Funding Council for England (HEFCE) under its Fund for the Development of Teaching and Learning (FDTL) in order to develop modules which would help first-year undergraduates studying for English degrees to acquire advanced-level communication skills. This emphasis on *advanced*-level skills for native speakers was imperative from the start of the Project – the work is not concerned with 'remedial' English or teaching English as a foreign language – and the Project Team specifically sought to integrate the teaching of these skills into disciplinary study, thereby promoting acquisition by all students.[5]

At this time the skills agenda was becoming increasingly – and often vehemently – vocalised in educational and political arenas. In 1997, Lord Dearing published his long-anticipated report on higher education, *Higher Education in the Learning Society*, part of which highlights the importance of skills acquisition in higher education programmes and argues that institutions need to be explicit about the skills developed as part of any specific programme (NCIHE, Sections 9.17, 9.21). The teaching, learning and assessment of such skills, the Report suggests, is fundamental to the concept of lifelong learning advocated by Dearing's committee. These recommendations subsequently altered the ways in which institutions described their courses, to include learning outcomes and 'transferable', 'key' or 'graduate' skills as well as subject content.

In December 1997, the Council for College and University English (CCUE), the subject association for the study of English in higher education, made an initial response to Dearing's recommendations in its report, *The English Curriculum: Diversity and Standards*, published by the Quality Assurance Agency for Higher Education (QAA). This report argued that there already existed among the subject community 'significant agreement on the definition of core skills and threshold standards expected of English undergraduates' (Council, 1997, p. 1) and documented those skills which are essential to the successful study of the subject as being:

> knowledge of the canon of English literature, a knowledge of the historical, intellectual and cultural contexts of literature, theoretical approaches and subject methodologies, presentational skills, oral communication skills, writing skills, powers of independent learning, flexibility of mind, a capacity for self-reflection, conceptual grasp, analytical skills, critical reasoning and the ability to engage in discussion of ethical and other human values.   (p. 3)

Three years later, the centrality of these skills to the study of degree-level English was reiterated by their inclusion and amplification in the *English Benchmarking Document* (Quality, 2000), which lists fourteen generic and graduate skills that graduates in English should possess, including:

- the ability to present sustained and persuasive written and oral arguments cogently and coherently;
- the capacity to analyse and critically examine diverse forms of discourse;
- competence in the planning and execution of essays and project-work;
- the ability to handle information and argument in a critical and self-reflective manner;
- skills in critical reasoning. (Section 3.3)

It was within the context of these public debates and government policies regarding the learning and teaching of skills, then, that the Speak–Write Project was established and developed during its initial stages of research, design and dissemination.

▶ The preliminary research

The first phase of the Speak–Write Project's work was founded upon research into the ways in which written and oral communication skills were then being taught and assessed within English degree programmes at a range of educational institutions across the country. The Project Team – Simon Avery (Researcher), Cordelia Bryan (Project Leader) and Rebecca Stott (Course Designer) – were particularly interested in how academics perceived the problems of students' communication skills, what training students were provided with, and how skills were being developed and tested, so that this wider perspective could then inform the design of the proposed new modules at Anglia Ruskin. During the academic year 1997–8, therefore, Simon Avery and Cordelia Bryan conducted a series of interviews with teaching staff at the universities of York, Leeds, Nottingham, Middlesex, Oxford Brookes and Sheffield Hallam, as well as with staff in secondary schools, sixth-form colleges and Further Education colleges. Over 200 first-year undergraduates in Anglia Ruskin's own English Department also completed a questionnaire on language and communication skills so that the Project Team could assess how students themselves felt about their capacities and needs as academic writers.[6]

In general, it was felt by staff and students alike that there was a clear need for greater facilitation of writing and communication skills development. Nearly all staff interviewed felt that standards of writing ability had declined somewhat across all sectors, and that particular problems were to be found in the areas of argument construction, paragraphing, and choice of appropriate register and diction, as well as syntax, punctuation, sentence construction and the mechanics of spelling, hyphenation, use of the apostrophe and correct formatting for quotations. Interviewees pointed to the wider range of students now entering higher education and the resulting wider range of ability as one reason for this perceived decline – a range which is set to increase to fulfil the government policy aim of encouraging 50 per cent of school-leavers into university (Department for Education and Skills, 2003, pp. 57, 59) – as well as factors such as the syllabus pressures engendered by the National Curriculum and league tables in schools, and the need for university students to work in order to fund themselves through their degree programmes, thereby restricting the time they can spend on traditional forms of academic reading and writing. Moreover, all staff emphasised the need to encourage students to reflect *actively* on their learning and progress as part of the development process. Overall, then, the findings confirmed many of our own views about students' abilities and requirements, and particularly the need for a pedagogical model which would enable students to develop communication skills effectively and comprehensively.

▶ Developing the Speak–Write model

As the Dearing Report makes explicit, there are two key means of delivering graduate-skills training: first, 'by embedding . . . in existing programmes as a vehicle for development', and secondly, 'by creating parallel modules of "skills development"' (NCIHE, 1997, Section 9.22). Drawing upon an investigation conducted by the Open University where both approaches were assessed and evaluated (Hodginson, 1996), the Report committee summarised the advantages and disadvantages of the differing models. Whilst the parallel model – where skills are taught in generic modules additional to degree courses – involved limited initial costs, it was thought to have minimum impact on the overall programme since many students would elect not to take such provision. In contrast, the embedded model, whilst having high initial costs for the training of subject tutors and redesign of the curriculum, would have a maximum impact on the programme since all students would be required to undertake skills-related activities (NCIHE, 1997, Section 9.23). Like the Dearing committee, the Speak–Write Team believed that teaching writing is both far more effective and perceived as far more relevant by students when conducted within a subject-specific environment rather than through separate skills modules, which threaten to be overly generic and pose a danger of reducing skills acquisition to the lowest common denominator. The following discussion of the programme we developed therefore demonstrates our interpretation of how this concept of embedding writing instruction into the curriculum could best be put into practice.

The main focus of the Speak–Write Project's work during the period 1997–9 was the development of two semester-long modules originally entitled *Varieties of Speaking and Writing I* and *II*, which focus on the acquisition and development of advanced communication skills within the discipline of English studies.[7] The two modules, later re-named *Introduction to Critical Argument* and *Introduction to Writing*, became central to Anglia Ruskin's English degree in 1998. They stretch across the whole of the first year of the programme and are compulsory for *all* English undergraduates, whether taking single or combined honours, since the skills acquired are crucial not only for successful academic study but also for future employment. The modules aim to develop students' abilities and competencies in four key areas:

- grammar and language awareness (first half of semester A);
- stylistic analysis and writing/re-writing (second half of semester A);
- oral presentation skills and effective seminar participation (first half of semester B);
- effective essay writing (second half of semester B).

Given the wide range of student backgrounds, abilities and qualifications on entry – an increasingly common range in the higher education marketplace and particularly in the post-1992 university sector – it was important to develop a model of learning and teaching and a mode of delivery which would enable all students to progress effectively and with confidence and motivation throughout the four sections of the programme. To this end, the Project Team abandoned the traditional lecture/seminar format which was the fundamental structure of most modules across the English curriculum, and, drawing upon both staff experience and the insights of published research,[8] replaced it with a practical, 'hands-on', weekly two-hour workshop where students work in small groups of five or six on a variety of tasks and exercises. This emphasis on small-group work effectively shifts the focus away from the conventional teacher-led approach – what Graham Gibbs terms 'closed teaching' where learning outcomes are all but completely defined by the teacher (Gibbs, 1992, p. 6) – and redefines the teacher's role as one of facilitator. Within this environment, students are encouraged to work both independently and collaboratively, pooling their ideas in a pro-active manner so that there is greater potential for the learning experience to become one of transformation. Certainly this student-centred approach – which was well received by both the first and subsequent cohorts of students on the modules[9] – encourages a more *holistic* mode of learning where students build connections between the pieces of information they assimilate and the skills they develop, thereby allowing them to achieve greater understanding, higher levels of motivation and potentially higher grades. Indeed, as Paul Ramsden argues, '[t]he supreme purpose of small group work is to encourage students to confront different conceptions and to practice making sense *for themselves*' (Ramsden, 1992, p. 168; emphasis added).

The pedagogical model which underpins each week's work subsequently amalgamates analysis with practice. First, students are given the fundamental information about a topic – on register, for example, or complex sentence structures or the ways of achieving an effective conclusion to an essay – which is explained in language which is accessible and user-friendly, although without reducing the complexity of the issues raised. Secondly, they undertake a number of exercises in analysis where they examine particular texts in relation to the ideas they have been reading and discussing. Then thirdly, they reinforce their understanding by working with the ideas themselves through structured exercises or a piece of their own writing. In the first week of the stylistic analysis and writing/re-writing section, for example, students learn about the effects of different personal and house styles and then analyse these in relation to a variety of texts, before writing their own piece in the house style of a guidebook or particular magazine. In each week's work, therefore, there is a movement from structured, more formal exercises to freer, more creative tasks, an approach which has proved both popular and effective with Anglia Ruskin's students. Moreover, by incorporating a wide range of exercises of varying complexity and difficulty, students can move forward at their own pace and build up their skills regardless of the level of ability with which they enter the course.

Additionally, the course offers students the opportunity to explore a wide range of written and spoken texts from different historical periods and cultures. Many of these are literary texts – as might be expected from a course designed for English undergraduates. However, students also examine different forms and styles, such as critical essays, children's fiction, political speeches, business writings, advertising and personal letters, in order to explore, for example, the relevance of different registers, the employment of rhetorical structures, or the exploitation of diction and sentence structures. Both contemporary cultural phenomena and established literary works, therefore, offer ways of appreciating different styles and modes of writing within different contexts and with reference to different audiences.

Teaching and learning grammar and language awareness

The first module starts with a six-week block on grammar and language awareness, which helps students gain an understanding of the underlying principles of language use and serves as a foundation for subsequent work on stylistic analysis and academic writing skills. A crucial problem in designing this part of the course, however, was how best to engage students in the theoretical material and terminology required whilst simultaneously overcoming dominant perceptions that the study of grammar is abstract, intimidating and tending to 'prescriptivism' (Crystal, 1995, p. 194).

In keeping with the pedagogical model of the course overall, then, the course designers sought to produce material which is both informative and engaging by emphasising the study of grammar *in use* and demonstrating how grammar is essential to effective communication in a wide range of contexts – in journalism and advertising as well as in more literary texts. Students therefore explore the forms and functions of different sentence types (simple, compound, complex, compound–complex), phrase constructions, word classes and issues of punctuation, acquiring the necessary terminology and skills of analysis before applying this understanding to their own work. For example, in week two, students learn about the internal structures of clauses – including verb elements, subject elements, direct and indirect objects, subject and object complements – and analyse these in a variety of passages. In week six, they are introduced to a range of strategies for achieving organisational coherence and cohesion in paragraphs, before analysing these in extracts from literary works, and then working with them in their own writings. As a final task, which encourages reflection upon their engagement with the material, the students are asked to write a short commentary which discusses the choices they made in their writing and any problems they encountered in undertaking the task. Throughout this section of the course, therefore, students are encouraged to explore and investigate grammar not abstractly and divorced from practice but as it is used in the living language and in a variety of contexts and formats, an approach which aims to achieve, as J. B. Biggs and K. F. Collis suggest in their analysis of the relations between teaching approaches and learning outcomes (1982), greater student engagement and understanding, and a more holistic grasp of subject matter.

Teaching and learning stylistic analysis and writing/re-writing

In the second part of the module students build upon what they have learnt in the section on grammar and language awareness by focusing upon the development of their skills in stylistic analysis. Again, the fundamental objective is to raise awareness about techniques of writing and therefore to assist students in the development of their own writing abilities. By analysing the *processes* of writing in a range of literary and non-literary texts, therefore, students are able to learn from established practitioners and understand how a range of principles for effective prose writing can be relevant to a variety of forms and contexts.

Students begin this section of the course by considering what style is and by learning about stylistic elements such as diction, sentence structure, word order, rhythm, sound and rhetorical devices. They then analyse style as a means of understanding the processes of effective writing and explore the intricate relations between style choice and rhetorical purpose. In examining the conversational style of a section of Lawrence Sterne's *Tristram Shandy* or the account of the same political event as it is recorded in different newspapers, for example, students learn that writers need to be flexible in choosing diction and an appropriate register and in adapting their work for a specific target audience.

Once students have gained this understanding, they then work on the techniques of writing in a strong, clear style. The emphasis here is on clarity, immediacy and accessibility, and on a range of strategies for avoiding convoluted, impenetrable prose. This section of the module emphasises that clear English is not basic or juvenile English but can be used to convey complex ideas with accuracy and subtlety. It is an approach that will be beneficial not only to the construction of a clear line of argument in students' academic essays, but also in drawing up business reports and other documentation they might encounter in future employment.

During the remainder of Module One, students examine more complex styles with an emphasis on techniques for making their own writing fresher, more original and more engaging, and maintaining clarity whilst employing more demanding vocabulary and grammatical structures. They pay attention to the problems associated with cliché and 'purple prose', for example, and explore a range of techniques for increasing impact, conciseness and accessibility through processes of redrafting. Attention is also paid to the effects of *rhythm* in prose, so that by the end of the first semester students will have gained greater subtlety and awareness in both their skills of analysis and their skills of writing and composition across a variety of formats and contexts.

Teaching and learning essay/academic writing

The second module of Anglia Ruskin's first-year course focuses on oral presentation and essay/academic writing. Thus, the study of essay writing follows on directly from a six-week section where students have learnt to give an effective oral presentation with an emphasis upon the use of rhetoric as a method by which a case can be made persuasively and structured effectively. As with the earlier sections, the development of oral communication skills is promoted through a combination of analysis and practice so that students study, for example, the rhetorical effects in dramatic speeches from Shakespeare or current political speeches, and examine the importance of selection and ordering of appropriate evidence, word choice, register and sound patterning.

When they embark on the specific essay-writing section of the course, then, students are able to appreciate how many of the skills they have used in building an effective oral presentation also apply to an effective *written* presentation. They explore the need for careful structuring, a strong argument and purposeful selection of evidence within written academic work, as well as the importance of a suitable register, objectivity in tone, cautiousness in making claims and a heightened awareness of the target audience. Again, a wide variety of examples is used for analysis, including essays by literary critics and sample student essays, and attention is paid to the effective construction of paragraphs, the importance of strong introductions and conclusions, and a range of editing strategies. The students are also encouraged to analyse their own written work and assignment questions as part of the emphasis upon relating the study to their own practice. This final work on essay/academic writing, by consolidating many of the previous approaches and issues raised with regards to other forms of writing, therefore provides an extremely strong foundation for the development and enhancement of students' writing at higher levels of study.

Evaluation

In placing *Introduction to Critical Argument* and *Introduction to Writing* as the core, compulsory modules of the level-one provision, Anglia Ruskin's English Department believes that the development of advanced-level communication skills is crucial to effective work at higher education level. Through the workshop model of analysis and practice the modules aim to move students away from a 'surface' learning approach to writing development towards a 'deeper', more reflective and potentially transformative approach (Ramsden, 1992, p. 46). Indeed, this idea of student self-reflection lies at the very heart of the course in the use of journal-workbooks, in which students record their progress in writing competencies through the inclusion of drafts, completed work and commentaries on what they have achieved and where they feel they still need to do more work. Further student autonomy in assessing development in writing is provided by the encouragement of peer feedback and assessment amongst the student group as they are asked to read each other's work, comment upon it, grade it using a set of established criteria, and justify that grading. Certainly, in its predominant reliance on formative assessment methods, the course foregrounds what the Assessment Reform Group has aptly termed 'assessment *for* learning' rather than the potentially more judgemental 'assessment *of* learning' associated with summative assessment (Assessment, 1999, p. 3).

Questionnaires and focus groups conducted with several cohorts of Anglia Ruskin students who have taken the modules reveal that the majority of students enjoy the course and feel that it substantially improves both their writing and their analytic abilities (Speak–Write, 1999).[9] The materials from the course – available in the first four Speak–Write books: *Grammar and Writing*, *Writing With Style*, *Speaking Your Mind* and *Making Your Case* – have been welcomed by many in the English subject community as a means of teaching advanced-level writing skills through disciplinary study – in Chapter 7, for example, Aled Ganobcsik-Williams relates using Speak–Write materials at the University of Derby – and they have subsequently become the foundation for the work undertaken in the second, 'continuation' phase of the Speak–Write Project.

▶ The Speak–Write Project, Phase 2

In 2000, Tory Young was appointed as Curriculum Consultant and Co-Director of the Speak–Write Project with Rebecca Stott. The first aim of the Speak–Write team upon completion of the initial research phase was to circulate its findings and innovative teaching materials to the wider English subject community. HEFCE's FDTL granted funds for one year's dissemination, and the resulting curriculum consultancy initiative then gained continuation funding first from the Royal Literary Fund (RLF) for two years and then from the English Subject Centre until December 2003.

The RLF and European Social Funds also enabled a writer, Vicky Williamson, to join the team to carry out a new research project focusing on the kinds of writing humanities graduates undertook in writing-intensive professions (Young, 2004). This research was used to develop a module on *Professional Writing*, materials from which will also be published as a book in the Speak–Write series by Longman. Student interest in writing modules at Anglia Ruskin continued to increase and in 2004 resulted in the development of a Combined Honours Writing degree pathway containing both Creative and Professional Writing modules. A Single Honours Degree in Writing was launched in 2006.

While the Speak–Write Project's research was expanding into workplace writing and the Writing pathway was being developed, Tory Young was carrying out the Project's aim of disseminating findings and teaching materials to the wider subject community. She was invited by colleagues in English departments from across the country and the sector to give presentations on the work of the Project and to tailor materials to suit existing modules and curricula. One department she worked closely with was English and Drama at Queen Mary, University of London, and through this connection she was invited to attend the Cornell Consortium for Writing in the Disciplines (WID), described by Mitchell and Evison in Chapter 5 of this volume. Participation in the Cornell Consortium and Queen Mary's own programme of WID workshops brought a new perspective on embedding the teaching of writing within subject disciplines: the most effective method of improving the writing of all students is to teach writing as part of the disciplinary content in all modules. According to the WID perspective, a fully embedded model of writing instruction would be a degree programme consisting of writing-intensive subject courses. Learning from WID theory, Tory Young came to see that the Speak–Write model, as a separate set of writing and communication modules tailored to the discipline of English, does not comprise a fully embedded model of writing instruction.

At the same time, drawing upon both WID theory and Lea and Street's (1998) UK-based critique of models of writing provision, she became convinced of a different perspective on the idea of student writing as a 'problem'. In 2002 she invited Jonathan Monroe, Director of the John S. Knight Institute for Writing in the Disciplines at Cornell University, to Anglia Ruskin to lead a symposium on prioritising the teaching of writing as a way of learning, and indeed of shaping, a field of academic study. 'Writing to learn and not learning to write' became a useful formula to challenge the rhetoric – upon which the Speak–Write Project's work was originally premised – that links literacy with student failure and falling standards of student writing.

Committed to pursuing the concepts of fully embedded writing provision and the creation of an institutional culture in which student writing is viewed not as a problem but as a tool for learning, Tory Young continued in her role as the Project's writing consultant. Through this work she came to understand that setting up writing-intensive degree programmes is an impossible goal for lone figures – many of whom are in the position of disenfranchised practitioners – to effect without institutional support. Young's consultancy research further revealed that it is the financial and institutional constraints under which academics work that cause the most frustration for those who wish to revolutionise the method and the image of teaching writing in UK higher education.[10]

▶ Conclusion

It remains the main aim of the Speak–Write Project to continue to raise the profile of the teaching of writing within the English subject community and to model a successful way of teaching writing within an English degree course. As this chapter discusses, however, the consultancy phase of the Project has shown that for the Project's staff to work as WID consultants at

Anglia Ruskin or at other universities, support will be required at the institutional level. As the chapter also demonstrates, as a result of the Speak–Write Project at least one English department – that of Anglia Ruskin – has replaced the idea of student writing as a 'problem' with the concept of student writing as a legitimate subject for study at degree level. It is time, we feel, for institutional managers and government policy-makers to recognise and understand this paradigm shift and to enact higher education policies and funding structures that are supportive of student writing development.

NOTES

1 Anglia Ruskin University was formerly Anglia Polytechnic University (APU).
2 This commendation is evidenced, for example, in unpublished feedback from a range of subject specialists in 'old' and 'new' higher education institutions who were asked to judge the quality of the course materials during the design stage, and in the positive reaction to the Speak–Write approach from those institutions who have subsequently used the consultancy service (see the discussion of Phase 2, pp. 94–5).
3 Stott and Chapman (2001), Stott and Avery (2001), Stott, Young and Bryan (2001), Stott, Rylance and Snaith (2001) and Young, Price and Williamson (forthcoming 2007).
4 See Bryan (1998), and also the General Introduction to this volume for examples of such views.
5 The term 'advanced skills' needs clarification here. Drawing upon the Dearing Report (NCIHE, 1997) and publications by CCUE and QAA (see further explanation in the chapter), the Speak–Write Team defined 'advanced skills' as the development of high-level written and oral communication skills (including presentation skills), the ability to analyse effectively and systematically a range of complex text types, and the ability to engage in critical reasoning and practices of self-reflection.
6 A full report on the interview findings is available in Bryan (1998). The staff interview questionnaire is reprinted in Avery (1998, pp. 41–3).
7 The two modules were initially designed by Rebecca Stott and Peter Chapman of Anglia Ruskin's English Department.
8 See, for example, Brown and Atkins (1988, pp. 50–90) and Ramsden (1992, pp. 1–119).
9 Unpublished research data derived from student questionnaires and focus groups contains evidence for this positive reception.
10 A fundamental institutional constraint is illustrated by the following comparison: drafting and revising student essays and the opportunity to write without being assessed are key to writing-intensive modules at Cornell. However, at Anglia Ruskin as at many other UK institutions, academic staff are discouraged from reading drafts of student writing because the requirement of student parity of experience means that doing so can be problematic. The exception to this practice occurs in Creative Writing modules, where drafting and revision is an

accepted process. This division between 'Creative' and 'Academic' writing is perplexing: it perpetuates the paradigm that marries critical writing with grammar and creative writing with 'self-expression'. It is also difficult to reconcile with much linguistic and literary theory of the twentieth century, which places in question the basis of such a distinction as well as the neutrality of academic writing. It is one of the ways – to paraphrase Deborah Brandt – that dutiful writing can be taught and instilled whilst its latent powers are constricted and controlled (Brandt, 2001, p. 148).

7 Building an Academic Writing Programme from within a Discipline

Aled Ganobcsik-Williams

▶ Introduction

This chapter describes the establishment of an undergraduate writing provision in the English department at the University of Derby. Academic Writing instruction and support began in 2003 in reaction to concerns voiced by successive external examiners regarding the poor writing skills characteristic of the weaker students in the English programme. As the University does not have an institution-wide writing programme, the onus was on the English teaching team, of which I am a member, to respond to the criticism of the quality of its graduates by researching, designing and delivering writing instruction from within the discipline. The University's administration has been supportive of our endeavour to develop the Academic Writing component of our degree, in part, as I shall explain, because the English department's desire to improve students' academic performance by addressing their writing skills is coterminous with the administration's priorities, themselves a reflection of national governmental agendas.

I believe the example of the English department at the University of Derby will be of interest to similarly resourced departments and programmes, showing what can be done with institutional support and the commitment of the teaching staff to writing pedagogy. While it is too early to judge definitively the success of the writing tuition, positive feedback from students and encouraging comments by external examiners are early indicators that the 'in-house' approach is proving to be an effective method of teaching writing in the discipline. We have been able to tailor writing instruction to the particular needs of our students and have been able to ensure a degree of coherence to what has been an evolving provision. Moreover, I will suggest that building a writing programme from the bottom up – effectively making writing support an issue of professional development for teaching staff – has benefited the degree programme as a whole, and not just the lowest-achieving students. The work of researching, designing and delivering writing support has had positive knock-on effects in terms of staff development and has also enriched the entire programme. This chapter will detail this model of writing support and then discuss some unresolved problems and tensions with the approach we have adopted.

▶ Institutional context

The nature of higher education in the UK has changed fundamentally over the past two decades. At the same time as participation has both increased and widened – with students now entering higher education with very different levels of prior attainment and preparedness for study – there has been a demand that universities provide evidence of teaching quality in the form of measurable educational outcomes. Ron Barnett (1994) usefully characterises these changes as symptoms of a more general change in the relationship between higher education institutions and society, a change he describes as the 'incorporation' of the university into society at large. The university, Barnett argues, from being relatively autonomous of wider societal ideologies, has had increasingly to adopt the values and vocabularies of 'the mainstream of society' (pp. 3–4). Hence, in discourses on and of higher education, references to terms such as 'value added', 'outcomes', 'efficiency' and 'competence' testify to the university's assimilation of the attitudes and frames of reference of the economic state (pp. 3–4, 157–8). Barnett's conceptualisation of the transformation in higher education is convincing because it explains some of the broad trends in UK government higher education policy since the mid-1980s, including the making of higher education more accessible, more accountable and more socially and economically relevant. These trends, in turn, may explain the emphasis on the teaching of skills in higher education, an emphasis evident in public discourse on higher education from (at the latest) 1980 onward (Drew, 1998, pp. 7–10).[1]

The University of Derby, for example, a post-1992 'new' university, can justly claim to have made widening access and societal contribution (in the sense of preparing students to contribute to the world outside the academy) two of its institutional priorities.[2] With respect to widening participation, the University's *Corporate Planning Statement* of July 2003 refers several times to the institution's dedication to the principles of open access (University of Derby, 2003, p. 1) and makes clear that the University targets for recruitment precisely those students traditionally excluded from higher education: 'The University has identified improving *access* for students and the *retention* of students from across the full spectrum of socio-economic groups as its top priority. It particularly wishes to attract the students with learning potential who may not have intended to give any consideration to further learning after leaving school' (p. 3) (emphasis in the original). The

Corporate Planning Statement also acknowledges more than once that 'the improved retention of students is . . . a vital corollary of widening participation' (p. 3). This emphasis on retention appears to anticipate that many of the students the institution recruits may not be adequately prepared on entry for the demands of university study. This implied admission obliges the institution to provide a high level of student support, which it makes available by offering academic skills modules and special needs assistance, for instance.

The University's commitment both to improving access and to enhancing the relevance of the degree is evinced by a new Skills Framework approved by its Academic Board for implementation in all academic programmes from September 2006. The Skills Framework is designed to assist academic departments to identify a range of key, academic and employability skills within their curricula and to help them draw up a strategy for teaching and assessing those skills, thereby ensuring a consistent approach to student skills development within the institution.[3] There are two fundamental purposes of the Skills Framework for teaching: to help students in the transition from school to higher education study and to facilitate their progression through the degree programme. In addition, the teaching of transferable skills is intended to enhance the employability of all graduates by making explicit to both students and employers the skills and competences acquired during the course of a degree.

The national skills movement, as already intimated, has helped to frame education policy for at least two decades. Although this policy is sometimes viewed as educationally reductive in focusing unremittingly on transferable and employment-related skills, the way in which the skills agenda is being implemented at the University of Derby will, I believe, have a positive impact in assisting students' adaptation to their new learning environment. More narrowly, it could be argued that the focus on skills in higher education has been conducive to the development of the English department's Academic Writing provision. Specifically, by framing Academic Writing in terms of the development of key skills – such as written communication, or information and communication technology (ICT) – that help the retention and employability of students, the English team has been able to bid for internal funding from the University's student retention and e-learning budgets. These monies, not explicitly ear-marked for writing development, have been used to release staff from teaching responsibilities and this has allowed time to research and develop the writing component in the English curriculum. Thus, although there is not a great deal of extra money available at the University, within the current national context of funding for higher education the administration has been supportive of our efforts to establish an Academic Writing component to the English degree.

▶ Building writing support

As mentioned in the previous section, the University of Derby offers academic study skills modules. Nevertheless, this generalist provision is not enough on its own to guarantee an acceptable, degree-level, standard of writing competence – at least in the view of the English programme's external examiners prior to 2002. My purpose here is not to make an argument about the relative efficacy of the 'skills' approach to teaching writing. As other contributors to this volume suggest, it may be that it is the position of such modules in the curriculum, rather than their content or teaching method, which makes them unreliable as a way of tackling student writing: the optional nature of academic skills modules may lead students to perceive them as marginal to the curriculum. When approaching the issue of Academic Writing support, therefore, English teaching staff agreed that the University's existing writing skills provision needed to be *supplemented* by concerted attention to student writing development from within the discipline.

The main difficulty for the English department in developing writing tuition and support was one of resources: of staff time and of staff expertise. First, the number of English staff is relatively small (less than five full-time academic staff members) and each full-time member of staff teaches eight modules in an academic year, with an average student-to-staff ratio of forty to one. Hence, there was not much staff time available for additional activities, such as designing and delivering writing support. There was also a problem of knowledge or expertise. The English degree at Derby is a theoretically-informed Literature degree and none of the full-time lecturers is a specialist in the field of English Language, Linguistics or Composition and Rhetoric. Undertaking to provide writing tuition and support, therefore, required researching current theory and practice in the field of student writing development. As Tomic and others in this volume describe, there are many print and online writing guides, and I want to mention here some of the resources that helped us think about the shape of our own programme of writing support.[4] Within the UK context there are available both student writing guides (such as Crème and Lea's *Writing at University: A Guide for Students* (2003), Peck and Coyle's *The Student's Guide to Writing: Grammar, Punctuation and Spelling* (1999) and Anglia Ruskin University's Speak–Write publications), and pedagogical development handbooks for staff (such as Coffin et al.'s (2003) *Teaching Academic Writing: A Toolkit for Higher Education*). It is fair to say, though, that the Anglia Ruskin University English department writing pathway, as detailed by Young and Avery in Chapter 6 of this volume, provided the main model for the writing support we sought to develop in the English programme at the University of Derby.

Based on our initial research into writing pedagogy and models of writing support, the English staff decided on two courses of action: the development of a three-module writing sequence – to be phased in by level, beginning with the first-year module in the 2003–4 academic year – and the offering of one-to-one writing tuition. Because of limited resources, the three writing modules are restricted to the Specialist English degree students,[5] and the first two of these modules are a requirement for all Specialist English students. Our rationale for requiring the writing modules is that a high level of competence in written communication should be expected of all English graduates. We believe that writing instruction helps all students – not the weakest students only – reach their academic potential. Individual tuition is open to all students taking English modules and through this provision we attempt to meet the concerns of the external examiners regarding the poor writing of the lowest-achieving students. One-to-one tuition effectively supplies extra support for the Specialist students and provides a minimum level of support for students on the Combined Studies programme (CSP) who choose to take English modules.

In 2003 one first-year and one second-year module were replaced by a required, two-year writing sequence. These dedicated modules for Specialist English degree students integrate the teaching of both general and discipline-specific writing skills into the English curriculum. The first-year module, for example, teaches generic academic skills, such as documenting and referencing sources, summarising, analysing and evaluating others' arguments, and planning and structuring students' own arguments. The module is 'general' in the sense that we do not focus solely, or even primarily, on literary texts, but ask students to read a variety of genres and text types. However, writing skills are taught within the context of English studies; hence, while we talk with students about the conventional requirements of academic discourse, we may provide discipline-specific instantiations of these expectations. During the module, the students produce a summary, an annotated bibliography and an argument paper, so that each assignment builds – in terms of skills and potentially in terms of content – on the previous one. The module is workshop-based and the emphasis is on practising and honing students' own writing skills. In addition, we guide students through writing process stages, by discussing and helping them to apply pre-writing strategies (brainstorming, planning, writing a proposal, identifying research questions) as well as techniques for revising.

The purpose of the second-year writing module, which ran for the first time in 2004–5, is to teach students critical thinking skills and critical reading strategies, because we believe that, within the context of our discipline, careful and detailed interpretive reading is a pre-requisite of sophisticated analytical writing and also because these thinking skills can be related to the

University's Skills Framework. As in the first-year module, the thinking skills taught are also 'generic' in the sense that the module does not focus on literary texts only, but on material from a wide range of disciplines and in a number of genres. Again, as with the first-year module, the design of the module allows class time for students to practise and hone their own analytical and writing skills.[6]

In contrast to the Anglia Ruskin University first-year writing module, which teaches the fundamentals of English grammar, we do not in these modules spend much time discussing grammar, clause and sentence construction, or punctuation, though these were the problems most often cited by external examiners. It is in the one-to-one tuition that we attempt to meet these concerns. From 2003, one member of the English teaching staff was released from teaching one literature module to be able to offer one-to-one writing support. Although one-to-one tuition is, in theory, available to all English students, both Specialist and CSP, a referral system is used to ensure that those students who are at risk of failing receive essay-writing support. The remit of the writing tutor includes every aspect of students' writing, including those elements (interpreting essay questions, brainstorming and planning, documenting and referencing sources, and developing arguments) addressed in the first-year Specialist module. However, one-to-one tutoring is especially well adapted, we believe, to discussing with students the mechanics of grammar and punctuation, since these are often best taught in the context of each student's own work. Thus one-to-one tuition complements the first-year writing module and attempts to address directly the externals' concerns about poor standards of grammar and punctuation in the writing of lowest-achieving students from both the Specialist and CSP programmes.

In order to extend the scope and enhance the quality of writing support, in 2004 the English department applied to two sources of internal funding. The subsequent award of money was used to release staff from teaching duties in order to allow time for research and development of the Academic Writing component of the degree programme. First, we were awarded money from an e-learning development fund to enable the staff member responsible for the dedicated writing sequence time to develop a significant e-learning component within each of those modules. The money does not need to be used to design full distance-learning modules, but may be used to enhance the content and delivery of the writing modules by blending into them networked learning opportunities. As the member responsible for the first-year and second-year modules, I found that the task of improving students' writing skills is not incompatible with the task of teaching them to manipulate information and computer technology, so that the time devoted to developing e-learning opportunities was also time given to developing the writing provision. I learned, for example, that there are a number of online resources available for teaching about referencing and plagiarism, and I had time to explore these resources and utilise the best of them in the networked classroom.[7] Also, some classroom activities can be equally or more effective when practised online: the recording of responses, one of the benefits of a networked classroom, can enrich an activity like peer critique, for instance, in which we ask students to apply the assessment criteria for the assignment to the writing drafts of their peers. Overall, then, as a result of this development there are advantages to the English programme as well as benefits to the students, since we are able to meet the students' and institution's demands for educational relevance by combining two highly desirable key skills (ICT and written communication).

Secondly, we were granted money from the University's retention fund, which we used to develop an early-assessment writing exercise to enable us to more quickly identify students who might be at risk of failing because of poor writing skills. This diagnostic exercise is in the form of a short writing assignment holistically graded, which is completed by all Specialist students by the fourth week of the autumn term. The retention money has also allowed us to extend one-to-one writing support without cutting back on the number of Literature modules we offer: the additional funds allow us to hire part-time hourly-paid staff to release full-time staff members from teaching three Literature modules in the academic year in order to devote time to one-to-one tutoring. It is worth emphasising that we decided that permanent rather than hourly-paid lecturers should provide writing support. By undertaking to provide one-to-one instruction ourselves, we hope to send the message to students that the English programme values writing support and believes it to be one of the most important services we offer to students.

This last point takes up a theme I emphasised at the outset: that the response of the English department at the University of Derby to the 'problem' of student writing has primarily been one of staff and curriculum development. As a by-product of ongoing research and discussion among the English team about the importance of writing support, a third tier of writing support is beginning to emerge within the English programme – in addition, that is, to the dedicated writing modules and the one-to-one tuition – which is to embed writing pedagogy into the English content curriculum. Hence, we have begun to spend classroom time in modules across the English programme on activities such as peer review. We have also started to make time for classroom activities that require students to write, believing that this facilitates students' learning of course content as well as giving them practice in expressing ideas. Finally, we make a concerted effort to include comments about students' writing performance in the feedback we offer on assignments. These and other activities tend to shift the emphasis from teaching course content to teaching learning strategies. I do not want to make too much of this: the strategy of embedding the teaching of writing is something that has begun in an *ad hoc* way and only by some lecturers. The implementation of the University's Skills Framework, however, will require that the embedding of academic skills within the content curriculum will have to be more widespread, and will have to be formally articulated in our programme aims as well as in individual module descriptions.

▶ Conclusion

This chapter has suggested that there are certain advantages to building writing support from within a discipline. Every organisational model has limitations as well as advantages, however, and I want briefly to discuss in conclusion what I see as unresolved issues with our Academic Writing provision as it currently exists.

The first issue is that of the sustainability of individual writing tuition. It is not clear at this point whether the one-to-one tutoring provision will, or ought to, be continued in its present form; as I have noted, it is currently staffed by full-time lecturers. Since the tutorial scheme is financed with money from an annual retention fund to release staff from teaching duties, the English department would have to re-apply for those monies in order to maintain the provision. Of course, it may be possible that one-to-one tuition could be funded out of a separate budget for part-time, hourly-paid lecturers. There is a broader issue here, though, of whether or not one-to-one tutoring is actually the best use of the time of English teaching staff. While I have suggested that the use of full-time lecturers as writing tutors constitutes a strength of the provision, it could also be argued that this arrangement is not the most efficient use of resources, especially if the writing tutorial scheme is under-used. We have considered, therefore, the possibility of using hourly-paid lecturers as writing tutors or of training a small number of hand-picked student peer tutors. However, neither of these options resolves the problem of under-utilisation. For while student take-up of one-to-one tutoring is quite good at certain times in the academic year – just before coursework deadlines, for example – there are still plenty of slack periods, times when the writing tutor is under-employed. To some extent we have been able to encourage students' attendance of writing tutorials and to monitor their attendance – this being especially true of the Specialist students, who fall more directly under our jurisdiction than the CSP students – but we cannot in the last instance force them to attend writing tutorials.

Students' attendance at writing tutorials becomes a problem for us particularly in relation to teaching grammar, since, as I have noted, it is in one-to-one tutorials that we have chosen to address the issue of poor grammar and punctuation. Moreover, recently one external examiner suggested that faulty grammar and punctuation were reason enough to reduce a student's grade by one class; that is, reason to reduce a first-class (A grade) degree to an upper second-class (B grade) degree, for example. The English teaching team, therefore, has a responsibility to ensure that we do reach the students who need assistance – and very few students would not benefit from assistance – with this aspect of their writing. In view of this, a more efficient way of reaching students, as well as a better use of resources, would be to have a required grammar module in the first year of the degree programme, on the model of that taught at Anglia Ruskin University, and to make room for this module by cutting a first-year literature module. This would be my own preference. Replacing a literature module with another language module in itself presents no difficulty; the challenge has always been one of how to use existing resources – building in Academic Writing in place of parts of the content curriculum – rather than of securing resources to expand our curriculum. The problem in doing so is that it would begin to change the nature of the English programme, shifting the balance, albeit slightly, between literary studies and what could be termed 'expressive competence'. For this reason, this change could not be made until the next programme re-validation cycle. Nevertheless, such a shift in emphasis would clearly fit well with the University's Skills Framework for teaching.

The second issue is that there is a problem, currently, of the lack of inclusiveness of the English department's writing provision, which fails to adequately cover Combined Studies (CSP) students or non-native speakers of English. With regard to the CSP students, we do not allow them to take the three writing modules, and although they can take advantage of the one-to-one tutoring, their attendance is less easy to monitor than is the attendance of English degree students. Nor do the CSP students complete the early diagnostic exercise. All of this may raise the question, from the point of view of external scrutiny, of how we guarantee the same quality of written work from the CSP students, who comprise well over half of the students we teach. It is possible that the implementation of the University's Skills Framework may help to resolve this dilemma for us by requiring a consistent approach to students' acquisition of key skills across academic programmes. Certainly the PDP, or 'Personal Development Plan', is one vehicle through which students can be encouraged to reflect on and improve their writing skills.[8]

With regard to non-native speakers, the University is making a concerted effort to recruit students from other countries and these are usually students whose first language is not English. Although these international students invariably possess high-level intellectual skills, the problems they pose as regards writing instruction are of a different kind from those of the native

English-speaking cohort. This raises the question of the responsibility of disciplinary staff. The English department's writing provision has worked well so far, but the introduction of a substantial number of non-native speakers to the degree programme does seem to require an additional level of support and one with which the English subject staff are not yet fully trained to deal.

The final issue I want to touch on is a possible tension between outcomes. As the module leader for the first- and second-year writing modules, I expected to experience a tension in planning the module between the tasks of teaching students to think and write and the task of teaching them to manipulate information and computer technology. In practice, I have not found this to be the case, but have found instead that designing reading and writing exercises with the specificity needed for online delivery has prompted me to design better teaching materials. However, there may be a tension in the expected outcomes of the English department's writing schemes. Because of the use of internal funds tied to specific outcomes (retention and e-learning), the success of the current writing projects will be judged by criteria other than the improvement of students' Academic Writing skills: the one-to-one scheme will be measured in relation to retention figures, for example. This might pose some problems. Student retention, for example, can depend on a number of factors that have nothing to do with writing support. One indicator of this tension is that we have yet to develop formal ways of measuring and recording the success of the writing programme. Although we do have subjective testimony, in the form of student feedback and external examiners' comments, that students' writing competence has improved, it is not possible to attribute this improvement to writing support solely. Hence, we urgently need to find ways of measuring the efficacy of the current approach to writing support. To convince both prospective students and University administrators of the validity of our writing provision, my colleagues and I require hard evidence that writing instruction improves the academic performance and assists the intellectual progression of *all* students in the English programmes, and gathering such evidence will be the next task to which we will turn.

NOTES

1 Barnett may over-simplify the process of transformation. John Pratt (1997), in *The Polytechnic Experiment: 1965–1992*, draws attention to the different historical missions of the 'old' universities and 'new' (post-1992) universities, which are often former polytechnics, and argues that while historically the traditional universities were 'aloof' from social concerns and 'exclusive' in their student body, polytechnics were always orientated towards the demands of wider society (pp. 8–10). In the mid-1960s the UK government embraced a 'dual system' for higher education, comprising universities and polytechnics. Pratt suggests that the

actual purpose of the polytechnics was to provide access to higher education for the working-class population traditionally excluded from higher education, although the ostensible purpose was to recognise that 'twin traditions' of higher education co-existed: an 'autonomous sector' and a 'service' or 'public sector' (p. 8). The dual system formally ended in 1992 when polytechnics were given the right 'to acquire the title of "university" and to award their own degrees' (pp. 7, 1). In light of Barnett's analysis, dissolving the distinction between universities and polytechnics was as much an acknowledgement that all institutions of higher education now had a responsibility to serve the needs of society as it was a formal recognition of autonomy for polytechnics.

2   Unlike the majority of new universities created in 1992, the University of Derby was formerly a college of higher education, not a polytechnic.

3   The University has named 12 types of skills to be taught and assessed. These comprise six key skills (Communication, Application of Number, Problem Solving, Working with Others, Information Technology, Improving own Learning and Performance), two academic skills (Research and Information, Thinking) and four employability skills (Opportunity Awareness, Self-Awareness, Decision Making, Transition Learning).

4   There are many online resources for assisting the teaching of writing. Two of the most helpful for our purposes have been the UniLearning website at the University of Wollongong, Australia (http://unilearning.uow.edu.au) and the 'Thinking Writing' website at Queen Mary, University of London (www.thinkingwriting.qmul.ac.uk).

5   At the University of Derby, English is offered as a specialist degree and as part of a combined-subject degree. Approximately 100 students are enrolled in the three-year Specialist English degree and over 200 students take English modules as part of the Combined Studies degree programme. It is important to point out that not all students enrolled in the English degree programme have weak writing skills. Nor is it true that those students most likely to struggle are non-traditional students, those who had given no thought to higher education on leaving school. In our experience it is not true that academic achievement follows from a conventional student background. Mature students, who comprise 20 per cent of students in English and who enter the programme through Access courses, Further Education colleges, or franchise programmes – which is to say, without traditional A Level qualifications – are among the highest-achieving students in our degree programme. Indeed, as confirmed by external examiners and by the award of Arts and Humanities Research Board (AHRB) postgraduate scholarships, the highest-achieving students in our programme are equal to the highest-achieving students anywhere. These students are often highly motivated and quickly equip themselves with the skills to succeed at university. Nevertheless, even these students are assisted in achieving their potential by explicit attention to the development of their Academic Writing skills.

6   The third-year module, offered for the first time in 2005–6, is an optional individual writing project.

7   There are many university websites designed to instruct students about referencing and citation, and some of these also include online plagiarism self-tests. Two

examples are those at the University of Essex (www.essex.ac.uk/plagiarism/ Contents.htm) and at Hong Kong University (http://ec.hku.hk/plagiarism). Coventry University, too, has a detailed guide to the Harvard referencing style (http://home.ched.coventry.ac.uk/caw/harvard/index.htm). Also, the University of Derby has developed an internal interactive website for teaching students about plagiarism.

8   Following recommendations by the Dearing Report (NCIHE, 1997), from Autumn 2006 the UK government's Quality Assurance Agency for Higher Education 'requires all universities to offer personal development planning and progress files for all undergraduates at each stage of their programme' (Cottrell, 2003). PDP is 'a structured and supported process undertaken by an individual to reflect upon [his or her] own learning, performance and/or achievement and to plan for [his or her] personal, educational and career development' (Quality, 2001, p. 2).

8 Engineering Writing: Replacing 'Writing Classes' with a 'Writing Imperative'

Alison Ahearn

▶ Introduction

Civil engineers leave long-lasting marks on the world, and engineering arte-facts from ancient civilisations are easier for most to interpret than writing from those civilisations, if they had writing at all. From a long history of engineers creating landmarks and infrastructure, we have obtained a stereotype – perhaps a true characteristic – of the civil engineer as someone who 'does', not someone who 'describes'. Engineering's professional institutions, however, blame many ills in the profession on poor communication skills, and writing courses are a requirement for Civil Engineering degrees. Students of Civil Engineering at Imperial College London, for instance, have been 'taught' writing skills since 1977. This chapter reviews the relationship between Civil Engineering students and writing at Imperial College London, and suggests that motivating students to want to write is more useful than teaching them writing. As the co-ordinater of writing tuition for first-year students, I describe my attempt to make writing tuition subservient to a writing imperative, and draw conclusions about the general effectiveness of this model, the refinements needed, and the function of a 'writing imperative' in a student's experience of university studies.

▶ Engineers and communication

Why do we teach writing to our students? In addition to generic good reasons for teaching writing to students of any subject, Civil Engineering departments must comply with requirements of external bodies who govern the profession. The Joint Board of Moderators require communication skills to be taught to students.[1] The Engineering Council, Institution of Civil Engineers, Institution of Structural Engineers, Royal Academy of Engineering and a host of other bodies have produced reports recommending improvement in communication.[2] However, the question remains: why do institutions put such store on communication skills, including writing? Understanding the answer to this question requires attention to the wider context of the engineering industry.

Socially and politically, engineering in the UK has a wonderful history yet British engineers, particularly civil engineers, are invisible in a way that is inexplicable given the visibility of their work. The Industrial Revolution allowed Britain to prosper and its empire to spread: often the engineering legacy is one of the more kindly-viewed legacies of empire because railways, sewers and roads have lasting use. Today, most Britons live in engineered, 'man'-made environments and the UK has a greater wealth of preserved engineering artefacts than many countries. It is, then, a source of great frustration to the civil engineering profession that the status of engineers in Britain is so low that it is unlikely that readers of this chapter can name a single living British civil engineer. The artefacts of civil engineering are so familiar that they go unremarked (unless they fail) and their creators go unrecognised. This is true of the work of many professions but civil engineers create structures that are highly noticeable: all modern landmarks are engineering creations. The symbols of cities, such as the Tower Bridge for London, the Eiffel Tower for Paris or the Opera House for Sydney, are the work of civil engineers. How many know that Eiffel was an engineer (and, if they know that, how many know that the design of the tower was the work of another engineer?). So we have a profession that feels frustrated and tongue-tied. In order to gain recognition, one must be talked about, written about, be the subject of communication. The profession decided long ago that if engineers communicated better, they would be better recognised. Irrespective of any syllogism lurking in this idea, UK university Civil Engineering departments attach great significance to fostering undergraduate students' communication skills.

What type of communicators do we have amongst Civil Engineering students? At Imperial College London, the average A Level score of first-year Civil Engineering students is 28 out of 30, although scores of 50/30 are not unknown due to the propensity of some students to do extra A Levels to ensure selection for the degree. The students are numerate, many having Maths, Further Maths and Physics as their subjects. Few have been required to write prose or practise expository writing since their GCSE courses.[3] Up to half speak English as a foreign language. Thus, extremely able students may find themselves struggling to produce quality work when prose, rather than mathematics or diagrams, is the vehicle of communication. Even where English is not a problem, students tend to lack awareness of the norms of academic forms of writing. Tackling this problem has proved difficult, and it should be noted that Imperial College London, is a specialist science, technology and medicine institution that does not have any undergraduate degree where writing is a mainstream subject. Given their preference for mathematics or diagrams as a means of communication, it has been easy to stereotype (or characterise) Engineering students as either process-oriented, content-driven, mathematically-correct or graphical communicators. Process-oriented students are interested in 'how to' not 'why to'; content-driven students are preoccupied with the topic to the exclusion of the reader's needs; mathematically-correct students prefer single right answers that are 'beautiful' rather than those messy, fuzzy, contextual, multiplicit answers familiar to social scientists; whilst graphical communicators feel that the right diagram or table or chart will speak volumes without the need for prose explanations: a picture is worth a thousand words, provided it has sufficient data points. Some students exhibit more than one characteristic. Some exhibit all.

Further, Engineering lecturers are people for whom writing is a tool for presenting their Engineering knowledge to a peer group or students: they tend to identify as engineers for whom writing is a by-product, rather than as writers for whom writing is an end product. Some, exceptionally, write for the press or, more commonly, for television.[4] With this view of Civil Engineering students and the profession's concerns about communication understood, it is possible to look at the teaching of writing at Imperial College London.

▶ Teaching writing in Civil Engineering at Imperial College London

Until 1995, first-year Civil Engineering students took a stand-alone writing course which required them to engage in coursework tasks such as writing a business letter on an imaginary small construction project. Students who could write well were underwhelmed and rattled off their coursework in minutes whereas students with poor writing skills merely received confirmation that their writing skills were weak. Little could be changed in student outcomes as the course was too short to allow weak writers to practise sufficiently to improve their skills, and able writers resented having to do 'an English course'. As the course did not involve fundamental aspects of Engineering, *per se*, it had been the victim of timetable raids over the years and was a poor creature compared with the course originally created in 1977. It did have a sister course that looked at non-technical concepts such as ethics, quality and business, which was intended to place Engineering into its non-technical context. In 1995 the two courses were replaced with one holistic course of 40 hours' tuition, *Engineering in Context 1*, dealing with context issues, soft skills and communication. This larger course provides more opportunity for students to test skills, note deficiencies, and improve them, either in the first year or in later years in sister courses.

Sister courses are vital to the success of the *Context 1* course, ensuring that it is seen as integrated into the mainstream of the Civil Engineering syllabus. *Context 1* is taught by me, a non-engineer who specialises in construction law and is passionate about improving students' appreciation of their non-technical professional obligations as engineers. The students enjoy being taught by people who display passion, and remark upon it; I believe that it gives them permission to be passionate too, which helps when trying to create a sense of imperatives. *Engineering in Context 2*, a second-year core course created by Dr Julian Bommer, is taught by engineers and builds on the first-year course by combining technical and non-technical issues through a series of case studies and role plays. The *Context* courses are presented as sisters to the *Creative Design* courses that run in the first, second and third years of the degree course. These courses are assessed through coursework only, without formal examinations, so students know that marks cannot be obtained through mathematics and formulae; for some that is a threat but for others it is a welcome relief. *Design 1* and *Context 1* have had shared site visits, assessed through joint coursework involving students in presenting their learning on a given issue using anything except a 'PowerPoint' presentation. Apart from saving the lecturer and class from the boredom that is associated with many PowerPoint presentations, this challenge to students has resulted in some of the most scintillating, imaginative and clever presentations possible, in the form of plays, debates, chat-show spoofs, satire and instant workshops. Such student-led efforts often far exceed lecturers' expectations. In 2002 this activity received special commendation as a teaching method in the report of the Joint Board of Moderators,[5] who, coincidentally, visited the Department in the month following the presentations. Although there is debate as to whether students learn more from such 'highlight' events or simply remember them fondly, it can be argued that boring presentations are no more likely to assist learning than memorable ones. Indeed, from a *Context 1* perspective, the most significant learning outcome from the site visit presentations has been students' improved or vindicated belief in themselves as communicators.

A key aspect of the new form of teaching of writing within *Context 1* is that it acknowledges the intellectual credibility of the students, despite deficiencies in writing skills demonstrated by some (or many). Indeed, if some students' initial attempts at writing were shown to an outsider, the outsider would find it hard to credit those students with the type of academic ability that their mathematical subjects show them to have. The problem with the previous 'bolt-on' writing course was that students lost their status as good students if they happened to be weak as writers; for talented students, the social adjustment of moving from top of the class to mediocre is difficult, even though they know that they must be competent to have been selected for their course. Students who have been top at their schools may not have realised that they could be middling or bottom-grade students once they move into highly-selective courses such as Civil Engineering at Imperial College London. Self-esteem relates to motivation, and motivation can only be weakened when a bolt-on course picks on a student's weakest skill and merely confirms it.[6] Ideally, any course should help a student identify the means of improving skills, but this is difficult in an environment where a crowded, hectic timetable is compounded by a heavy coursework load featuring 'number-crunching'. Students have few hours available for optional extra coaching in writing and communication skills and they resent, or ignore, any requirement to spend hours practising these skills when writing carries few marks and is not the primary aim of the degree.[7]

Overcoming resistance to practising writing involves creating an imperative for students to want to write and to want to write effectively. The essential coursework in the current version of *Context 1* is a major report that is devised, executed and reported by the student, utilising teamwork, independent inquiry, critical thinking and academic audience-orientated writing. Students are given a brief which can be simplified as follows:

1 Students must advance our understanding of Engineering in its non-technical context.
2 Students must use both secondary (library) research and primary (original) research.
3 Students must use a referencing system.
4 Student teams must submit a portfolio reflecting on their experiential learning from the project and each student must submit a self-reflective 'personal learning summary'.
5 Students must make an oral presentation to their peers and write a self-critique in light of the feedback obtained from peers.

For most students, such a brief is a challenge. The nature and duration of the work make it a task equivalent to a final-year undergraduate or MSc project, although the standard of attainment expected is lower. The brief is given in week 3 of the course and reports are submitted in week 22. It takes most students at least four weeks to determine and narrow their question. Teamwork is encouraged and teams are able to run the work as a project, with systems for maximising efficiency, as befits future project engineers. Timetabled workshops provide support, including opportunities for student teams to meet and focus on a task. An outline of the classroom support is set out later in this chapter in Table 8.1. The significant difference between these classes on writing and the old course on writing is that, having done the research, students are motivated to want to know how they can present their work to its advantage. Further, many students are keen to write more than the word limit, as they want to do justice to their research work. From this, it can be seen that writing has moved from being a trivial chore to a privilege to be fought for with the teacher (who resists on the grounds that marking would be impossible if each student wrote 10,000 words).

▶ Discussion of the 'imperative' experience

What are the advantages of embedding writing into such a significant piece of coursework, for students who are totally inexperienced in Academic Writing? Many students need coaching on style, tone and permissible vocabulary but, because they are the discoverers of the knowledge they wish to impart, they are keen to find out about the rules governing how to write up their work. Great emphasis is placed on proper structuring and format of the document although no templates are provided: this is to discourage a donkey-work approach to tasks but this policy may require review. Mitchell et al. (2000) points out that there is an irony in the aversion of tutors to giving stylistic and structural advice for writing when students are alerted to structure and style in their practical work as a matter of course (p. 88).[8]

Context 1 students are asked to consider the requirements of their audience (a non-technical academic in an Engineering department). Writing without templates, it is possible for a whole team to mislead themselves as to the norms of Academic Writing; ironically, good teamwork can prove counter-productive when students exercise collective creativity as to the academic forms of writing. For instance, some teams choose to leave out vital academic and scientific elements such as a description of their methodology; this is despite advice on the need to prove a valid approach to both secondary and primary research. Such problems underscore the need to provide strong assignment guidelines if giving students the freedom to work without templates.

Fortunately, most students are well motivated to write up their work. Despite the huge effort they put into their research on their self-defined topic, many recognise that their learning about the process of research and presentation is of far greater significance than their discoveries on the substantive topic of their investigation: this intellectual move beyond the 'content' of the writing to a metadiscourse on the process of writing up research does not fit the stereotype of formulae-orientated Civil Engineering students. These considerations of 'form' and 'novelty' accord with Kaufer and Geisler's (1989) view that novelty is a strong feature of Academic Writing assignments. The *Context 1* writing assignment is novel in the students' first-year studies: there is no other similar coursework. However, the major report project is conventional in terms of Academic Writing norms because it requires students to 'warrant' their work by the use of references to conventionalised realms of knowledge (secondary sources) and to 'render transparent' their assumptions, definitions and reasonings (Mitchell et al., 2000, p. 89). These processes are new to most students in their first year of study.

Students report the project as a personal challenge, daunting at first and satisfying upon completion. A number of students report amazement that senior figures in industry and academia are willing to engage intellectually with 'mere' first-year students, through interviews and consultations. From the point of view of empowering students to consider themselves as 'fit to write', the major report assignment can be evaluated as a great success, relying on students' comments in their portfolios and learning summaries, and on the work that they actually produce.

Regarding communication skills, students learn the value of personal contacts, selection of sources, keeping references, barriers to communication with the public, qualitative research methods and a variety of other issues, varying from project to project. For instance, in 2001–2, students' reflections on secondary research produced a variety of comments on the usefulness of the internet as a source of information: some students soon realise the difference between low-grade information and high-grade knowledge, while others are astonished that anyone would use a library with 'old books' that are 'hard to find' when they have the web at their disposal. Fortunately, the library service at Imperial College London, has developed a scheme of user education and, since 2003–4, students have been provided with guidance and expert librarian advice on defining the limits of investigation and reportage. This has been done in the timetabled classroom workshops (lecture hours) using WebCT software as a vehicle for students to do online exercises in the retrieval and referencing of sources.

Also, in my parallel role as an Educational Development Lecturer for the College, I have initiated the latest version of the imperative-oriented approach to teaching Engineering writing on the basis of four key ideals. These ideals are personal to the author but derive from experience and general reading on the subjects of Science Communication, Rhetoric, Writing and Educational Development.

1. Replace the 'marks imperative' with a 'rhetorical imperative'

Student-writers need a rhetorical imperative. Numerate students can gain marks more easily in mathematics-based subjects than in writing-based subjects. They therefore must be presented with a situation in which they actively seek to learn to write as a means of showing off their academic work.

2. Replace content-consciousness with audience-consciousness

The rationale behind the push for communication skills education in Engineering includes the need to reach out to the public. This underlines the requirement for teaching an audience-orientated approach to writing, as opposed to a content-conscious approach. If replacement is impossible, awareness must be a substitute aim.

3. Require students to take authority over their writing, not just authorship

Students who write for an expert audience are usually confined to asserting authorship of their writing: the authority for the content belongs to the experts whose work they cite, and students may be citing their own lecturer/examiner, who may be the 'world expert'. Students who design their research and report it can take authority as well as authorship. Therefore, the element of primary research is fundamental to giving students a reason to demonstrate authority as well as authorship.

4. Require creativity

Generally, in the first year of study, students cannot make original contributions to their teachers' knowledge of classic areas of physics, maths or mechanics. With the major report, students choose their own topics; they define their own questions. They are compelled to be creative in finding answers because the lecturer has never attempted any investigation of their chosen topic. They know this, believe this, and act on this because they are in control of their own project and make their own choices. In order to be creative, one must have the freedom to be creative. A problem with this approach is the question of how to get students to balance creativity with the need to provide credible, valid research. Clear guidelines and advice are needed, which must not detract from students' freedom to create their project.[9]

Application of the ideals can be seen in Table 8.1, which sets out a description of tasks facing students on the major report. The middle column indicates the type of classroom activity that assisted students in engaging with the task in 2001. The final column indicates the providers of the assistance. As the course co-ordinator I attend, even if I do not teach, all classes. The course is refined each year and varies in detail. When the course was first revised it included guest lectures from Sir John Egan and Professor Stephen Glaister, which provided confirmation to the students that their endeavours and studies are meritorious: Sir John Egan authored a government report

Table 8.1 The major report project

Student has to . . .	Student is supported by . . .	This support is provided by . . .
Discover complexity. Seek inspiration for a topic for report	Narrative of an engineering disaster told by client who suffered £70m loss	Sir John Egan (ex-Chair, British Airports Authority)
Choose topic	Secondary research, guided talk and library tour	Librarian and lecturer
Find team, gain confidence	Moot (construction law role play)[10]	Law lecturer (Ahearn)
Write proposal	Critical thinking. Primary research talk	Workshop (Ahearn)
Write plan	GANTT chart exercise[11]	Workshop (Ahearn)
Use social science methods	In-class survey work	Transport economist Professor Glaister
Collate work-in-progress	Reflective learning	Reminders throughout course (Ahearn)
Follow staged completion process	Showing work to tutor and/or team	External reassurance
Use oral communication	Peer criticism and feedback	Workshops (Ahearn)
Write report	Coaching classes	Workshop (Ahearn)
Write reflective portfolio	Discussions and critiques	Course co-ordinator (Ahearn)

that is revolutionising the construction industry and Professor Glaister is a noted transport economist. With the advent of the library-user education project, guest lectures have given way to integrating the librarians' user-education web and lecture programme. As an illustration of the logic behind the classes, Table 8.1 shows the 2000–1 model. Later models are variations of this.

The outcomes of the major report in the team-based version run since 2000–1 are that the majority of students demonstrate:

(a) **passionate interest in their topics and reports**, to the point where some do far more work than required. This indicates that a time budget may be necessary to enforce critical decision-making about the process of research: students who become over-passionate tend to exhibit poor audience awareness in their write-ups, being too close to their topic to maintain judgement about presentation.

(b) **assertion of authority over the material**. This seems easiest for students who combine good secondary research (literature survey) with the development of their own views, tested against the views of an expert, culled from an interview. These students are generally able to define their own territory in their arguments and display a strong sense of purpose in their writing. Such students tend to provide a structure to their writing which is driven less by description of 'what I did' and more by explanation of 'the significance of what I did'.

(c) **a sense of nobility and a desire to strive to change the world for the better**. There is little opportunity for Civil Engineering students to share their sense of higher purpose with each other or with their lecturers, given the mathematically-focused nature of most of their degree study. For this project, a significant number of students opt to study topics about helping society. This sense of vocation may be a stronger rhetorical imperative than Civil Engineering staff appreciate and should be investigated further.

(d) **appreciation of complexity**. Students find soon after they begin their projects that they must narrow down the field of enquiry, as even narrow questions tend to have complex answers. Students who find their projects too complex must be reassured that learning about complexity will be rewarded in the same way that other products of the project will be rewarded. The freedom to fail to obtain the goal self-set by the student is important, so long as the student sees the significance of being able to learn from failure, and writes the project up constructively. In short, students need to know that excellent expository writing about a failed project can merit a high mark.

(e) **a shift from 'what' to 'why'**. The drive to describe 'how' or 'what' rather than 'why' seems deep-seated in some Engineering students. The *Engineering in Context* course was introduced in 1977 in an effort to address this, but it has been taken further, from 2001–2, with more emphasis in mathematics classes on Engineering relevance and attempts to integrate coursework for technical subjects and Creative Design modules. The hope is that this shift in the culture of the Engineering department may help students to refocus their writing in later years.

(f) **an academically acceptable approach to writing**. Some groups adhere to rules about academic forms of writing, and write their major report like university students. Others write in their own, authentic voice and are equally passionate about their subject; street language and contractions are lexical indicators of this voice. This raises a difficult point: is it better to encourage students to find their own voices when writing about Engineering, or is it the lecturer's duty to ensure they know how to conform to standard academic forms of writing? Does pursuit of standardised writing quash a student's authority over his or her own writing? An element for consideration is that many passionate but colloquial students tend to adopt a positivist view of science and of the insistent meaning of facts. Making students aware that 'the facts do not speak for themselves' (Dillon, 1991, p. 76)[12] justifies, in my view, the imposition of academic style and structure.

(g) **content–audience balance**. This remains the most unstable outcome, for the reasons mentioned previously regarding the culture of content-consciousness in the Engineering department as a whole. In short, students often get away with being content-driven when writing for an expert audience.

Although the major report assignment is team-based, each chapter is authored by an individual team member. It is useful to note the variety of topics investigated. Table 8.2, column 1, provides examples from when the revised course was first run, when students came up with their own topics and then tried to find a group to join. Broad topics are a team's general topic, whilst specific titles are examples of sub-topics investigated by a student.

In 2003–4, this selection process was revised to allow students to commit to a group with a key-word topic and to use that as a launch pad for finding individual topics. Table 8.2, column 2, lists the topics around which students created their groups in 2002–4. These topics resulted from a hectic brainstorm session by students and were not teacher-led. This revised method of choosing topics has speeded up the process, allowed more opportunity to troubleshoot and provided more peer support for students who find the freedom to self-define their own project daunting.

▶ Conclusion

Is it pointless to teach writing to Civil Engineering students? Taking a pragmatic view, for able students deficient in writing skills, writing classes can be demoralising if they simply underline deficiencies. In the Department of Civil and Environmental Engineering at Imperial College London, we have found that students demonstrate greater keenness to write when their writing is

Table 8.2 Major report topics (2001 and 2002–4)

Column 1	Column 2
Aesthetics in Engineering (e.g. What makes a bridge beautiful? Must form follow function?)	London Transport
Devastation caused by Engineering	Waste management
What if an earthquake hit the UK?	Renewable energy
Stadia (e.g. the political function of a sports stadium as a venue for rallies)	Non-renewable energy
Drinking water law, pricing, conservation and public utilities	Landmarks
History (e.g. of specialisation of Science and Engineering, history of suspension bridge design)	Environment
Engineering the High Street: Why is Gap cool and C&A not?	Infrastructures
The music of Mathematics	Docklands
Timber's viability as a material of the future	
A Greek's perspective on earthquakes	
Engineers in the developing world: ethics, NGO funding, educational impact	
Extending a London Underground tube line: implications for local council, community and London Underground Ltd	

incidental to the work they have done in advancing their teachers' knowledge of Engineering. Their zeal for this work far exceeds students' zeal for coursework on the old course, *Written and Oral Communication*. That is not to say that in *Context 1*, writing is not discussed, debated, lectured upon or demanded; on the contrary, students seek information about how to write, why to write, and when to write, in what manner and to what standard.

Nevertheless, some students are so unfamiliar with Academic Writing that they switch off from the academic requirements and tussle only with the job of getting their new knowledge onto paper. These students need much more guidance but of a different type from that absorbed by the majority of students in the lectures that provide support for writing up a project. As an extra form of support, a Royal Literary Fund (RLF) Writing Fellow joined the department from 2001 to offer one-to-one sessions that help students to think about what it means to write for an academic audience, and to grapple with the idea of tailored expository writing.[13]

Does the writing imperative work as a substitute for a generic writing class? The major report idea was taken from a curriculum guide developed at the University of Sydney by Dr Caroline Baillie,[14] but it has developed into a different creature in the *Context 1* course by being adapted for the needs of Civil Engineering students in the setting of Imperial College London. Other universities' interest indicates that it is novel to give first-year students an assignment that mimics a final-year project or even an MSc dissertation. While one purpose of the major report assignment is *learning about writing by doing writing*, its larger purpose is *learning about one's own ability to exceed one's expectations, including the ability to write seriously as an academic.*

Can we summarise the imperatives for writing in the major report? Dias describes the 'social motive for student writing' as epistemic, 'oriented towards knowledge' (Dias et al., 1999, p. 65), so the characterisation of the project as akin to a dissertation or thesis fully embraces the social motive. The use of teams and team reports creates an imperative for groups of students to discuss what it means to write up a report, leading them to think through the mechanics of writing as well as the content of the report. It has to be noted that students can mislead themselves on the assignment, so the teacher's checks and, if necessary, interventions, are important. The major report provides a rare opportunity for Engineering students to wrestle with the idea of a rhetorical imperative: because the student is the 'authority' on the topic, the reader cannot draw on another body of knowledge to make sense of the student's report so the student must be persuasive. Again, the student mimics the position of a doctoral student, who moves beyond the expertise of his or her supervisor to claim expert authority. The *Context 1* student takes authority as well as authorship with the major report. Students write because they persuade themselves that writing matters. They discover that knowledge deserves to be presented to the world in writing as effectively as possible, as inspiringly as possible and as convincingly as possible. When they seek to write their major reports, most students have discovered knowledge that they find exciting, that they wish to share. Whilst their writing skills may not always rise to the occasion, their aspirations to be better writers seem to soar. Does this aspiration survive beyond the project?[15] Further research is required to answer this question, and for that, further Engineering courses with writing imperatives are needed.

NOTES

1   In the US, technical writing tuition for engineers has had a stronger development (Kynell, 1996).

2   These include reports by Finniston (Great Britain Committee, 1980), Latham (1994), Ridley (1996), Egan (Construction, 1998), and addresses by incoming

presidents of the institutions. The Latham and Egan reports were targeted at industry, rather than academia and the professions, but many reforms focus on improved, non-adversarial communication between parties to construction projects.

3 These students have much in common with students studying Dance or other practical subjects (Mitchell et al., 2000).

4 Professors John Burland (who saved the Leaning Tower of Pisa) and Chris Wise (who co-designed London's Millennium Bridge) are exceptions, each having a variety of television documentaries and appearances to their credit.

5 The Joint Board of Moderators (which includes the Institution of Civil Engineers and the Institution of Structural Engineers) visits every 5 years to accredit Civil Engineering degrees as professional qualifications.

6 Mitchell et al. (2000) notes the same in Dance students: 'While dance students in a university setting are confident about their own practice, with its starting point of physical movement, . . . they are often uneasy about the formal writing tasks they encounter' (p. 86).

7 See Dias et al. on Architecture, a similar discipline in which the focus is on a 'non-verbal process' (1999, p. 5).

8 Mitchell et al. (2000) refers to students who are taught style and structure in Dance, but an analogy can be drawn to Engineers who study structure and design (p. 88).

9 The tension between creativity and learning academic forms of writing is characterised by Dias et al. (1999) as a result of the dual social motive affecting students' writing genres: the epistemic motive versus the institutional motive to sort and rank students (p. 47).

10 The moot was a courtroom role play undertaken by students, with only four hours of preparation. A 'moot' is a microcosm of the main project: the students grapple with an unfamiliar topic and procedure but find they can do it, thereby gaining confidence in their non-mathematical abilities.

11 The Gantt Chart, developed by American engineer Henry L. Gantt in 1917, is a graphical project management tool used 'to show scheduled and actual progress of projects' (KIDASA, 2005).

12 Dillon (1991) refers to the socio-constructivist view espoused by Latour and Woolgar (p. 76).

13 See Lisa Ganobcsik-Williams's General Introduction to this volume for an explanation of the RLF Fellowship Scheme.

14 Dr Caroline Baillie later joined Imperial College London, and gave personal input to the initial ideas for the creation of *Context 1* and, also, for Dr Julian Bommer's course, *Engineering in Context 2*.

15 It is hoped that this question might be answered by future investigation into the quality of the final fourth-year reports produced by students who completed the *Context 1* class in their first year.

9 If not Rhetoric and Composition, then What? Teaching Teachers to Teach Writing

Rowena Murray

▶ Introduction

It is often, perhaps generally, assumed that university lecturers know about writing; they know how to write and they know how to use writing in their teaching: 'Successful university lecturers are likely to have spent many years developing acceptable ways of constructing their own knowledge through their own writing practices in a variety of disciplinary contexts' (Lea and Street, 1998, p. 163). In fact, many lecturers are unsure not only of how to help students improve their writing, but also of how to improve their own practice and output. Many are completely unaware of scholarship and research on Rhetoric and Composition, Student Literacies, Writing for Academic Purposes, Writing Across the Curriculum and Writing in the Disciplines. However, there is evidence that those lecturers who do avail themselves of writing development and support – and it has been thoroughly argued that both are essential (Boice, 1987) – transfer what they have learned to their teaching role (Murray, 2001).

This chapter reports research on seven strategies lecturers at the University of Strathclyde have used to facilitate student writing. Taken together, the first six examples demonstrate that a range of writing strategies were deemed relevant to students' needs: freewriting, structuring and visualising. The final example, enabling writing for undergraduate dissertation writing, shows how lecturers can draw on skills they already have in order to run a writing workshop, a session where student writing is the focus. The use of these lecturers' own voices is designed to show the interchange of theory and practice in this area; in fact, both are so closely woven together in each example that it is difficult to separate them.

▶ Context

At the University of Strathclyde, as at many UK universities, educational development for academic staff is provided by the Centre for Academic

Practice (CAP), established in 1989. As a Senior Lecturer in the CAP, I provide support and development on, among other subjects, Academic Writing. Having been trained in the teaching of Rhetoric and Composition at the Pennsylvania State University, I draw on both UK and US traditions of teaching writing.

Working with lecturers across the university, I have developed a range of activities and strategies to support lecturers as they develop new teaching activities to help their students improve their writing. In the course of this work, I have observed that lecturers have very little knowledge of existing scholarship on Academic Writing. This is not to say that I would position them as deficient or negligent; rather, I would argue that many lecturers are very willing to learn about such scholarship and to use it in their teaching, once they have been introduced to it, once its relevance to 'problems' they see has been revealed and once they have been supported in innovations in their teaching to improve student writing.

Lecturers at the University of Strathclyde can access both formal and informal modes of development in the CAP: they can attend credit-bearing courses or short, informal workshops. There are also extended collaborations, in which a staff developer and a lecturer work together over several months to address students' writing needs. Lecturers who participate in staff development do so voluntarily, although some, for example new lecturers in their 'probationary' years, are required to undertake the Certificate in Advanced Academic Studies, which includes an optional module on Academic Writing. This course is part of the University's provision of formal training for academic staff, which is rapidly becoming a requirement in UK higher education.[1]

▶ Background: lecturers learn about writing

This chapter presents a selection of staff development work focused on improving student writing, and reports on the diverse uses lecturers at the University of Strathclyde have for writing activities in their teaching. Once lecturers have developed their understanding of writing they can add to their repertoire a broader range of writing activities and a growing understanding of the pedagogical foundations for them. This suggests that lecturers should experience more writing development opportunities, formally or informally, so that they can in turn develop their students' writing.

The examples I detail in this chapter represent a range of interventions, which were formulated either pro-actively or reactively. Some of the lecturers had experienced writing development training themselves; some had very little knowledge of writing development. There are therefore two groups of lecturers in this selection of examples: those who completed a formal course on Academic Writing as part of the Certificate/Diploma in Advanced Academic Studies and those who had no post-school writing development experience. The first group had learned writing strategies with the aim of improving their own Academic Writing practices and had then adapted these to their teaching. The second group, in one or two highly-condensed tutorials on the scholarship of writing prior to designing a writing lesson, intended to solve a specific problem they had identified in their students' writing. The first group were educated about Academic Writing; the second had a comparatively superficial education in the subject.

▶ Writing development for lecturers: seven examples

The purpose of these snapshots of writing development is to illustrate the lecturers' experiences through extracts from their first-person accounts. Perhaps more importantly for writing development scholars these examples indicate what constitutes 'learning' for these lecturers. Although some of these perspectives may be tried and tested, and even old in the context of writing scholarship, they are new and meaningful to these lecturers. The seven examples are characterised by the lecturers' own representations of writing development, as follows:

1   writing in class as 'a dynamic';
2   writing outside the 'boundaries' of assessment;
3   writing as a process;
4   writing as a communal activity;
5   writing tasks throughout the project;
6   helping the student to visualise each stage of writing;
7   a writing workshop.

These seven examples were drawn from a spread of academic disciplines, including the Sciences, the Humanities and the Social Sciences.

1   Writing in class as 'a dynamic'

This example shows the direct effect of the lecturer's own writing development training on his or her uses of writing in teaching. The word 'dynamic' suggests a new, for this lecturer, interactive approach to writing, embedding it in a student-centred learning process:

For example, when I've finished a class and got them to write 50 words on the learning from that class. . . . I'm more confident and committed to . . . I insist that undergraduate classes write in class (five minutes). This is a dramatic change. Prior to this it was lecture discussion notes. . . . Writing has now become second nature. *I use writing in class as a dynamic:* writing in different forms, with different purposes, linking back to the assignment, summing up, making links. Also with dissertation students: we discuss and I prompt them to write there and then. Therefore I'm more assertive in saying, 'Shouldn't you be writing that down?'

This lecturer connects such 'writing in class' with writing for the assessment; in fact, writing has been given a place and purpose at several stages in the course. By contrast, the lecturer in the following example draws a distinction between the two.

2 Writing outside the 'boundaries' of assessment

The interaction of reflective writing and assessment writing is addressed in this example:

It was felt that introducing reflective writing activities into the classroom – looking at the writing process in an active, experiential way, *outwith the 'boundaries' of assessment* – would make students adopt good writing habits. Students would, it was hoped, do regular, sustained writing, where they planned and structured material and checked it before submission. Students would effectively become their own editors and take control of their writing. . . . Activities such as reading books, memorising notes or copying styles from exemplars would be exchanged for activities such as classroom debates on [writing] style, reflective writing exercises and role play. . . . The key change was that little time was spent during these sessions talking about actual assessments.

The relatively sustained reflection, by this lecturer, on the value of writing that is not for assessment, suggests that here the traditional tension between assessment and almost any form of pedagogical innovation is being resolved.

3 Writing as a process

Reconstituting writing as 'a process' is no longer a ground-breaking insight to theorists of Academic Writing (Kent, 1999). However, many subject lecturers find it to be so. For instance, it has opened up the following lecturer's mind to new possibilities:

Once employed in education I found I was writing more, and more varied, documents, ranging from course and syllabus material to course notes for students, but *I had never considered my writing as a process* which could be improved. It was just something I did. . . . The second and more surprising outcome is that I've found something I can do well, that works for me and that I can see me taking forward, both as a tool for my personal writing, and as a method I will suggest to students to aid their writing. I have already suggested Freewriting to a Project Student who was struggling with how to approach writing his report. I did not give it a name, but merely suggested that he should write down the topics he wanted to cover in each section, and then write down everything he knew about that topic for five minutes, without considering structure or punctuation. Then to go through it with his highlighter pen and pick out the useful bits and use them as bullet points for his final write up. His feedback has been very positive so I think that one will be used again.

This extract shows how this lecturer took a lesson learned about his or her own writing practice and adapted it to help students with their writing, adapting terminology to suit the context.

4   Writing as a communal activity

The next example does not describe a specific innovation; it shows the lecturer identifying a student writing problem and working out an explanation for it:

Postgraduate students frequently fail to recognise *science as a communal activity*, and not the work of excellent researchers working in isolation. Central to this activity is consideration of interactions between first-person perspectives . . . I encountered a marked resistance from my two [postgraduate student] co-authors to writing. It was easy for them to delegate this role to their male supervisor as outside their 'reality'. To both, the supervisor had a role based on greater experience and less need to keep a grasp on 'reality'.

This lecturer has a different frame of reference from the other examples, connecting to a different set of references including Psychology, Philosophy and Psychotherapy, as opposed to Academic Writing specifically or higher education generally. For this lecturer, seeing writing as a 'communal activity' is a key step in students' writing development. For science subjects, this may be a particularly relevant framework. The challenge may lie in getting students to see it that way, or in developing activities that help them to achieve their goals and the development goals their lecturer has chosen for them.

5 Writing tasks throughout the project

Again, what seems new to this lecturer may seem like one of the oldest chestnuts to writing scholars:

> One of the major skills which is neglected during a PhD project is developing a student's ability to carry out Academic Writing (Torrance et al., 1992). Learning to write for an academic audience is a difficult process (Jackson, 1991; Moses, 1985). With practice students can improve but the student needs to understand that learning to write is an essential component of PhD study. . . . Writing for publication is probably the most rewarding type of Academic Writing. However, giving a student small *writing tasks throughout the project* may help to make writing up the thesis less traumatic for both student and supervisor.

Perhaps the challenge for writing developers working with university lecturers is to enable such 'basic', fundamental, personal reflection on writing. The examples reported in this chapter are first-person accounts, and illustrate the different frames of reference that lecturers bring to writing. Without such reflective opportunities would these perspectives be explicitly articulated at all? Would the practices of Academic Writing be made visible to students?

6 Helping the student to visualise each stage of writing

This realisation that lecturers need to be given time for guided reflection about writing takes us to the question of how the process of Academic Writing can be made visible for students:

> This report proposes a more structured approach to the written dissertation . . . seminars will . . . focus on a key issue relevant to a particular stage in the process of conducting the dissertation. The meetings will *help the student visualise each stage* and identify and clarify emerging questions throughout the process. . . . Students will be able to individualise the supervisor's general advice at each stage, dependent on their thesis. Emphasis will be on student involvement and contribution through discussion and illustration by examples of past work. Students will be encouraged to discuss their work within small groups. In many instances discussion of proposals can lead to a far clearer understanding. In small groups students will be encouraged to give each other feedback and

advice – thus capitalising on peer support which hopefully will continue outwith the sessions.

This example shows the movement from reflection on writing by the lecturer to a curriculum design that includes writing. The 'visualisation' is to be done by students, a process to be stimulated and supported by the lecturer and peers.

7 A writing workshop

Building on the previous extract, this example shows more specifically how a lecturer in Physiotherapy will carry out a dissertation-writing workshop, using graphical representations to aid visualisations:

> This approach aims to give both students and supervisors/tutors a method for approaching what is often a daunting writing task. The process of visualising the structure of the project report has proved helpful in early discussions with students. Group discussions of project reports can both enable students to address their concerns and save supervisors valuable time. The supervisor acts as facilitator, introducing a structured approach to writing and enabling students to adapt it to their projects. Integrating the dimensions of projects, including time, writing and conceptualisation helps students to develop an understanding of the type of writing that will be involved throughout the project process. It enables them to begin writing at an early stage in the project.

An interesting feature of this example is the ease with which this lecturer adapted existing teaching skills to what was essentially a writing workshop. The skills of facilitation blended well with the discussion of writing. Enabling students to take the initiative in both their research and writing tasks was a coherent focus. Consideration of the conceptual – not just practical – shifts required throughout the project was seen as applying to both research and writing. The role of writing at different stages in the project was clarified.[2]

▶ Discussion

These examples cannot be taken as an 'agenda' for development. They are simply a collection of experiences. It may be that the seven key learning points extracted from these lecturers' accounts may serve as prompts for other lecturers, helping them to conceptualise writing in their disciplines. Taken together or individually, these examples are not discipline-bound; the strategies they use can be adopted in other contexts. One of the reasons for not specifying the discipline base of each example reported here is to make the point that these processes could be occurring in any one of a range of disciplines.

Taken together, the seven examples suggest that writing development, and lecturers' responses to it, can be very individual. Lecturers' new views on writing are very much tied to their experiences as learners. It would be difficult, therefore, to pull these examples together into one framework, such as Writing Across the Curriculum (WAC) or Writing in the Disciplines (WID). Although for some, particularly those working outside the UK system perhaps, WAC or WID seems like the next logical step, I believe it is unlikely that a sustained, systemic programme of those types will take hold in UK higher education at this time. Perhaps as a new generation of academics comes through, having experienced more in the way of training for teaching in higher education, this will change.

However, academics have to take responsibility for knowledge about writing in their disciplines – their own writing and their students'. More importantly, staff who can make the connection between their own writing and writing development, and their students', are most likely to make progress in the uses of writing in their disciplines, although, again, the risk is that, as with this chapter, writing development remains no more than a series of individual 'examples'.

What these examples can be taken to indicate, however, is that what constitutes new knowledge about writing for these lecturers is quite old knowledge for scholars and practitioners of writing development. This suggests that wider dissemination of writing development practice and research, of the contextualised type, is required.

Similarly, it is not new to include reflective writing in personal and professional development contexts (Bolton, 2001). Reflective writing of various forms is now well established in the health professions, for example, at both undergraduate and post-qualification levels. However, opportunities in academia for such first-person writing-about-writing as practised in the examples reported in this chapter are rare (Boud, 1999). Perhaps lecturers could engage in extended dialogue about writing, through the medium of email exchanges with a colleague who knows the scholarship or through structured reflective writing in module assessments. In these ways sustained reflection is possible and lecturers have time to contextualise their reading and thinking about writing in their disciplines.

Finally, these examples supply a further argument for the writers' group, a forum for sharing insights on writing with peers that has proved successful in helping lecturers to develop writing for scholarly publication (Murray and MacKay, 1998). Members of such groups frequently exchange ideas for helping students with their writing, as lecturers translate their learning about writing to their teaching of writing (Murray, 2001).

▶ Conclusion

The question in the title of this chapter, 'If not Rhetoric and Composition, then what?', brings with it a structural question for UK higher education: 'If not the Composition Unit, then who?' Who will provide this development, this teaching about writing for teachers in higher education?

Units like the CAP may have the expertise to provide the necessary development, but can subject departments bring a more coherent view to writing development in the disciplines? Will the staff development initiatives reported in this chapter coalesce into a series of discipline-specific writing programmes, like those offered in some US universities? Or is the key question one of timing? My own learning about writing, for instance, took place when I was a graduate student at the Pennsylvania State University writing programme; for lecturers in the examples presented in this chapter, learning about writing took place when seeking to improve their own Academic Writing practices, when looking to help undergraduate students learn to write better and/or when supervising postgraduate research and writing.

It was not the purpose of this chapter to argue that all lecturers should develop all of the perspectives covered in these examples, although there is evidence that this can occur more easily and more quickly than many expect. Rather, the point emerges that writing development appears to be quite individual for lecturers. It may be less discipline-based than idiosyncratic, that is, it is perceived as particular to the individual lecturer by the individual lecturer. This may say something about the perceived, or alleged, autonomy enjoyed by academics. Alternatively, it may reveal the vulnerability of the discipline base; the traditional discipline-based perspective is quickly eroded in this context. What these examples also contribute is insight into how lecturers are attempting to make writing practices visible for students, as the examples make visible writing development processes.

A positive interpretation would be that these examples show how quickly academic staff can pick up on writing strategies for learning purposes. The last example shows how staff can use teaching skills they already have for developing writing in a student-centred way, making writing part of the learning environment. These experiences suggest that there is fertile ground for writing development.

A negative interpretation would be that writing is still seen to be so marginal, relative to the academic disciplines, that only those lecturers who already have an interest in it are likely to engage in personal or pedagogical development or reflect formally or informally on what they do and why they do it. In addition, where there is a residual stigma attached to writing development, where it is seen as remedial, those students who have writing difficulties are often positioned in the margins. Although writing is central to learning, and although writing is central to most forms of assessment, there is no systematic, well-founded approach to teaching writing in UK higher education. There is not yet a culture of taking writing to a higher level for higher education.

I believe the phrase 'embedding writing in the disciplines' is an impersonal construction which depersonalises the process of transformation that is required if writing development is to become central to teaching across the disciplines. Who is to do this embedding? Lecturers' perspectives have to evolve if students are to be taught about writing in the disciplines. The examples in this chapter suggest that this may be a highly personal, if not personalised, process. While lecturers in some disciplines do experience a fair amount of writing development, through mentoring during the PhD, for example, others do not. Providing support and development for students and lecturers, through units like the CAP, is one way of improving both the teaching of writing and scholarly output in UK higher education.

Finally, it should not be assumed that the lecturers represented in these examples have 'completed' their writing development in any sense. It would be safer to assume that they will continue to develop as writers and as teachers of writing. This lifelong learning will depend on the resources provided for staff writing development and on the acknowledgement of its direct, positive impact on student learning.

NOTES

1   For information about national policy on teaching qualifications for academics, see the Higher Education Academy website (www.heacademy.ac.uk/).
2   This dissertation workshop is described in more detail, including the lecturer's extended first-hand account, in Thow and Murray (2001).

Part III

Responding to Other Models

Introduction

Lisa Ganobcsik-Williams

The authors in Part II have explored Academic Writing theories and pedagogical practices that are being developed in UK universities, and in doing so have made reference to approaches drawn from other higher education contexts. The chapters in Part III describe and evaluate models of Academic Writing support developed in other countries, and are written by teachers and scholars within whose higher education contexts these models have been put into practice. The chapters in this section either advocate the adoption by UK practitioners of models developed in other contexts, or suggest that UK practitioners can learn from problems encountered in implementing particular models of writing support.

As Part II has shown, a strong tendency has been to look to well-established US models for formulating approaches to writing pedagogy. However, the first chapter in Part III reminds readers that Academic Writing has also been taught in Australian universities since the early 1990s, and demonstrates that the Australian example has much to offer UK higher education.[1] In this chapter, Jan Skillen reviews the history of approaches to teaching writing developed by staff in Learning Centres in Australian universities, and identifies a model of embedded writing instruction through which writing is integrated into the curriculum of content subjects as a result of collaborative curriculum development. Allowing students to acquire writing skills relevant to the discipline as they acquire the content knowledge of the curriculum, it makes the teaching of writing inseparable from the teaching of a subject – and a joint responsibility between disciplines and writing teachers. Although sharing characteristics of WID and WAC, the Australian 'transformative' model has developed independently. This chapter suggests that this model of teaching writing has measurable effects on student performance as well as a positive impact on teaching practice and curricula.

Speaking from a US perspective, John Heyda in Chapter 11, Joan Mullin in Chapter 12 and Mary Jane Curry in Chapter 13 describe a number of benefits – and expose some important drawbacks – that underlie US models of writing instruction. Heyda provides a detailed description of first-year or 'freshman' composition, the general writing course for students commonly taught in US colleges and universities. Written by an educator involved in the teaching and administration of first-year Composition for many years, this chapter takes a hard look at institutional motivations for requiring this course of all first-year students and argues that the generalist course does not prepare students for disciplinary writing demands. Heyda laments that US institutions' focus on this model has resulted in fewer resources for other approaches to grow more fully.

Mullin continues the discussion of US writing provision in Chapter 12, which outlines obstacles that are being encountered by those involved with improving the teaching of writing in both US and UK higher education: open admissions to less academically-privileged populations; the belief that writing can be mastered through a single course or single series of courses; and a disconnection between reading, writing and critical thinking. The chapter shows the consequences of US responses to some of these challenges, and analyses how a failure to question deeply embedded assumptions about the teaching of writing has led to an 'industry' of solutions that needs to be examined closely before being adopted by other higher education systems.

In Chapter 13, Curry looks at the implications for writing pedagogy of moves to widen participation in higher education. She examines the 'skills' conception of learning and argues that the view of academic modes of communication as divorced from their social context and separable into discrete skills does little to help students to join specific academic discourse communities. Drawing on the history of access in the US and grounded in data from an ethnographic study of a pre-university-level writing course at a US community college, the chapter illustrates the pitfalls of using a discrete 'skills' model to teach writing.

In the final chapter of the book, Bonnie Devet, Susan Orr, Margo Blythman and Celia Bishop discuss one other major US model: the writing centre.[2] This model is touched upon by Mullin in Chapter 12, who explains the fruitful connections that can exist between tutorial centres and WAC and WID programmes. In Chapter 14, Devet, Orr, Blythman and Bishop raise an important question about the extent to which models for teaching writing can be transferred across cultures and institutional structures. Their chapter interrogates the use of student peer tutors in developing other students' writing in the US and UK, and advises readers of the need – emphasised throughout the book – to adapt Academic Writing theories and pedagogical models carefully to local institutional contexts. In this chapter the authors place themselves in dialogue with each other; a move which effectively highlights the aim of scholarly exchange that is fundamental to Part III and to the book overall.

NOTES

1   As part of the Commonwealth system, Australia and the UK share cultural similarities, many of which are reflected in their higher education systems.

2   There is increasing European and UK interest in the US writing-centre model of offering university students dedicated one-to-one tutoring in Academic Writing – so much so that the National Writing Centers Association, established in 1983, has changed its name to the International Writing Centers Association (IWCA) in recognition that university writing centres are now being set up in a number of countries (see http://writingcenters.org/). It was noted in the general Introduction to this volume that the European Writing Centers Association (EWCA) was founded in 1998, and also that the Royal Literary Fund Fellowship Scheme, established in 1999, has highlighted the need for one-to-one writing tuition in UK universities. In addition, in Autumn 2000, 93 per cent of UK university staff responding to a national survey about student writing indicated that 'a university writing centre offering one-to-one tutorials in writing and communication' would be a 'useful' or 'highly useful' form of student support (Ganobcsik-Williams, 2004, pp. 28, 47). Despite these developments, the writing-centre model remains very new in UK higher education. There was an attempt to establish a writing centre at Newcastle Polytechnic (now Northumbria University) as early as 1979 (Hebron, 1984, p. 92), and another in 2002, at the University of Glasgow, Crichton Campus. In 2003 a writing centre was set up for students at Liverpool Hope University with a start-up grant from HEFCE, and in January 2004 a centralised 'Writing by Appointment' programme was put in place at the University of Dundee; both initiatives have been successful and continue to expand. The Centre for Academic Writing, established at Coventry University in 2004, is the first UK university writing centre whose mission is to provide both one-to-one writing tutorials for students and staff development in the teaching of writing. See Ganobcsik-Williams (2004, pp. 29–31) for further information on the history of one-to-one writing tutoring and writing centres in UK higher education, as well as a map of writing provision in UK universities.

10 Teaching Academic Writing from the 'Centre' in Australian Universities

Jan Skillen

▶ Introduction

Few Australian universities prior to the 1990s provided students with formal instruction in Academic Writing despite the fact that learning was assessed, for the most part, via academic essays, reports and theses. This situation was based on the assumption that instruction was unnecessary, that students at this level of education already had adequate writing skills acquired during secondary school. With the massification of the tertiary education system in the 1970s and 1980s this assumption was questioned and it was argued that students commencing university lacked the high-level language and literacy skills necessary for university study. As in UK higher education today, this perceived lack of skills has mostly been ascribed to a changing student body that was becoming more culturally and educationally diverse than was previously the case (Higher Education Council, 1992, quoted in Baskin et al., 1997, p. 66). Universities responded by creating learning centres to provide remedial assistance to those students seen as 'at risk' because of a lack of skills.

This chapter focuses on the provision of writing instruction offered by learning centres, using a model of practice that puts instruction in writing at the 'centre' of the university, a model that has been put into effect at the University of Wollongong and in a growing number of universities in Australia.[1] In this 'transformative' model *every* new student is seen as in need of acquiring the generic and specific writing skills of the disciplines he or she is moving into, and explicit instruction is seen as necessary for students to acquire those skills in a timely manner. The model is based on a number of premises. One is that written, academic English in all its disciplinary versions is a different variety of English from the English used for everyday communication by the majority of students. Another is that university students are adult learners and unlike children, who do not require explicit teaching in the acquisition of another language or language variety, will more quickly acquire the genre and linguistic idiosyncrasies of academic English through explicit instruction. Yet another is that teaching is most successful when it is effectively contextualised. The main strategy of the model is thus to provide 'explicit' instruction from within the discipline subjects that students are studying, ensuring that a majority of students will have a chance to learn about the generic and specific writing skills of the disciplines they are moving into and that writing instruction is not peripheral but central to study in the disciplines. This chapter will describe this model and provide evidence that it is able to enhance student learning in a number of ways. It will also suggest that the transformative model can have a positive impact on institutions because it operates on and with disciplinary curricula and thus directly influences teachers and teaching. The chapter will also argue that teachers of writing themselves gain by this model because it places them at the 'centre' of the intellectual work of the university, instead of at the periphery.

▶ Models of writing instruction

Although writing instruction was sometimes offered formally by English or Communications departments as subjects for credit or informally by individual lecturers during the teaching of their own subjects, the provision of explicit teaching in Academic Writing as a university-wide phenomenon with the overt backing of the institution arose with the introduction of learning centres in the early 1990s.[2] In these centres, writing instruction evolved over time: from early 'remedial' models of instruction[3] to 'integrated' and 'transforming' models of instruction;[4] each model responding to the student populations of the time and reflecting the level of responsibility taken by institutions for the development of students' writing skills.[5]

The oldest of the models was a 'remedial' one in which teachers in learning centres[6] provided instruction, via classes or one-to-one consultations, to students from non-English-speaking backgrounds, or 'equity' students from a range of disadvantaged backgrounds, or the general student who was motivated enough to seek opportunities for improvement. While this form of remedial support undoubtedly produced significant learning outcomes, it was limited to small numbers of students because of the comparatively small number of staff within each centre. It was also generic, as, isolated from other disciplines and their curricula, Learning Developers could not offer writing instruction suitable for every genre in every discipline, or provide advice that would always be in accord with the subject,[7] the discipline or the academic staff concerned. More importantly, it categorised the provision of writing instruction as remedial, with most students and staff seeing such support as necessary only for those students whose skills were poor.

Later or more sophisticated manifestations of writing instruction escaped the remedial tag by moving into curricula[8] and evolving into an integrated model in which the teaching of writing was integrated into content subjects within the disciplines, where writing was taught as part of the general teaching of those subjects.[9] The philosophy underpinning this integrated approach is a developmental one that centres on the belief that the writing skills required in the secondary system are qualitatively different from the wide range of skills required in the university system, and that therefore all students need to acquire new sets of literacy and learning skills pertinent to academia generally and to their fields of study specifically.

This integrated approach to teaching writing is supported by both Education and Linguistics. Ramsden's (1992) work in tertiary education, for instance, suggests that the acquisition of skills is most effective when instruction in those skills is placed within a specific context of study, and that teaching is effective if students see the direct relevance of what is being taught or studied. Newport's (1990) work in Linguistics suggests that explicit teaching is needed (or that conscious learning strategies need to be instituted) for adult learners of a new language (p. 551). Given that disciplinary discourses are varieties of English different from standard English and that students may never have been exposed to such language varieties, the typical tertiary student is very much like the adult second-language learner. This situation is also complicated because the language variety being learned is a written as well as a spoken one, providing even more of a rationale for explicit teaching: even children who are adept second-language learners require explicit teaching in *written* codes, registers or genres (Berkenkotter and Huckin, 1995). Berkenkotter and Huckin suggest that without explicit teaching, the majority of students must use the slower, lengthier process of osmosis or 'immersion in the discipline and a lengthy apprenticeship and enculturation' (1995, p. 13) to become competent in the written registers and genres of their disciplines, not a useful strategy within the restricted time frame of a degree programme.

Linguistic and learning theories also inform or provide the framework for the teaching practices employed in much of the integrated writing instruction taking place in Australia. One important theory informing our teaching is Systemic Functional Linguistics (SFL), a grammar of English that is descriptive of the structure and function of language at a number of levels, including that of genre.[10] It allows us to ensure not only that writing instruction is contextualised, but that it also provides students with awareness of the linguistic devices that are characteristic of Academic Writing and enables them to have conscious control over their use. These devices include the following:

- **modality** – allowing writers to express the level of certainty in claims, e.g. 'the results *may* indicate that . . .';

- **nominalisation** – allowing writers to increase the density of information in a sentence by turning verbs into noun constructions, e.g. the sentence '*The building was constructed using this new technology*' becomes the nominal '*The construction of the building using this new technology . . .*', which can act as the subject noun phrase of a much denser sentence;
- **thematic development** – allowing writers to construct cohesive and logical text;
- **the passive voice in thematic development** – allowing writers to direct the readers' attention to what happened rather than onto who did something, e.g. '*The hand-washing practices of hospital staff* were evaluated over a two-week period' or '*The research team* evaluated the hand-washing practices of hospital staff over a two-week period.'

Learning theories also provide the framework for the specific practices employed in our integrated teaching. Theorists such as Kolb (1984) highlight the learner's need for learning to be scaffolded around exposure to information, the opportunity to experience or experiment with that new information, feedback about this experience and time for reflection after feedback. This learning imperative is the underlying principle behind some of our teaching practice, specifically the use of staged or iterative tasks that allow experiment and feedback cycles following explicit teaching. Theorists and practitioners also point out learners' need to *see* an example of what it is they are to achieve (Poskitt, 2002); exemplars enable students to learn faster and more successfully. Annotated exemplars of the kinds of texts students are trying to achieve are used as a central part of our teaching; when an assessment task requires students to write in a new genre (for example, an Engineering design report), an exemplar text that is annotated to highlight certain issues relevant to the teaching forms part of the teaching and learning resources used in the class.

Given such integrated teaching, students see the content of the discipline and its associated writing and learning practices as equally important aspects of the discipline, instead of as separable and separate elements. Overall, the integrated model when it occurs as part of the general teaching of a content subject is a successful strategy for teaching disciplinary writing (and other associated skills) to large numbers of students, because it:

- contextualises the teaching within a disciplinary learning environment, making the content of that teaching more immediately useful and 'real' and making it relevant to students' needs and interests;
- provides instruction which is an indivisible part of studying a subject;
- efficiently and equitably provides instruction to all students studying a subject;

- provides cost-effective instruction because more students can be taught than in the traditional learning centre;
- provides teaching at the right time in relation to learning and assessment;
- gives students conscious knowledge of and control over the structural and rhetorical devices of the target genres;
- achieves significant development in skills for ALL students within a cohort.[11]

▶ A transformative model

A variation of the integrated model in which integration is carried strategically, rather than haphazardly, throughout a department, faculty or institution, is a transformative one, one that can have benefits beyond those achieved by individual students. The following discussion focuses on a transformative model currently in use within the University of Wollongong. The model involves collaboration between writing teachers, or Learning Developers, who are based in the learning centre, and staff at all levels of the university: faculties or schools, departments or disciplines, and discipline lecturers.[12] The collaboration revolves around the development of curricula that teach not only the explicit subject of study but also the skills implicit in the study of that subject. This includes a revision, if necessary, of assessment practice within curricula to ensure a match between learning objectives and assessment strategies, and the use of formative as well as summative assessment to maximise learning opportunities in terms of both skills and content. Such collaboration necessarily involves the Learning Developer in more than the teaching of writing, and the subject lecturers in more than the teaching of their subject content. Both partners become involved in issues to do with Academic Writing generally; with disciplinary discourse specifically; with the discipline content of the subject; and with teaching, learning and assessment concepts and practices. It is in this process of collaboration that the value of this model is found.

The goals of collaboration with faculties or schools are to identify the desired professional or discipline-specific skills of graduates of a particular faculty, and to identify core subjects for all disciplines of the faculty within which teaching and assessment of skills could be integrated into the teaching of content. Such collaboration provides one way for faculties to implement their own and their institution's policies with regard to graduate skills, particularly writing skills. Not only does this collaboration provide the opportunity for Learning Developers to teach writing in a strategic way that impacts on large numbers of students, it also acts as a catalyst for cross-disciplinary discussion and analysis of common objectives within and across disciplines.

The goals of collaboration with disciplines or departments are usually similar: to identify the desired generic and discipline-specific skills of graduates and to develop practices that ensure that those skills valued by the discipline are acquired by students within the time frame of their degree. This involves enriching degree courses so that a core subject at each year level (or, if necessary, a number of core subjects) includes the teaching of skills. This collaboration provides instruction that is tailored to the needs of the discipline as well as the curriculum and is integrated into the curriculum in a logical and sequential manner that mirrors the growing demands of study and assessment tasks in the curriculum. It supports students' sequential, cohesive acquisition of skills alongside the acquisition of content knowledge, which aids the enculturation process that constitutes studying a discipline.

The goals of collaboration with subject lecturers are to provide the teaching of writing skills that are implicitly or explicitly assessed within that lecturer's curriculum and that are necessary if students are to achieve at their potential in that curriculum. Prior to the teaching, the collaboration involves an analysis of the subject's content and learning objectives, assessment schedule, types of assessment and marking schema, and any necessary revision of any of the above. It also involves the design and production of learning materials, the development of strategies for teaching writing (and critical reading, thinking and learning skills), and the development of marking guidelines and marking workshops. It is at this level of subject integration that the previous two levels are implemented.

▶ Significant learning outcomes

Evaluation of the transformative model in terms of learning outcomes for students has been carried out in a number of subjects at the University of Wollongong. These evaluations have shown that the model produced a more effective and faster development in students' writing skills than a model without skills instruction integrated into curricula. One example of these evaluations was carried out in two consecutive, first-year, core Biology subjects (BIOL1 in the first semester and BIOL2 in the second semester).[13] In these subjects, curriculum development involved redesigning assignments to allow for the staging of assignments and for peer evaluation, and explicit teaching of study skills, reading and writing in the genres of the discipline. Evaluation involved comparing two cohorts,[14] an 'integration' and a 'no integration' group, and a semester-long longitudinal evaluation.

Control group evaluation

This evaluation was based on the results achieved in a report-writing task by two cohorts within BIOL2: one group had experienced one semester of writing instruction, integrated into the curriculum in BIOL1; the other group, entering Biology for the first time in BIOL2, had experienced none. The reports were assessed by Biology lecturers using a Biology report-marking schema adapted from the MASUS procedure, a tool for assessing Academic Writing developed at the University of Sydney (Bonanno and Jones, 1997). The marking criteria focused on using information (Criterion A), structuring and developing text (Criterion B),[15] Academic Writing style (Criterion C),[16] grammatical correctness (Criterion D) and presenting data (Criterion E). To ensure that methodological factors in the marking process such as parity between markers were controlled, the Learning Developers and discipline staff collaborated to adopt the following strategies:

- a marking handbook to be used by all markers was developed using annotated exemplars from student assignments to fully explicate each criterion and sub-criterion;
- a marking workshop was held to discuss the criteria; and
- cross-marking of a range of student reports was carried out.

The results showed that the cohort who had writing instruction integrated into their curriculum achieved ratings that were statistically higher in three criteria (A, C and E) than the control group who had no integrated instruction (Figure 10.1).[17] This was the case despite the fact that the 'no integration' control group had entered university with higher Tertiary Entrance Ranking (TER) scores than the 'integration' group.

Longitudinal evaluation

A longitudinal evaluation was also carried out to assess the effectiveness of the instruction. It was based on two assessments in BIOL2, the first early in the semester and the second towards the end of the semester. In the second assessment, the same strategies used in the marking of the first assessment were used again to ensure parity and reliability. Analysis of the ratings achieved by students in each criterion and sub-criterion showed that the cohort (350 students) improved significantly in all five areas (Figure 10.2).

This longitudinal evaluation also included analysis of the development of the two sub-groups in this cohort: the original BIOL1 cohort that consisted of Science majors and the new students who joined that cohort in BIOL2, Health and Behavioural Science (HBSc) majors. This analysis

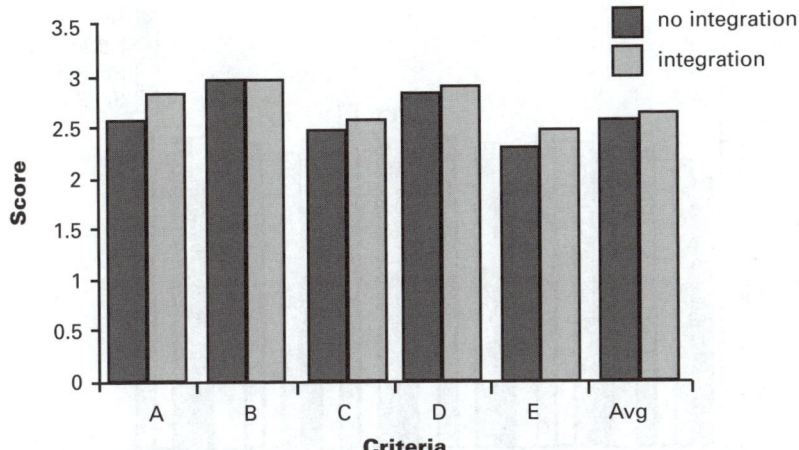

Figure 10.1   Comparison of mean results in each criterion area between 'integration' and 'no integration' groups

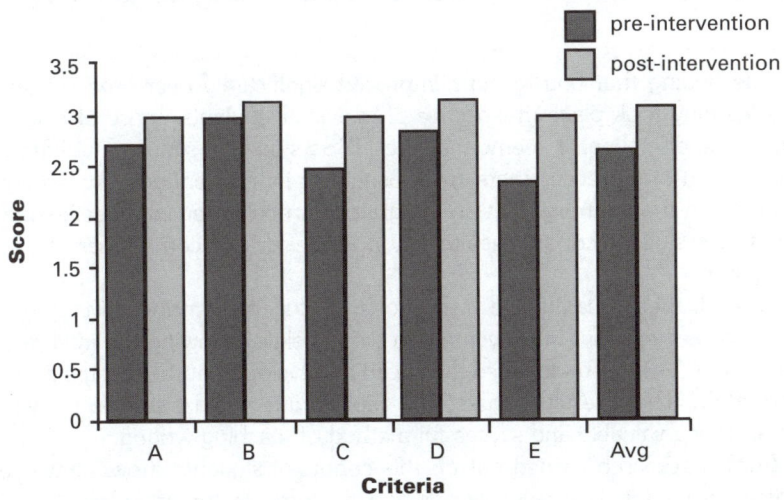

Figure 10.2   Comparison between pre- and post-intervention scores

was considered necessary, given the superior university entry scores of the HBSc students, to identify whether or not the source of significant improvement by the whole cohort originated from both the sub-groups or only from one. Analysis showed that both groups improved significantly in each criterion area, with particularly significant improvements in Criterion C, D and E (Figure 10.3).

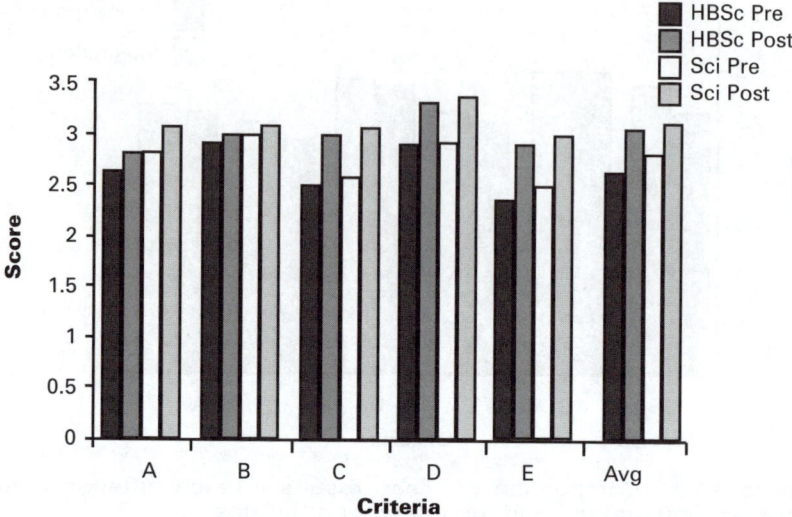

Figure 10.3 Sub-group performance pre- and post-intervention

The finding that both groups improved significantly over time suggests that learning took place irrespective of individual students' sense of belonging to the discipline. It seems that the HBSc students' status as visitors to Biology did not prevent them from acquiring its conventions. The results suggest, on the contrary, that an integrated curriculum encourages learning across the student cohort despite any possible lack of commitment to the discipline.

Overall, these quantitative evaluations of students' writing development identified a significant improvement in writing skills following the integrated instruction. They also identified the speed of development that occurs during integration. These results suggest that explicit, integrated instruction in writing skills is a valuable and successful method of teaching writing.

Further research carried out on this cohort of students shows that integrated instruction is a valuable addition to curricula for other reasons. A follow-up study (Hampton, 2002; Hampton et al., 2003) which evaluated the impact of this model of instruction on students' performance demonstrated that in the year of integration and the year following integration, both success and retention were improved in this cohort in comparison with cohorts who experienced no integrated instruction. This finding is supported by previous research in which the benefits of teaching skills inside curricula were felt both in terms of skill levels and in terms of content knowledge, leading to higher grades and higher retention rates (Stoodt and Balbo, 1979).

The transformative model thus not only helps students to reach their potential within the subject of study but also influences their continuing success within the discipline. It can be argued that the model provides a platform for the acquisition of the learning, language and literacy skills that help to ensure student success.

▶ Impact on teaching, curricula and teachers' role

An underlying philosophy of the model is that institutions have a responsibility for teaching skills as well as content; this is realised in the practice of teaching skills inside curricula in a way that signals their relationship to the disciplines being studied and recognises that skills are best learned within a disciplinary context. This practice is not only successful in teaching students about the discourse of their disciplines and in ensuring their acquisition of that discourse, it also appears to have beneficial influences on teaching within the institution,[18] on the curriculum itself, on the role of the teacher and on teachers themselves.

The model affects teaching in a number of ways. Most importantly, teaching becomes more student-centred because students' needs as learners become a central concern. Often, the primary concern in standard teaching is the disciplinary content of the curriculum and the amount of content that can be 'squeezed' into a semester. Once disciplines or lecturers commit to this new model, the concern becomes how learning can be achieved and, therefore, how teaching must take place. The model, in effect, becomes a vehicle for encouraging discipline staff to reflect more consciously on teaching and learning and it provides the collaboration and support for this to happen. The result is often a change in the way teaching takes place, with more active learning encouraged and more opportunities allowed for iteration or staging of assignments (Skillen et al., 1999; Trivett and Skillen, 1998). Evaluation of the model has suggested that general teaching strategies such as iteration 'have been very positive and have improved learning outcomes' (Lecturer in Biological Sciences, formal evaluation comment, 2000). These changes in teaching are often implemented to encourage skills acquisition but their value in assisting the learning of content is soon realised (James et al., 2004).

The model also has an impact on the curriculum. Most noticeable is the change in what is valued and taught. The model changes the nature of the curriculum to encompass the skills of the discipline as well as the discipline knowledge itself. One could argue that this knowledge is just being taught more fully, as it can be said to encompass the skills as well as the content of the discipline. The curriculum also adapts to encompass the process of learning as well as what is to be learned. This results from the more frequent use of formative assessment, which encourages learning, assesses how much and what has been learned and provides feedback to students about their learning.

The role of the teacher and, indeed, teachers themselves are also enhanced by the model. The role of the teacher changes to become that of teacher of skills as well as content, and also that of a collaborator in learning. This change in role can occur because the focus on more active learning strategies in class and on engaging students in the process of being peer markers alters the nature of classroom interactions. Thus the model expands teachers' perceptions of teaching. Indeed, it has been said that the staff development that results from working within the model 'is practical, positive and empowering' and that 'teaching [is] significantly improved' (Senior Lecturer, Faculty of Arts, formal evaluation comment, 1999). Most importantly, the model also extends teachers' conscious knowledge of the discourse of their disciplines (James et al., 2004). In an evaluation in 2000, a respondent noted that 'the most useful part [of this model] for some staff was the provision of a language with which they could articulate student strengths and weaknesses [in tertiary literacy]' (Lecturer in Nursing, formal evaluation comment, 2000).

This extension of teachers' skills can be an important bonus because while teachers may be skilled in the literacy conventions of their own disciplines and may recognise good exemplars of writing in the discipline, they are not necessarily conscious of what they know about the grammar of academic language generally or of their discipline's language specifically. Nor are they necessarily able to articulate what they know. This model allows them to become conscious of what they know and skilled in teaching students more explicitly and expertly about the discursive and structural characteristics of writing within their discipline.

▶ What the model means for teachers of writing

This modus operandi of the transformative model also affects teachers of writing themselves. Older models of writing instruction that involved only remedial one-to-one work with students placed writing teachers at the periphery of their institutions, resulting in little recognition for the intellectual work in which they were engaged.[19] This model, on the other hand, helps to enrich the contribution teachers of writing can make to university intellectual life and places them, along with discipline teachers, at the centre of the intellectual work of the university. One reason for this centrality is its collaborative nature, making the intellectual work that teachers of writing are engaged in highly visible and thus recognised by other academics within the institution as well as by students. At the University of Wollongong, for example, this recognition has come in the form of commendations in university teaching awards, and inclusion in university and faculty policy-making.

Another reason for the model's placement of teachers at this 'centre' may be the positioning of writing instruction *within* content subjects within the disciplines. This instruction within content subjects at university,[20] where the impact on student success and retention across whole cohorts of students is entirely visible to others, provides teachers of writing with more credibility than non-credit-bearing writing subjects taught from a learning centre where the positive learning outcomes achieved by students are not easily visible to the rest of the university community or are not seen as resulting from learning centre teaching. It may also provide more credibility than stand-alone, credit-bearing subjects in writing because, again, the visibility of the teaching and the collaboration required in the provision of writing instruction *within* content subjects ensures other academics are exposed to the language, learning and literacy expertise of teachers of writing. With a growing majority of Learning Developers highly qualified in Linguistics, this expertise is a powerful contribution to a teaching team's capacity to teach and talk about the language and literacy conventions of a discipline.

A final reason for placing writing teachers at the centre is that this model's positive impact on learning and teaching makes it a valuable contribution to the core business of the university community. At the University of Wollongong, for instance, the teaching carried out by writing teachers within Learning Development has resulted in them being short-listed in national teaching awards, awards not just for teachers of writing but for university teaching generally. This could be said to be recognition of our contribution to the 'core' business of universities and recognition that while the overt focus of this work is about Academic Writing, the enrichment of teaching and student learning is this model's end product.

▶ Conclusion

The transformative model is a shift in the remedial paradigm previously adopted by learning centres or Learning Developers to one that is a paradigm in the developmental tradition. This developmental transformative model is giving all students within a cohort, not just disadvantaged students or less capable students, the opportunity to acquire the generic and discipline-specific literacy and learning skills suitable for the new contexts they are entering. It is creating valid, effective and equitable learning support that recognises the need for all students to acquire these skills if they are to successfully negotiate new disciplines and new contexts, and that recognises that students acquire these skills best when they are taught alongside content. The collaboration needed for the integration of instruction in skills into mainstream content curricula, the hallmark of the transformative model, is also having an impact on institutions. It is enriching teaching and curricula, and creating teachers who are skilled in teaching and assessing the literacy or discursive aspects of their disciplines. In achieving these outcomes, the model is also allowing Learning Developers, as teachers of writing, to impact more positively on their institutions and is effectively placing them at the centre of the intellectual work of the university, instead of at the periphery.

NOTES

1   An unpublished Unilearn survey (3 June 2004) indicated that learning centres in more than half of all Australian universities are teaching in this way to some degree. The common use of this model was also attested to at national Learning and Academic Skills Conferences held at Flinders University, South Australia (2003), and at the University of Wollongong, NSW (2001) (see http://learning.uow.edu.au/LAS2001).

2   Webb (2002, p.14) notes, however, that some universities did set up learning centres/academic skills centres much earlier than this. The Australian National University is one example. One reason suggested for the lack of writing instruction prior to the introduction of learning centres is the early discipline specialisation that occurs in Australian higher education (Webb, 2002), which leaves little room in a degree programme for generic subjects unrelated to a particular discipline or profession.

3   See Skillen and Mahony (1997) for a description of this evolution.

4   See McLean et al. (1995), Skillen et al. (1999) and Webb (2002).

5   The terminology of writing models such as Writing Across the Curriculum (WAC) and Writing in the Disciplines (WID) is not common in Australia, although there are overlaps in practices between the integrated model discussed here and WAC and WID. The influence of these US models has been limited because, as Tapper (2003) points out, '[i]n Australian universities, US models of Writing Across the Curriculum need considerable adaptation if they are to get off the ground, and [when they do] often focus on communication skills rather than [on] writing alone'. Distinctly WAC terminology and practices have been used in a number of universities in Australia though, most notably in the School of Communication at the Queensland University of Technology where the first Australian university WAC programme was set up in 1993 (Petelin, 2002); and at the University of Melbourne, where a Communication Across the Curriculum (CAC) project was established in 1997 (Tapper, 2000, 2003).

6   Teachers in learning centres are usually academic staff and are variously called Learning Developers, Academic Skills Advisers, or Study Skills Advisers. Their main focus is on the teaching of writing but they also have a more general role in learning and language. In fact, the interest in learning is primary: the focus

on writing exists to support students' ability to learn from reading and to provide evidence of their learning in written assignments and examinations.

7   In Australian higher education, the word 'subject' is equivalent to the terms 'class', 'module' or 'unit'.

8   Some movement of the teaching of writing into curricula occurred earlier; the University of Sydney, for example, began this move in 1991 (Jones, 2004).

9   See Hicks et al. (1995), Garner and Edwards (1995) and Skillen and Mahony (1997). Sometimes, integration into the disciplines occurred as special 'communication' subjects, although this type of integration is not the focus of this chapter.

10 See Halliday (1994), Swales (1990) and Jones (2004). This theory also informs practice in the teaching of writing in Australian primary and secondary education.

11 Supplementing this model with some form of generic support via a learning centre is also important. Putting in place multiple types of provision ensures all students are supported.

12 The goals of collaboration are outlined in more detail in Skillen et al. (2001).

13 See Skillen et al. (1999).

14 The 'integration' group was the original BIOL1 cohort and the 'no integration' group was a sub-group who joined the BIOL1 cohort in the second semester of BIOL2.

15 The teaching related to Criterion B included elements such as genre and the control of theme and rheme (see Halliday, 1994) to achieve cohesive text at the sentence and paragraph level.

16 The teaching related to Criterion C included the use of passive voice to focus readers' attention in the appropriate direction, and the use of formal as opposed to informal vocabulary.

17 In this semester only minimal instruction was given in Criterion B and no instruction was given in Criterion D.

18 This beneficial influence is being researched more fully at the University of Wollongong, although initial evaluation suggests that its impact on teaching is considerable (see James et al., 2004).

19 This lack of status and exclusion from the mainstream has also been noted in writing centres in US universities (Grimm, 1996).

20 These are subjects such as 'Molecules, Cells and Organisms', a core subject within the discipline of Biology.

11 Sentimental Education: First-Year Writing as Compulsory Ritual in US Colleges and Universities

John Heyda

▶ Introduction

Long required of first-year undergraduates, freshman composition in the United States has grown into a vast, sprawling enterprise. According to a 2001 study, 97 per cent of colleges and universities surveyed have a core writing course, with 64 per cent reporting a two-course requirement (Moghtader et al., 2001, p. 464). Converted to numbers of students in first-year writing courses nationwide, these percentages yield startling enrollment data. Sharon Crowley (1998) writes that in 1994–5, 'nationally there were at least four million students enrolled in the freshman composition course'. This meant 'some one-hundred and sixty-thousand sections of freshman composition were offered, if schools limited enrollments per section to twenty-five students – as they typically do' (p. 1). Figures from the National Center for Education Statistics (2002) add close to one million to Crowley's total, reporting 13,155,000 enrolled by 2000, and based on projections for degree-granting institutions, 'between 2000 and 2013, total enrollment is projected to increase 19 percent, to 18.2 million' (National Center for Education Statistics, 2003). Applying Crowley's enrollment-per-section calculus, one can imagine something like 235,000 sections, or modules, of first-year writing by 2013. Figures such as these boggle the mind. Here is a course approaching 200,000 sections a year, with higher annual enrollments than just about any other university course on the planet. Yet for all these big numbers, and perhaps because of them, Composition has had only a limited part to play in the undergraduate curriculum.

Though more and more first-year writing programs claim to prepare students to write and read academic prose, those with well defined links to the academic disciplines remain in short supply. Some programs housed in departments offering graduate degrees in Composition and Rhetoric have forged such ties, but at the vast majority of colleges and universities first-year writing has formed few alliances with undergraduate curricula. I would argue that the culprit here is the universal requirement. This mandate generates tens of thousands of sections of Composition every year but withholds the resources needed to establish first-year programs as viable gateways to academic and workplace literacies. In truth, Composition instructors are expected to work wonders with students' writing in a semester or two but without the institutional support that would make their labors consequential. To teach students writing for subsequent work in the academy and on the job would require that Composition programs train, supervise, and support legions of instructors, an expense far greater than US colleges and universities have ever considered budgeting for. In fact, as the Moghtader et al. (2001) survey shows, Composition enjoys such support significantly less today than thirty years ago: 'the number of schools where Composition courses are taught only by full-time faculty has dramatically declined; the number of schools staffing Composition courses with [graduate] teaching assistants has increased slightly; and the number of schools employing part-time instructors to teach required writing courses has increased dramatically' (pp. 458–9).

Looking in on US higher education from abroad, one might be hard pressed to imagine requiring Composition of all students without committing, at the same time, to making the experience as relevant and useful as possible. Yet this is precisely the situation. I believe that maintaining the requirement as an unfundable mandate has prevented the first-year course from realizing its potential as a gateway to Academic Writing. Rather, the course has taken on a decidedly vocational character, emphasizing the practical, not intellectual, advantages of 'taking up the pen'. At its best, Composition is a stand-alone general writing course geared to the production of university-level essays. At its worst, it is a writing-by-the-numbers charade demanding only that students crank out five-paragraph themes with precisely-placed thesis statements and topic sentences.

Historically, the combination of unmanageable enrollments and vocationally-oriented instruction gave rise to a 'current-traditional' pedagogy that became the course's hallmark. The following account illustrates the vocational, skills-and-drills character of current-traditional teaching:

> Current-traditional pedagogy discriminated four genres: exposition, description, narration, and argument (EDNA). It idealized a single format – the five-paragraph theme, which after a brief introduction that stated its author's thesis, presented three highly prescribed paragraphs of support, and concluded. Students were taught current-traditional principles of discourse through teachers' analyses of professional examples, and they were then expected to compose paragraphs and essays that displayed their observance of those principles.   (Crowley, 1998, p. 94)

What students had to say in their writing came to matter very little: 'what matters in current-traditional rhetoric is form. Current-traditional pedagogy forces students to repeatedly display their use of institutionally sanctioned forms. Failure to master the sanctioned forms signals some sort of character flaw such as laziness or inattention' (p. 95). The current-traditional program maintained control of the first-year writing classroom for decades. As James Berlin observes, in *Rhetoric and Reality* (1987), 'Current-traditional rhetoric has been . . . in the last hundred years . . . the dominant rhetoric overall. For the majority of English teachers, it has been a compelling paradigm, making it impossible for them to conceive of the discipline in any other way' (p. 9).

I begin with these daunting enrollment figures, and with the domination of current-traditional teachings, to point up first-year Composition's vulnerability to repetition, routine – even regimentation. With tens of thousands of sections to cover every term, the course's ongoing susceptibility to the vocational has been thoroughly institutionalized, yielding a stultifying sameness capable of crushing experimentation and innovation. Richard Ohmann (1976) captured this ritualizing character of the course in *English in America*, noting that the student, 'whose name is legion, has little impulse to make his thoughts public . . . . Composition is for him a matter of time-serving, doing what the instructor requires, submitting to a mild, necessary indignity' (pp. 141–2). It is all the more remarkable, then, that this course has survived as a requirement, not to mention that the terms of its survival are caught up in their own forms of repetition and routine. In 'The Abolition Debate in Composition: A Short History', Robert Connors (1996) contends that Composition's very history can be read as a repeating cycle of calls for its abolition and reform:

> [C]omposition over the last century has been marked by alternating periods of what I will call reformism and abolitionism. During reformist periods, freshman comp, though problematical, is seen as the thin red line protecting the very life of literacy. Abolitionist periods are times during which at least some English teachers call for the end of freshman composition, declaring the large sums expended on this all-but-ubiquitous course a gross waste.   (p. 47)

Perhaps most astonishing is that, while over the last few decades Composition scholars have leveled largely successful challenges against the course's vocational character, its ritualizing aspect has survived, emerging in a far more positive light than one might have imagined possible. In *Composition in the University*, Crowley (1998) speaks of this phenomenon, characterizing the first-year writing course as 'a sentimental favorite in America, like big bands and Colin Powell' (p. 228).

In this chapter, I contend that in the period since Crowley's book first appeared, the compulsory first-year course has only solidified its position as a 'sentimental favorite', in spite of the dismantling of much of the old course and program apparatus. I argue that at a time when first-year writing could be breaking free, at last, from the sentimentalizing power of longstanding ritual practices, the maintenance of the universal requirement all but guarantees perpetuation of Composition as ritual. I examine recent calls for abolition of the universal requirement and resistance to these calls. I claim that US higher education institutions have more reasons than ever to resist calls for abolishing the requirement, and that this resistance represents as big an obstacle to curricular progress as the first-year course has yet faced.

▶ First-year Composition: administration and pedagogy

I have taught first-year writing for over a quarter-century, directing my university's first-year writing program for two of those years. During this time I have seen Composition and its administration put through big changes. In the 1960s and 1970s, I saw Composition serve as a gate-keeping course, a blunt instrument for weeding out freshman class undesirables. In the 1980s and 1990s, it was refashioned as a gateway course, employed as a delicate instrument for raising students' consciousness about matters ranging from cultural pluralism to identity politics. From the standpoint of the administration of the course, I saw Composition's massive first-year writing programs change as well, from tightly controlling to only loosely monitoring individual sections. Teachers began choosing their own textbooks, writing their own syllabi, teaching the course as they saw fit. Results from Moghtader et al.'s (2001) survey bear this out: only 4 per cent of 'Composition instructors use a syllabus written by the program director' and a mere 7 per cent go with 'a syllabus written together by all instructors', while 55 per cent use 'syllabi they have written themselves'. We learn, too, that 18 per cent of 'Composition instructors use the same text' and another 12 per cent 'choose texts from a pre-approved list', while 39 per cent 'select their own texts' (2001, p. 465).

There is one key feature of the first-year course still in place, however: the universal requirement, which mandates that students take at least one semester of Composition, regardless of their major field of study or degree program. While the requirement has remained firmly in place, what instructors have required of their students has changed significantly. As a result, the history of Composition since the Second World War has been about key changes that have led to 'deregulating' the course while at the same time ensuring its survival as a requirement. Until well into the 1970s, Composition featured a rudimentary 'think first – then write' pedagogy that trained students in a top–down model for writing papers on demand. As Crowley (1990) notes, 'the model tacitly assumed that any thinking student should be able to get her writing right on the first go-round. She needed no assistance with invention proper; indeed very little could be given her. What teachers could do was lecture about how a finished discourse should look.' Students were schooled to follow 'a neat linear progression: select, narrow, and amplify'. This gave rise to the ubiquitous current-traditional assignment: 'From the following list, choose the topic that most appeals to you. Construct a thesis, develop support, organize your ideas, and draft an essay – in that order' (pp. 147–8). Students sat in rows, facing a teacher who lectured on such gripping topics as 'patterns of organization', 'outlining', and 'purposeful details'. They had no choice but to pay close attention, as teachers rarely permitted them to revise their papers once submitted.

While the cursory model Crowley describes hangs on to this day in programs of a more remedial bent, it was supplanted thanks to two major shifts in curricular orientation, the first of which saw the emergence of writing-process pedagogies in the 1970s, the second the arrival of a post-process challenge in the 1990s. Until the 1970s the course relied, largely, on students' following the current-traditional model. That began to change in the 1970s with the advent of expressivist approaches, and picked up steam in the 1980s with the popularizing of 'write to learn' pedagogies. One-draft assignments gave way to the teaching of 'process' or multi-stage writing featuring instruction in invention and pre-writing, composing, then re-writing. Students learned to work in peer groups, sharing drafts and practicing revision strategies; thus the production, reading, and discussion of student writing became the centerpiece of the course.

Instructors began encouraging students to revise their work, supported by portfolio grading. With portfolios, students' revision efforts could be tied to a final project requiring that they submit their best essays in a packet at the end of the semester. In this way, not all writing assignments were assessed, and students had time to revise through multiple re-writes. Expository, descriptive, narrative, and persuasive writing continued to figure prominently, though the dominance of these four modes of discourse began to lose their grip. New, more exploratory and reflective forms of writing began to win support as a more relaxed atmosphere took hold. Besides peer workshops and shorter, informal writing assignments, process activities have included free-writing, journal-keeping, and class discussions of students' writing. This freer writing began to emerge from students' personal interests and research rather than from assigned essay prompts.

These were halcyon days for Composition, the course at last appearing to have found its disciplinary focus, namely the study of the writing process and student texts. Research into student writing picked up accordingly. The new student-centered pedagogies had their shortcomings, however, and by the 1990s challenges to the 'process approach' began to expose them. Too often, putting student writing at the center meant that students only read texts produced by their peers. Consequently, genres narrowed to those that students could readily produce via the writing process taught in class, and, as process tilted toward personal writing, Composition came to favor topics drawn from private experience, thereby limiting writing's connection to the social. Process pedagogies' initial promise of escape from prescriptive 'think first – then write' models, therefore, began giving way to an all-too-prescriptive 'writing process'.

Challenging the process approach, post-process Composition theory that began to appear in the 1990s represents another significant shift in course orientation. It holds that writing is a public act, inevitably a social process, and not governable by sets of codified guidelines dictating a single, prescriptive 'writing process'. As Thomas Kent (1999) explains, in *Post-Process Theory: Beyond the Writing Process Paradigm*, 'post-process theorists hold – for all sorts of different reasons – that writing is a practice that cannot be captured by a generalized process or a Big Theory' (p. 1). The post-process classroom distinguishes itself from its predecessors in its greater emphasis on teacher–student collaboration and dialogue. Kent notes, for instance, that 'by working in partnership with their students, mentors would no longer stand outside their students' writing and reading experiences. Instead, they would become an integral part of their students' learning experiences' (p. 166).

▶ A baleful influence: the first-year writing course and sentimentalism

Just as the first-year course's administration and pedagogy have changed, so has the character of the sentimentality attached to the course. While the sentimental education dispensed by first-year writing and its rituals has long engaged its students and teachers, only in recent years has it touched the course's administrators. For them, sentimentality attaches to the universal requirement itself in ways that reveal much about the requirement's hold on the imagination of academic staff and administrators. What, then, accounts for first-year writing's claim on the sentimental imagination? How has a course with so many detractors managed to emerge, in the post-modern American university, as more of a sentimental favorite than ever? What does this emergence tell us about the obstacles facing those who now call for abolition of it as a requirement?

Composition has been on the American scene for a long time. Harvard 'began college-level composition courses in 1872' and in 1885 'English A, the name that has remained synonymous with Freshman English, was introduced' there 'as *the* freshman composition course' (Russell, 2002, pp. 49, 53; Greenbaum, 1969, p. 174). In 1900 English A, which had 'become the model for required freshman-composition courses around the country', was made 'the only required course' for undergraduates at Harvard (Russell, 2002, p. 50). According to Leonard Greenbaum's (1969) thumbnail history of the requirement, 'The Tradition of Complaint', almost from the beginning the course inspired negative sentiments. There is, for instance, the remorse of Harvard Professor Barrett Wendell, one of the course's pioneers, over his having 'exerted a more baleful influence upon college education in America than any other man in his profession' in setting 'this Frankenstein monster in motion'. At the end of his career, nearly a century ago, Wendell 'was frankly appalled when he heard the creaking of the huge machine inexpertly devised for teaching freshmen . . . how to write in their mother-tongue' (p. 175). By 1939, in 'The Failure of Freshman English', Oscar James Campbell was echoing Wendell's negative view and calling for drastic measures. 'I am convinced that Mr. Wendell was right,' he observes. 'I believe that the standard college course in freshman composition has done much more harm than good' (p. 178). Campbell goes on to call for the course's elimination, saying 'the greatest service that college teachers of English could render their profession and to collegiate education in general would be to urge the immediate abolition of this course everywhere' (p. 178).

Discontent with requiring such a course continued well into the postwar period. Greenbaum outlines over 50 years of in-house complaints about the course. One reads here of the mind-numbing teaching loads assigned to Composition's 'section hands', of the longstanding suspicion that students write no better upon completion of the course, of nagging disagreements over course goals and methods, of noisome calls to do away with the first-year course entirely, and so on. Missing in Greenbaum's record of complaint, though, is any real concern that instruction in writing had become all but synonymous with its ritualization in the first-year classroom. When you're calling for the abolition of the course, who cares about its rituals? It was not until the 1960s and 1970s, when the postwar baby-boom generation hit college campuses and enrollments exploded, that the first stirrings of positive sentiments about the required course begin appearing. Not coincidentally, it was also during this time that the rituals themselves began to change, with the 'endless drill in grammar and mechanics' giving way to the 'comfortable seminar taught by a tweedy professor' (Crowley, 1998, p. 228).

▶ Challenging the 'skills-course' model of Composition

Only about one-fifth of American 18-to-21-year-olds were enrolled in higher education at the end of the Second World War. By the end of the 1970s, however, this figure had risen to about one-half of the relevant age group. About 3.8 million were enrolled in higher education at the beginning of the 1960s; by 1970 about 7.8 million (Beverley, 1978, p. 68). These increases can be explained, in large part, by the 'promise' of higher education. In place by the 1940s, this 'promise' took students out of the labor market, postponing their school-leaving age while enlisting higher education in training them for re-admission to the workforce later on and at a level higher than they could have attained otherwise. To make the 'promise' pay off in this way, however, students were expected to 'learn the skills needed to accommodate to the first requirement of industrial labor: respect for authority, the self-discipline necessary to internalize the values of the labor process, and the place of the worker within the prevailing occupational hierarchies' (Aronowitz, 1973, p. 74). Clearly, higher education was moving toward the vocational as liberal education curricula declined in power and prestige. Following the war, ritualizing of curricula reached unprecedented proportions. Writing in 1956, William H. Whyte found students 'getting more and more . . . training in the minutiae of organizational skills, and that while it is hardly news that the US inclines to the vocational, the magnitude of the swing has been much greater than is generally recognized' (Whyte, 1956, p. 35). By the mid-1950s, then, it was evident that traditional curricula would play a reduced role in shaping higher education's 'promise'.

If higher education's newly-created promise had little to offer the traditional liberal arts curriculum, it had even less for first-year writing. Postwar vocationalizing had made obsolete Composition's original purpose, to 'select those who display the verbal signs of a governing class' and 'to teach them some of the verbal skills necessary for governance' (Ohmann, 1976, p. 134). With the abandonment of this purpose, first-year writing lost connection to its origins and began to fragment. By the time Rhetoric and Composition scholarship began to emerge, belatedly, as a field in its own right in the United States, this fragmentation had begun to show itself in a plethora of new course objectives: 'to introduce students to literary culture, to fight the corruption of thought and language, or simply to "teach students to think" or introduce them to scholarly ideas about language or teach them principles of rhetoric' (p. 134).

If first-year Composition was still a course in writing, this was more or less incidental; it was to become something more like an introduction to the sorts of skills – intellectual, organizational, and so on – that a semi-skilled, white-collar worker might have to employ on the job. This redesign of Composition as a 'skills' course might have swept all before it, too, had it not been for the upheavals of the late 1960s and early 1970s. With student activism of this period came demands for educational reform: open admissions, more relevant course offerings, the dismantling of degree programs and removal of required courses. Elective courses replaced requirements, and first-year writing, as the ultimate required course, became, quite naturally, a prime target of reform. Freshman composition courses were compressed into a semester or a quarter, or in some rare instances made voluntary. A 1973 survey of the requirement reported, for instance, that in 1967, 93 per cent of US colleges required at least one course in Composition and 78 per cent required at least two, but that by 1973 these figures stood at 76 per cent and 45 per cent respectively (Copperman, 1978, p. 108).

Writing teachers and scholars opposed to first-year writing as workforce training began to challenge the idea of Composition as a skills course. In the work of such pioneers of student-centered Composition as Ken Macrorie, William E. Coles, Jr, and Walker Gibson, skills-course Composition is condemned as authoritarian and illiberal. Macrorie's (1970) take on schooling as deadening and repressive appears especially in his attacks on 'Engfish', 'the phony, pretentious language of the schools'. For Macrorie this language finds its way into undergraduate writing because 'most English teachers have been trained to correct students' writing, not to read it' (pp. 1–2). Just how vocationalized the course had become is summed up by Coles (1969), who, interpreting the language used in a generic 'preface' to students 'beginning an actual text on rhetoric', observes that, in its tone, 'there is no reasonable demand for writing which cannot be articulated, nothing about writing which cannot be understood. . . . Writing becomes "effective" writing becomes Themewriting.' For the writer of the preface, ' "effective writing" is something one can learn to do "easily," . . . and which once learned will enable a student to write "brochures and manuals" and letters in the same way that he has written "term papers" and "essay examinations" ' (p. 141).

In challenging rote learning, Coles and Macrorie promote Composition teaching as a refuge or retreat from the authoritarian and hierarchical world outside their classrooms, with the hope that such an alternative might counter the stifling atmosphere at work in traditional 'teacher-centered' classes, where the teacher lectures and students take notes. Since the 1980s, their influence, along with the sway of other renowned student-centered teachers like Peter Elbow in *Writing without Teachers* (1998, first published in 1973) and Donald Murray in *Write to Learn* (2005, first published in 1984), has extended beyond the classroom and into first-year programs themselves. Through their influence, and as the vocationalizing of higher education has continued its advance, required, generalist first-year writing programs have grown more and more accommodating to the notion of the writing course as a refuge or retreat from 'illiberal' schooling. The first-year course can, then, be made to serve as a respite from an ever more skills-based curriculum, a glimpse into an alternative higher education environment, one without alienation and massification. By making the course a compulsory, first-year retreat, US colleges and universities have made of Composition something other than just a first-year writing course. They have made it a cultural rite of passage, a highly ritualized space in which students can try out new, more 'open' classrooms, and 'experience' the subjects they encounter by sharing and evaluating their feelings with peers in low-risk, low-enrollment settings. Margaret Mathieson (1975) observes that, 'the teacher's role in this' scenario is 'to be an open-minded person with whom one can trustfully roam' (p. 220).

Student-centered pedagogies and the classroom apparatus built to support them – in-class workshops, the writing of multiple drafts, discussions geared to eliciting student subjectivities – have given the first-year writing course a new lease on life. However it is structured within a college or university, the generalist 'writing requirement' has a stronger presence today than twenty-five years ago (Moghtader et al., 2001, p. 456). Given Composition's success in 'turning things around' at the first-year level, one might have expected the disciplinary field of Rhetoric and Composition to build on this success, extending the reach of writing instruction into the second, third, and fourth years of the undergraduate curriculum. Apart from a limited number of programs, this has not happened, however, and the perpetuating of the universal requirement has had everything to do with that.

▶ The new abolitionists

The appearance of the 'new abolitionists' in the early 1990s represents a notable turn in Composition's longstanding 'tradition of complaint'. At the time, Crowley observed that 'we might be able to alter the functions of Freshman English by altering its institutional status', and urged Composition teachers to work to 'abolish the universal requirement', and 'stop insisting that every student who enrolls in a two-year college or four-year university must take a required composition course' (1998, p. 241). Unlike the course's detractors cited by Greenbaum, who wanted simply to abolish the course, Crowley and the new abolitionists want to free Composition from being universally required so that it might take on new life. Crowley (1999) has presented a number of arguments for abolishing the requirement. First, '[t]he universal requirement exploits teachers of writing, particularly part-time teachers and graduate students. Currently, 90 per cent of first-year Composition courses are taught by marginally employed teachers.' Paid comparatively little per class, these instructors have no health benefits, job security, or the academic freedom that comes with tenure. Maintaining the massive underclass required to dispense first-year writing to all freshman students means that teachers of the course are locked into the lowest positions on the academic ladder, without hope of rising within the profession. In this regard, their position is practically the same as it was before World War II.

Another argument against the requirement is that students have to put a good deal of time and energy into the course, without clear benefit. Crowley (1999) notes that 'students' investment in a required course should be backed with some assurance that their efforts are useful or necessary'. Yet a 'curious silence' obtains regarding the 'measurable effects of the universally-required course'.

The first-year requirement presents curricular problems as well. Requiring the course is bad for the curriculum. Crowley cites difficulties in designing 'a course for a large amorphous audience when, moreover, the course fits into no discernable disciplinary or scholarly sequence. In curricular terms, the introductory Composition requirement comes from nowhere and goes nowhere.' Besides these problems, innovations are 'difficult to implement and sustain because of the size and impermanence of Composition faculties' (1999).

Perhaps Crowley's most compelling argument against the requirement involves the inevitable 'negative professional and disciplinary effects'. She observes that 'like it or not, university faculty, parents, and taxpayers still assume that the required introductory course teaches grammar, spelling, punctuation, and organization. Because of this, they view Composition faculty as literacy gatekeepers rather than as intellectuals.' Worst of all, 'the effort required to maintain the required course' prevents 'thinking of our discipline in more expansive curricular terms'. Freed of the burden of administering the requirement, 'specialists could begin to work toward installing writing instruction throughout the curriculum, toward strengthening and expanding writing centers, toward establishing departments of writing' (1999).

Crowley's arguments have provoked considerable debate and much opposition. In 'Reframing the Great Debate on First-Year Writing', Marjorie Roemer, Lucille Schultz, and Russel Durst question Crowley's characterization of the required course 'as backward and benighted', and contend that reading 'the first-year course as a site where the teaching is instrumental, the method is skill and drill, and the intended outcome is error-free prose is deceptive'. Crowley and others are then charged with depicting the course 'as it existed 150 years ago, or even 50 years ago, denying the tremendous changes that we have seen in the field' (Roemer et al., 1999, pp. 383–4). Of course, dismissing calls to abolish the requirement would be easy enough were they coming out of an uncomplicated view of Composition as mere 'skill and drill', and evincing the elitist disdain for first-year writing common among pre-World War II Literature professors. Were that the case, Crowley's arguments for abolishing the requirement would carry no more weight than decades-old calls to eliminate the course entirely. Abolitionists' arguments might be read then, as Roemer, Schultz, and Durst imagine, as 'an expressed desire not to work with beginning college students on Composition-related matters', and 'a corresponding preference to teach more advanced, engaged students on subjects more compatible with the interests and abilities of the college English faculty' (1999, p. 378).

In truth, 'new' abolitionists' views of the first-year course are considerably more complex than their detractors allow. Rather than calling only for the evacuation of first-year classrooms in favor of the greener pastures of upper-division coursework, abolitionists envision more systemic changes within institutions, including the creation of new undergraduate writing and rhetoric courses and majors, and development of more comprehensive Writing Across the Curriculum (WAC) programs and writing centers. Goggin and Miller (2000) note 'we offer very few undergraduate courses in rhetoric and Composition in less than a handful of undergraduate programs across the country', and observe that 'teaching our discipline both in introductory courses and in undergraduate minors and majors in rhetoric and Composition would effectively broaden the base of understanding, thus, reaching future administrators, faculty, parents, and taxpayers' (p. 99). No such systemic change is likely, however, while Composition's limited resources – in administration, in staffing, and so on – are tied to the first-year course. Given the compelling arguments for change advanced by Crowley and others, it is rather surprising to find rejoinders expressing so much mere sentiment in support of the status quo.

Even more surprising is that defenders of requiring first-year writing appear so fiercely attached to the course. Is there not, for instance, a good bit of sentimentality in the following tribute? First-year writing 'is our primary field site: the site which generates most of our scholarship and research, the site where we train graduate students to be teachers, the site that spawned Writing Across the Curriculum and other discipline-based writing programs, the site that inaugurated the field of basic writing. It is where we do our most visible work and where others learn from us' (Roemer et al., 1999, p. 385). It is as though, without the required course, no such changes could have come about – and as if, without its continuance, such pedagogical innovation cannot be sustained or developed.

Expressing indebtedness to the required course for its fostering advances in Composition studies presupposes, of course, that first-year programs have improved enough to provide the requisite support. Recent studies suggest that they have not. Bullock and Smith, in 1998, 'found that contrary to proclamations by many in Rhetoric and Composition about changes in the field, virtually all of the programs they analyzed were firmly rooted in current-traditional practices' (quoted in Goggin and Miller, 2000, p. 87). In 'Enlarging the Context', which details findings of his Ford Foundation study, Richard Larson finds 'a substantial majority' of first-year programs exhibiting 'one or more (usually quite a few) of the following characteristics: a heavy emphasis on the teaching of form . . .; relative inattention to processes of substantive invention . . .; lack of visible attention to quality of reasoning and to what makes for forceful arguments on behalf of cogent ideas' and 'a general lack of concern for the rhetoric of discourse'. Larson adds, soberingly: 'we confront a profession not yet ready to commit itself to defining carefully its goals in teaching and to finding out in a systematic and serious way whether its courses are attaining those goals' (Larson, 1994, pp. 120–1).

▶ Conclusion

Unfortunately for the cause of abolition, US institutions now have more reasons than ever to resist calls for abolishing the requirement. With high tuition costs and undergraduate education growing more impersonal and bureaucratized, the 'old college' aspect of general Composition, its small classes, hands-on instructional style, and lower-risk learning environment, make retaining the universal requirement irresistible. There is the small matter, too, of the required course's proven record as a profitable enterprise. Crowley (2000) notes that when she first proposed abolishing the requirement, she had not fully appreciated 'the extent to which universities had changed between 1975 and 1990 . . . universities got incorporated – they began to be run like corporations – to make money, to turn out more . . . and better "product" more efficiently and ever more cheaply'. With cutbacks in 'support of universities during the relatively hard times of the 1970s and early 80s' came 'vacant faculty lines . . . filled with part-time workers. When administrators realized that this temporary measure was a moneymaker, they made it a permanent feature of their hiring practices.' Few collegiate operations have turned out more product more cheaply and efficiently than Composition programs. Few have relied more heavily on part-time workers. As a consequence, it will be a long while before the American educational system sees the end of the sentimental favorite that is compulsory first-year Composition.

12 Learning from – Not Duplicating – US Composition Theory and Practice

Joan A. Mullin

▶ Introduction

Participants at recent writing conferences around the world have been pooling research to resolve similar problems in the teaching of writing.[1] University faculty from the US contribute to this discussion with over a hundred years of writing scholarship and practice. Since, as John Heyda details in the previous chapter, most writing in US higher education is taught through first-year writing courses in departments of English, or Rhetoric and Writing, US scholars have had a rich laboratory for studying how writing occurs, how to teach it, and how to assess its processes and products. Nonetheless, there is a cautionary tale for colleagues considering these studies and the practices they have engendered: the teaching of Composition in the US, built on nineteenth-century concepts, has become increasingly intertwined with multiple social, academic, political and, equally important, economic agendas. Combined, these forces have produced a disturbing disconnect between writing research and the actual practice of teaching writing, which only recently has begun to change.

The history of US writing instruction may seem problematic for that country only, but in 1999, colleagues at the WDHE conference in the UK reacted with anger and disbelief at higher education learning outcomes and assessment structures being discussed by government. In 2004, the Central European University's (CEU) writing center in Budapest reported an impending lack of support because its staff had not been able to prove to an administrator's satisfaction that they were accomplishing anything of merit.[2] Given their own complicated, 130-year legacy, US Compositionists who have tried to change attitudes towards Academic Writing find these situations all too familiar.

For many years, writing scholarship, textbooks, conferences, and scholarly journals in the US have examined student-writers and their processes. While such studies were in progress, however, a massive structure supporting instruction based on the traditional paradigm of generalist Composition teaching also grew. This instruction, focused on correct grammar, repetitive sentence exercises, and decontextualized rules, immediately engendered protests: in the 1890s the need for interdisciplinary writing instruction was argued (Russell, 2002), and in the 1930s social constructionists argued for the collaborative nature of writing that responds to context, not hard and fast rules (Haynes, 1996, p. 221). Yet because surface rules are easily seen (or not seen) on a page, traditionalists maintained that fixing these would produce better writers. This made sense to business, industry, and the general public, whose continued pressure fostered the essentialist view of writing that focuses on product, format, and surface correction. I would argue that for most of the past fifty years – and even yet – any new research that emerged which would counter the traditional paradigm has merely been accommodated within its frame.

In the 1990s, for example, research indicated that Ebonics, the American-English specific to African-American communities, had a distinct grammar and place in US discourse studies. Pairing this research with that on student empowerment and language learning,[3] the Oakland California School Board in 1996 declared that since Ebonics was the primary language of African-American children, it would be incorporated into the curriculum. This began the Ebonics Wars. For the public, and many teachers, the speaking and writing of African-American discourse in the classroom was 'proof' that the system was lowering literacy standards. Teachers were forbidden from using the publicly vilified techniques, and the incident fueled the 'English Only' movement – that is, the teaching of Standard Academic (white) American English. Twisting research to fit the traditional paradigm, the public equated 'Ebonics' with error – something to be eradicated through a traditional school curriculum.[4]

Rickford (1998) correctly points to 'deep-seated social and political fears and prejudices' that informed people's response to Ebonics. I would argue also that the existence of three conditions, fostered by economic outcomes of the traditional paradigm, helped the public maintain the status quo: parents and administrators objecting to Ebonics used as evidence for privileging their discourse the overwhelming presence of African-American students in remedial writing courses; years of writing placement tests allegedly demonstrated that African-American students were failures (not the system); and hundreds of textbooks outlined how English should be spoken and written (textbooks became 'Bibles' for the public). In this chapter I argue that these same three elements within US higher education – the discreet writing classroom, the placement test, and the textbook-driven curriculum – illustrate and serve as a warning for how the teaching of writing, despite the research and resources available, can become disconnected from the scholarship that should inform it.

▶ Cash cows and infighting: institutionalizing the discreet writing classroom

Historians of Composition in the US[5] note that for most who complained about student writers in the nineteenth century:

> Writing amounted to correct transcription of fully formed thought or speech, not the process of engagement with a subject or communication with a reader. The oral emphasis of the old college [post-1860s] was beginning to fade as writing became dominant, but it left in its wake 'the opinion that "reading and writing" can or should be completely mastered before the main business of education begins'. (Russell, 2002, p. 49)

Harvard's creation of Composition A in 1885 responded to calls for mastery before the 'main business of education begins'. While this course initially was meant as an interdisciplinary effort, the new and growing 'elective curriculum and departmental organization made a specific place for Composition courses where there had been none before, but no place for collegewide writing requirements outside the course structure. As writing became one subject among many, it ceased being a central part of all of them' (Russell, 2002, p. 63). Often perceived as remediation, the Composition course became further isolated in departments of English, which were charged with teaching it; for disciplinary faculty, poor writing and poor thinking were someone else's problem. Since no one explicitly introduced students to disciplinary writing genres, papers continued to worsen (Russell, 2002 p. 74). When students graduated, employers raised alarms about the poor quality of writing, and more writing classes were recommended, created, and required. This is the context which still shapes Composition programs in the US.

Today, numerous Composition classes prove a burden for English departments as well as a boon. The burden is in staffing and in managing the growing number of students taking required writing classes. Since most full-time English Literature staff do not want to teach writing, its teachers are now, as they were in the past, often hired because they have *a* degree rather than a degree in Rhetoric or Writing (Crowley, 1990, p. 141). This produces a two-class system within English departments of tenure-track faculty eligible for promotion and guaranteed health and retirement benefits and life-time employment, and part-time lecturers (contingent faculty hired to teach writing classes). The former, held in esteem because they produce academic research, continue teaching Literature, leaving the job considered remediation to those who have no university status.

There is, however, some advantage to the English department's responsibility for writing. Tenure-track faculty benefit from funds generated by increased student numbers; more funds mean more money for research, travel, sabbaticals, and graduate assistants. A department serving large numbers of students also gains academic status for serving the university as a whole. Having more graduate students means faculty teach graduate courses in their fields of study, and justifies asking for more tenure-track faculty to teach the increased number of graduate students. In US universities, the larger the department, the greater the potential it has to gain institutional power. English departments therefore make use of their valuable 'cash cow' – writing – to feed and grow their ranks.

Contingent faculty not only have no research responsibilities, but also have no incentives, or time, to keep current, investigate, read, or engage in scholarly questions:

> The truth is that after family responsibilities and more than thirty hours a week spent directly on the teaching of three classes of Composition, I have to think carefully and pragmatically about how I'm going to spend the precious remaining time. . . . [E]ven if I become more knowledgeable – read theorists, attend conferences, present papers, take additional courses – I will receive no additional institutional recognition of any sort. I will not receive a penny more in remuneration for the courses I currently teach, nor will I become eligible for a full-time position or additional employee benefits. In fact, no practical or professional benefit will result. (Schell, 1998, p. 64)

Some changes to this situation occurred in the 1970s when the term 'Composition Studies' came into use (Heilker and Vandenberg, 1996, p. 45). At that time, several prominent scholars switched their research agendas from the study of Literature to that of Rhetoric and Writing. New interest bloomed, and other scholars, spurred by the seminal work of Corbett (1965), Berlin (1980), Kinneavy (1984), and others, focused their attention on student-writing practices. As these faculty sought resources for their studies and began to lobby for funding allocations generated by Composition classes to be given to writing programs, internal departmental conflicts began. Sometimes, divisions of Composition complete with degree-granting programs emerged within a department; in other cases departments split (sometimes violently) and new departments of Rhetoric and Writing, or Composition Studies, were born. Mostly, however, Composition staff who had made the theoretical change necessary to rethinking writing practices found themselves fighting their own Literature colleagues for more writing faculty, research funds, and graduate students. They often had to fight for recognition of their scholarship, endangering their potential tenure and promotion. Requests for new full-time faculty and for benefits for contingent faculty were often and consistently refused. Instead, as classes of Composition increased, the number of full-time faculty remained the same and more part-time faculty were hired. Meanwhile, resources generated by Composition classes continued to support those not teaching Composition. In many institutions today, this situation has not changed.

For example, a typical US university might have as many as 126 classes of twenty-five students each to staff per term, and only two full-time faculty trained to teach Composition. These institutions might have 20 lecturers who teach four classes of writing per term, for two-thirds salary. Twenty additional classes might be taught by graduate students in exchange for tuition fees and a small stipend. A typical Composition Program might be given $100,000 for the remaining 53 classes, or less than $2,000 per course for each part-time staff member. Rather than arguing with the university for the hiring of tenure-track faculty or even full-time staff needed to teach all the students who take Composition, an English department will maintain this status quo, getting 'more bang for their buck [dollar]' by hiring cheaply and milking the cash cow. Such actions, repeated every year across the US, re-inscribe the idea that writing instruction can be done cheaply, need not be rewarded, and can be done without theoretical or professional development. Until the last decade of the twentieth century, conflicting economic agendas in most English departments kept new writing research from growing into practice by undermining the financial support necessary to make paradigmatic changes.

▶ **An industry of placement tests**

In the 1950s and 1960s, several state and national groups pressured university administrators by publicly decrying the decline of literacy. Without taking into account new populations in schools and new social and racial integration movements, administrators and legislators looked to intelligence tests developed by the US Army after the Second World War, and their derivative field, Educational Psychology, to resolve the problem of separating out those who could succeed in a traditional higher education system and those who could not. The idea that one could be tested for skill and intelligence spurred a profitable industry of educational measurement, and the call for learning outcomes and quantifiable assessment instruments increased over the next twenty years. The publication in 1983 of *A Nation at Risk*, written under the Reagan administration by the National Commission of Education, led to legislated mandates calling for standardized testing in primary and secondary schools across the country. The report suggested targeted funding for remediation and the concomitant identification and placement of students into levels of expertise, castigating a school system that had clearly failed according to traditional standards.

Today, standardized tests created by state agencies continue to be based on traditional notions of school learning, and school administrators address students' 'inadequate backgrounds' by teaching to the test. This means that students learn a formula for writing so they will pass the test. While tests are supposed to 'decrease the achievement gap in order to leave no child behind, the state testing program has a powerful effect on increasing the gap by restricting what students are allowed to learn' (Hillocks, 2002, p. 102).

These public policies affect how US higher education trains teachers and influence how prepared students are when they enter universities. Unfortunately, the university application process reinforces the quantitative and formulaic. Admission to higher education is determined first by a total score achieved in individual secondary school courses (a Grade Point Average), in conjunction with scores from standardized multiple-choice tests (SAT, ACT) created by large educational testing firms. Any one of the testing companies provides state schools with tests, scoring, and scorers – all for a fee. While many teachers devote significant class time to preparing students for college entry exams, there are also numerous books students can buy from companies to prepare them for the exams; students can also pay hundreds and even thousands of dollars to take test preparation classes organized by testing companies. Students' scores determine not only whether they will be admitted to a university, but what level of first-year Composition course they may take – or whether they might test out entirely. 'Testing out' is desirable because that means students do not have to take a writing class they see as unrelated to their major.

Recent tracking of the accuracy of both standardized tests and holistic scoring of in-house placement essays at the University of Toledo, Ohio, has demonstrated that student success in Composition is determined less by either placement scores or standardized tests.[6] Instead students' high school English grade seems to better predict in which class students should be placed. Yet the testing industry is so intertwined with schools and universities that admissions officers continue the practices that have spawned a money-making business closely tied to traditional ideas of performance testing. As a result, universities must shape courses to accommodate what students haven't learned. It is not unusual to have within the university curriculum a basic writing course, a level-one and a level-two Composition course; some institutions have an additional developmental writing course for which students receive no credit but which gives them entry to either the basic writing course or the first level of Composition.

Responding to growing critiques of machine-scored writing tests and resulting curricula, testing companies now require a writing sample that demands a student write quickly, with limited resources, to an unknown writing prompt:

> Each essay will be scanned into computers and read by at least two scorers. A force of 3,000 scorers, mainly moonlighting teachers, is being deployed at 15 regional centers. Scorers must read an average of 220 essays in eight to 10 hours. Some will read many more. Others will drop out, exhausted, their brains befuddled by incomprehensible sentences and impossible-to-decipher handwriting. (Dobbs, 2005, p. A01)

The scoring used for 'the new SAT essay comes pretty close to the worst end of the spectrum. A point no one has brought up is the rules that raters have to follow governing the time they spend reading. It averages out to 2.4 minutes an essay. . . . And this is the use that the industrial–educational complex makes of a century of serious investigation into writing evaluation?' (Haswell, 2005). Worse yet, the writing portion of the test only counts for 30 per cent of a student's overall score – the other 70 per cent is based on a multiple-choice grammar quiz. Yet the cycle continues, with testing companies providing extra income for teachers, training them, setting the conditions under which they assess, and thus influencing the instruction for the next year's students.

▶ Texts for teachers: the textbook-driven curriculum

In the early 1900s, Composition instructors were scrambling for teaching tools; 'the textbooks that survived were not the most innovative or subtle or exploratory: they were those that were the most teachable' (Crowley, 1990, p. 141). By the 1960s, complex theories of rhetoric dissolved into basic formulas controlled by four textbook companies that had founded a profitable market (Connors, 1989, p. 234), a market that has continued to grow. Today, US writing teachers get deluged with sample texts that include three standard text-types used in Composition courses: a rhetoric (a how-to-write), a reader (a set of reading to which students respond) or a combined rhetoric and reader, and a grammar handbook. The printing of these texts has spurred a new partnership wherein publishers split some of their profits with departments who want customized texts for the thousands of students who buy them. Textbook decisions are vital not only because of the economics, but because, given the large contingent labor force teaching Composition, they are often the major tool for faculty development.

While it is the job of Writing Program Administrators (WPAs) to supervise Composition instructors, most do not have time to visit all classes, and evaluate teaching methods and outcomes, nor, in institutions where labor is unionized, do they have the right to do so. In addition, many programs have large numbers of graduate students teaching, whose classes are difficult to supervise in a 15-week term for WPAs with multiple programmatic responsibilities. Quite often, to exert some philosophical cohesion and purpose, WPAs will recommend that a standard text be used in all Composition courses, which then doubles as a syllabus. But if an instructor is operating under a traditional paradigm, even texts guided by current theory will be undermined.

For example, there are excellent student texts that apply rhetorical principles to images. However, instead of using the text's explanation of logos, pathos, and ethos to deconstruct the image, place it in context, and examine its parts and impact, a 'traditional' teacher might require students to 'Explain what the image is saying to the audience and how you react when you see it'. In other words, the teacher does not understand the rhetorical terms herself and would evaluate student papers on whether they have accurately described the image and made some personal statement about their reaction to it . . . all in grammatically correct form.[7] The textbook, should the students have read it, is not only undermined, but actually serves to confuse those given very different directions by an uninformed instructor.

The practice of ignoring textbook theory in favor of a personal teaching belief also completes the cycle of textbook proliferation and production: the more dissatisfied the WPAs are with student outcomes, the more they search for a better text incorporating different approaches. The more textbook publishers hear of WPAs' dissatisfaction, the more they seek authors willing to write new texts. These books become syllabi for inexperienced or exhausted teachers, who may or may not respond to the new texts when viewed through their traditional perspectives. Having conducted over 12 program reviews in the last four years, worked in 32 public school districts, conducted workshops for Composition teachers in four universities, reviewed hundreds of textbooks, and attended numerous writing conference presentations, I can guarantee that the traditional paradigm is alive and well.

Only in the last few years has this trend been challenged by well-known scholars in the field of Composition, who have created theoretically sound texts focusing on rhetorical principles of analysis, acknowledging the role of collaborative writing and learning styles within the writing process. Sensitive to the problems inherent in the teaching of Composition, these texts not only teach students new ways to think about writing, but teach staff to build on students' linguistic capabilities and change their teaching, assignments and evaluation methods to be more consistent with current research on writing.[8]

▶ Conclusion

The year 2003 saw the publication of *The Neglected 'R': The Need for a Writing Revolution*, followed in 2004 by *Writing: A Ticket to Work . . . Or a Ticket Out*, written by the National Commission on Writing in America's Schools and Colleges and published by the College Entrance Examination Board.[9] The 2003 report calls for a revolution in the teaching of writing – one that is supported by research and not by traditional notions of teaching. *Writing: A Ticket to Work . . . Or a Ticket Out* surveyed over 200 businesses, reporting on the poor writing skills with which students are entering the workforce. What is unusual about these reports is that they are supportive of new ways of teaching and thinking about writing and provide the kind of public explanation that Composition scholars have been unable to achieve by themselves. These reports have facilitated nationwide conversations between teachers and the company responsible for providing SAT and ACT college entrance testing. I believe such exchanges exemplify one of four lessons to be gleaned from the experiences of US Compositionists as outlined here. I recommend that any country's writing scholars contending with public misunderstandings about writing, working with diverse social and ethnic student populations, and stymied by academic colleagues' traditional notions about writing, should avoid such commercialization of their efforts and instead:

- use *academic currency* – research – to build a well-regarded body of interdisciplinary knowledge that informs the teaching of writing locally and globally;
- involve colleagues in *writing across the curriculum*, researching writing and mindfully teaching with it in their classes;
- establish *writing centers* to work with students, faculty, and community, bridging the research-practice gaps that otherwise occur;
- *engage the public* to change the perception of writing as a simple and finite set of skills.

The following four sections outline these recommendations.

Building academic currency

Professional organizations and their resulting scholarship go a long way towards building world-wide knowledge that can construct a case for changing academic paradigms. Many scholars cited in this collection have provided studies supporting integrated writing instruction, which, as the Introduction to this volume explains, started in the US in the mid-1960s and was influenced in 1975 by James Britton's research from the UK (J. Harris, 1997, pp. 1–17). Yet more needs to be done. University administrators need to be drawn into writing conferences to see the growing scholarship. Mini-conferences can be held locally so students, faculty and alumni can report about their writing or research; teachers can exchange ideas; and administrators can be publicly applauded for supporting excellence (or convinced that they should do so).

It is also important to engage in practices that other scholars and administrators will recognize locally and nationally. Besides conferences, it may mean inviting to campus a prominent guest speaker, starting a journal, or getting invited to another institution to speak on your research on writing: all this should be publicized in whatever media will serve to educate faculty that writing research has changed over time, and that they may have to become part of the change if they want to improve writing in their students' course of study.

Writing across the curriculum (WAC)

Scholars need to stay closely connected to the teaching of writing in the disciplines so as not to ghettoize the study or teaching of writing. Perhaps one of the most destructive factors in the history of US writing instruction was separating writing from the disciplines, isolating it in English departments, and then separating its teaching from the work of full-time faculty. Once tenured faculty began studying writing, there still lay a huge gap between those who taught and those who researched, for researchers and teachers were not sharing their knowledge about student writing in productive ways. Unfortunately, Composition students continue to receive instruction that does not necessarily serve them well in other classes or in their workplaces. While this situation is finally changing, anyone addressing the teaching of writing should avoid at all costs isolating the work of writing into a substandard field; both the research and the act of teaching writing are interdisciplinary.

Myths about teaching writing dissipate as faculty see results of their WAC teaching methods (for examples, see Walvoord et al., 1997). By learning how to use 'writing-to-learn' activities as pedagogy, faculty provide students with opportunities to manipulate the language of a discipline, and learners become comfortable with it and understand how language is used (Fulwiler, 1987; Bean, 2001; McLeod et al., 2001). We now know that writing needs to be connected to disciplinary knowledge-making so that students have opportunities to practice a number of genres. Having students write often will give them numerous opportunities to form and resolve disciplinary problems with the appropriate language. Created to change attitudes about writing and provide faculty development, formal WAC programs can be situated centrally as a signal that no one discipline has sole responsibility for teaching writing.

Writing centers

The growing connection between writing centers and WAC programs is documented elsewhere,[10] but it should be noted that some writing centers are the locus for WAC programs. Writing centers can work across disciplinary/department lines and with all writers, from first-years to graduate students to faculty. Besides one-on-one instruction, centers may train graduate teaching assistants and undergraduates as writing tutors and attach them to classes tagged by WAC programs as 'writing intensive', that is, classes wherein writing is used as a pedagogy to teach content (Soven, 2001). Since writing center tutors work with writers across the academic curriculum, they are cognizant of the disciplinary differences that shape writing. They likewise are exposed to a number of poorly conceptualized assignments and minimally marked student texts that provide little or no feedback. Seeking to better their work with student-writers, writing center practitioners reach out to faculty: asking them about their assessment criteria (and thereby educating faculty that they should think about and articulate criteria); clarifying assignments (thus educating faculty that assignment guidelines ought to be clarified – and helping them do so); questioning the meaning of a scrawled assessment response (and thereby teaching faculty how to write useful feedback on graded assignments). Successful writing centers gain a global view of the institutional culture of teaching, learning, theory, and practice and can better understand how to use the currency of the academy (research) and the vocabulary of academics or administrators to explain writing to multiple academic audiences.

Because the market is smaller, there has not occurred a proliferation of writing center training texts, so they do not have the same controlling effect as in Composition programs. Often, training is more locally sensitive to conditions and populations, and directors incorporate in-house-produced materials that derive from tutors' real experiences. Writing centers certainly use Composition and WAC texts as references. However, while guided by them, writing center tutors continually interact with faculty in real classrooms with real writing assignments, actual expectations, and stated grading criteria. Writing center tutors are also prepared to help students negotiate traditional Composition pedagogy that fails to prepare them for the writing tasks ahead.

Educating the public

The UK's Quality Assurance Agency (QAA) seeks to enhance 'the quality of teaching and learning in the universities . . . for an employable pool of graduates' (M. Scott, 2002, p. 128). Scott points to the complex political forces operating behind the widening access policy in the UK, noting that some 'view it as a "dumbing down" of higher education' (p. 89). This dichotomy is all too familiar to US Compositionists and others. Strong writing research communities have emerged to overturn traditional teaching practices in Europe, South Africa, and Australia. Barton, Hamilton, and Ivanič's *Situated Literacy: Reading and Writing in Context* (2000) and Theresa Lillis's *Student Writing: Access, Regulation, Desire* (2001) provide powerful research for instituting new practices and text production. Study-support staff and faculty who promote writing center and WAC theory-practice, such as those at Queen Mary, University of London; the University of Wollongong; or Rijksuniversiteit Groningen, have adapted reflective, situated practices to their own contexts. However, they are fighting the same battles that US programs continue to wage: garnering resources for programs in universities that see writing as a form of inoculation. Scott articulates the hope, spurred by QAA initiatives, that a 'collaboration between writing teachers and teachers of the disciplines . . . can lead to new approaches to writing that go beyond general writing skills and assumptions that Academic Writing has to be either "taught" or "caught" ' (2002, p. 128).

Working together with faculty, establishing a research community, and creating a writing center are vital, but not enough. The general public – publishers, legislators, administrators, and local communities – must also undergo a paradigm shift if writing scholars hope to successfully implement instruction consistent with their research. In the US, writing centers have gone a long way towards effecting such a shift by extending their services to the community outside the university, in literacy centers, public libraries, and by working with employees in business and industry who need to improve their communication skills. Writing centers and Composition programs are working in high schools to change writing instruction through collaboration. Some writing programs have created urban after-school programs, helped people write their life stories,[11] and conducted on-site research in business and workplaces.[12]

Compilations of excellent student work can be published and distributed to administrators, legislators, and the general public – evidence that the way in which writing should be taught does have positive results. Surveys of alumni and current students can often provide evidence that students do need practice writing in all disciplines. Any publicity that can be generated from students reading their work, forum discussions of writing, or from business and industry roundtables with students to talk about writing, provide opportunities to discuss what has not worked and offer praxis that can.

Collaborating with the local community and government has become essential to changing the way writing is taught and to exercising control over our own curriculum and assessment. Such alliances can help undermine funding of irrational testing, produce useful textbooks, and stem the proliferation of traditional teaching methods. Working with those outside our own departments or divisions can reap funding for faculty development, which is so crucial to shifting paradigms. In these ways, colleagues around the world can avoid a decontextualized, ahistorical, 'skills' approach to teaching writing, one that flies in the face of over a hundred years of scholarship and duplicates practice that visionary writing departments and programs in the US seek to undo.

NOTES

1 See the Introduction and Chapter 14 of this volume for discussion of international writing conferences.

2 Drawing on support from Academic Writing colleagues around the world via the EATAW, EWCA, and WCenter listservs, the CEU writing center did not sustain the cuts to their program.

3 See Shaughnessy (1977), and Brodkey (1989).

4 For a summary of the controversy and outcomes, see www.stanford.edu/~rickford/papers/EbonicsInMyBackyard.html

5 See Kitzhaber (1953), Berlin (1984), and Russell (2002).

6 If a student's test scores are borderline, universities may administer a timed writing test with a prompt not previously seen by the student. The results determine which level of writing class the student needs, or provide exemption from a writing class.

7 This was an actual assignment brought by a student to the University of Toledo Writing Center.

8 See, for instance, Lunsford and Ruszkiewicz (2004), and Mauk and Metz (2004).

9 See www.collegeboard.com for more information on the College Entrance Examination Board.

10 See Barnett and Blumner (1999), and Mullin (2001).

11 The University of Texas, Austin, for example, has produced *Writing Austin's Lives*, a collection of stories that paint a portrait of Central Texans in 2003. Over 800 community members submitted memories that paint a vivid picture of the variety that makes up the community.

12 See Lunsford and Ede (1990), Hull (1997), and Rose (2004).

13 Skills, Access, and 'Basic Writing': a Community College Case Study from the United States

Mary Jane Curry

▶ Introduction

> As we move into the new century, skills and learning must become the key determinants of the economic prosperity and social cohesion of our country. Knowledge and skills are now the key drivers of innovation and change. Economic performance depends increasingly on talent and creativity. And in this new economy, it is education and skills which shape the opportunities and rewards available to individuals.
>
> (David Blunkett, UK Secretary of State for Education, Department for Education and Employment, 2000, p. 3)

In the past decade, as the pressures of the 'knowledge economy' have increased, a strong policy drive toward increasing participation in lifelong learning and higher education has emerged in the UK and other parts of the world (Woodrow, 2002). Although more students are participating in post-compulsory education, in general 'the students recruited have not come from a sufficiently wide cross-section of the community' (Kennedy, 1997, p. 3). Thus attracting and supporting 'non-traditional' students[1] remain important issues. Beyond recruitment, the nature of the educational provision offered to 'non-traditional' students (McGivney, 2001) is one key to whether students are successful in negotiating the communicative demands of the academy – chiefly through Academic Writing – and can persist in education. With an increasingly diverse student population, whether students' pre-existing forms of oral and written communication fit comfortably with those of the academy becomes crucial to students' success (Doloughan, 2001; Lillis, 2003).

▶ The skills discourse

UK government discourses often link widening participation to 'skills shortages' in the economy (Clarke, 2002; Coffield, 1999). The 'skills' discourse also informs the structure of the national curriculum into 'key skills'.[2] It carries through to the emphasis on study skills that many educational institutions have adopted in trying to prepare 'non-traditional' students for academic success. Similarly, tutors frequently express concerns about the Academic Writing of their students by referring to their perceived shortcomings in the traditional cluster of writing skills: grammar, spelling, and punctuation. That the notion of skills seems central to many of these discourses has prompted this response to what I see as a worrying trend in terms of efforts to prepare students to participate in the communicative practices of the academy. In this chapter I draw on a case study of the student experiences within a 'basic writing' course taught to non-native speakers of English at a US community college. By offering a rich description and analysis of the shortcomings of the skills model of teaching Academic Writing, I hope to highlight issues of concern to educators and policy-makers who are involved in widening participation in post-compulsory education in many contexts.

The recent history of widening participation in the UK shares similarities with the historical expansion of higher education in the US. An ideology of educational opportunity evolved in the US as the doors of the academy were pushed open, first around 1900, by the requirements of business and industry for trained workers, then at mid-century by government policy for veterans, and later, by demands from racial and ethnic minorities, women, and working-class students. After the Second World War, the Servicemen's Readjustment Act, popularly known as the G. I. Bill of Rights, provided access to higher education to three million veterans (Aronowitz, 1997). In the 1960s and 1970s, higher education again grew in response to the requirements of the economy, the Vietnam War, and students' increasing demands for access. Most of these students enrolled in state universities and local community colleges, which because of open access policies continue to be 'the most common point of entry into college for those groups that have traditionally been excluded from higher education' (Brint and Karabel, 1989, p. 35; Woodrow, 2002).[3]

UK further education (FE) colleges resemble US community colleges in that they are usually open-admissions institutions that fulfil multiple educational functions (Dougherty, 1994).[4] Figures 13.1 and 13.2 delineate the chief possible routes to and through post-compulsory education in the UK and the US respectively.[5] FE and community colleges are also allocated fewer resources than other institutions, yet are frequently the chief providers of education for English-language learners (ELLs),[6] as well as for students deemed to need remedial or 'basic' education in literacy and numeracy.

In an élite educational system, assumptions that students learned the discourses of the academy through 'osmosis, through exposure to the informally constituted community of scholars, academics, and their books' (Malcolm, 2000, p. 19) was based on 'traditional' students, who tended to

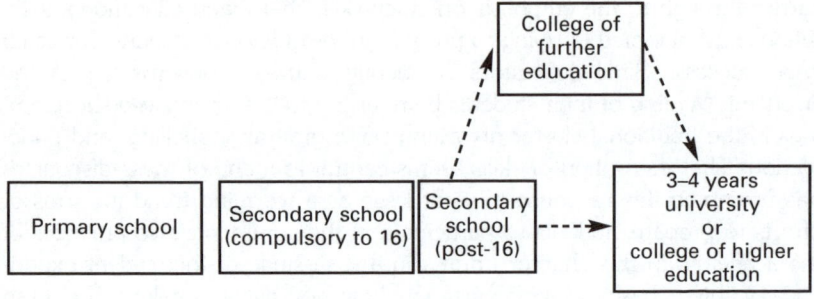

Figure 13.1 Routes through UK post-compulsory educational structures

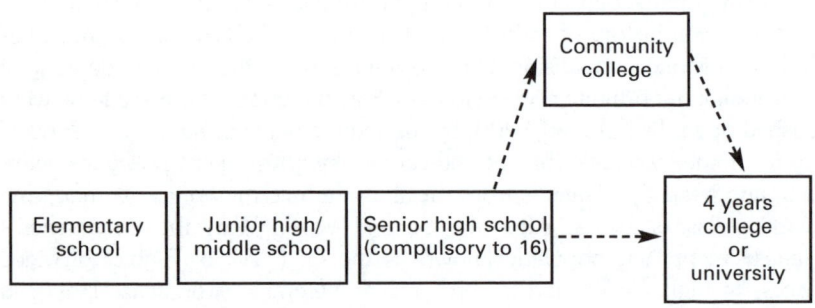

Figure 13.2 Routes through US post-compulsory educational structures

have both the family and academic background to ready them for the academic and cultural conventions of university (Gee, 1996). The increase in 'non-traditional' students entering further and higher education in the UK, South Africa, and other countries has prompted greater discussion about ways to teach Academic Writing, as evidenced by the growing number of publications, conferences, and academic associations dedicated to this topic (Coffin et al., 2003, pp. 1–18). Aspects of teaching Academic Writing under debate include using other text types besides the traditional essay, such as reflective journals; increasing students' awareness of the writing conventions of different disciplines; increasing the amount and variety of writing required within the disciplines; and providing stand-alone writing courses, thereby moving writing tuition out of study skills centers and into the mainstream curriculum. While these discussions are occurring in the academic field, a more traditional view of writing and literacy practices as discrete skills continues to hold sway in government discourses of education and economic development (Doloughan, 2001).

As a former teacher of English to speakers of other languages (ESOL) and of writing to native and non-native speakers of English in various adult education settings, I am interested in how (and if) students learn academic discourses. Given that the literature – and my own teaching experience – demonstrate that this process is complex and difficult, it is clear that academic literacy tuition requires knowledgeable teachers who have sufficient time to dedicate to the task. However, the working conditions of the multitude of part-time teachers at community colleges, adult education centers and, increasingly, universities frequently have a negative effect on the quality of education provided to 'non-traditional students'. These conditions may therefore militate against the aims of government and institutional policies to widen participation in post-compulsory education.

In this case study, of a writing course at a US community college, I examine the curriculum, including writing assignments; the tutor's feedback on student writing; and students' responses to the course. I contend that the teaching of writing as a set of discrete skills limited the participation of the diverse students in this particular class in the writing practices of the academy (Jones et al., 1999). Further, for the less prepared refugee students, the use of this model reinforced Academic Writing as an 'institutional practice of mystery' (Lillis, 1999) and functioned as a barrier to higher education. Before discussing the case study, I will review the relationship between the massification of higher education and the teaching of Academic Writing in the United States, where the study took place.

The history of writing instruction in the US is closely entwined with its social history, including increased access to post-compulsory education. From early on, writing instruction has comprised a distinct part of the curriculum in all strata of tertiary education, including élite universities (Rose, 1985). Indeed, 'freshman composition', or first-year writing, has become the most-required course at US institutions of higher education (Crowley, 1998). US students beginning their course of study often take placement examinations in writing and mathematics (Losey, 1997).[7] Students categorized as 'under-prepared' may then be required to enrol in pre-college, or 'basic' courses. English-language learners (ELLs) are often placed in these courses, either into segregated ESOL courses or into mixed classes.

Basic writing is intended to prepare students to pass tests that certify equivalence to secondary (high school) education, enrol in college transfer courses including freshman composition, or enter vocational training programs. Because of high drop-out rates in basic education courses and the difficulties that many students encounter in these and subsequent courses (Sternglass, 1997), debates about the functions and place of 'remedial education', including basic writing and ESOL, are ongoing. A central question is whether basic writers should be mainstreamed into higher-level courses or continue to be offered separate courses that 'shelter' students as they enter institutions of tertiary education. The 'abolitionist' view of basic writing sees it as perpetuating the segregation of non-traditional students (Shor, 1997). Proponents of retaining basic education point to the historical role it has played in supporting access to tertiary education for under-prepared students (Greenberg, 1997). Whilst in principle I support the maintenance of basic education as a way into tertiary education, I would advocate improvements in the quality of instruction provided to the students, and in working conditions for staff.

▶ The case study

The ethnographic study of one semester of Basic Writing 3 (BW3) took place at Monroe Community College, a US community college.[8] The course was offered free to students in the Alternative Learning Division (ALD). Such courses carry no degree credit, enrol the most non-traditional students, and are taught mainly by part-time tutors. BW3 was populated by 18 English-language learners, who came from Russia, Korea, Japan, Sierra Leone, Laos, the Dominican Republic, Taiwan, and the United Arab Emirates. Students' ages ranged from 18 to 'retired' (with no age given). Some students had taken Basic Writing 3 in previous semesters. The tutor, George Cleary, worked as a part-time tutor at multiple jobs – including teaching writing at Monroe Community College to native English speakers, and English to migrant Mexican farm-workers – and as a medical interpreter. He had taught English overseas for many years but had little experience or training in teaching writing to ELLs.

Basic Writing 3 displayed characteristics common to English as a second language and basic education courses at community colleges, including increasing numbers of ELLs (Smoke, 1999) and a reliance on part-time instructional staff (Brill, 1999). Less typical was the wide range of educational attainment levels and future goals among students: two-thirds had first degrees from universities in their native countries. Of these students, five also had postgraduate degrees, including three Russians with PhDs. Some of the well educated students were living in Monroe because it houses a large research university with which their family members were connected. Many of the students, including the focal students in the study, had aspirations to continue in tertiary education, whether at vocational, undergraduate, or postgraduate levels. Others, including three of the Russians, were retired and simply wanted to improve their English. Because of changing trends in immigration patterns, such student diversity is increasingly coming to characterize many institutions (Grubb et al., 1999), adding to the challenges of teaching a diverse student body.

The course met twice a week for a 15-week term, during which I gathered data through observations and audiotapes of the classroom, student questionnaires, and interviews, which I conducted twice with the instructor and once each with two administrators. I also interviewed six focal students in the first year of the study and one year later, and again three years later, with four of the focal students. I also collected writing samples, institutional documents, and the course textbook. The events of the semester challenged my initial goal of understanding how students learn academic argumentation. Importantly, the enacted curriculum in Basic Writing 3 shifted from a primary focus on writing to one dominated by an English grammar curriculum, as I explore below. Students clearly learned some aspects of the 'hidden curriculum' related to this shift (Curry, 2001), for example, that the tutor rewarded the questions they posed about grammar and word meanings.

After the first few weeks of the semester, students began to drop out, with 75 per cent of the students ultimately leaving the course (and in some cases, the college). The refugee students, who most needed assistance, were the first to drop out of the course and the least likely to re-enrol in basic writing or other courses. They cited difficulty in understanding the assignments and following what was going on in the course as the main reason for leaving. These students had full-time jobs and the least amount of time to come to the college to use the computers or seek academic counselling. In addition, many highly educated students dropped out of the course. For example, from frustration and boredom, Katarina, a Russian with a Bachelor's degree in engineering, left in the middle of the semester and waited until the following term to begin vocational courses in preparing tax returns.

The enacted curriculum of Basic Writing 3 evolved into a predominantly skills-based approach to writing instruction. For instance, Cleary, the tutor, frequently extracted the grammar and sentence-level writing exercises from the course textbook, leaving aside the more integrated activities that were based on the book's readings on contemporary issues. He supplemented these exercises with decontextualized fill-in-the-blank tasks focusing on grammar and punctuation that he had created for a composition/communications workbook that he was writing. Cleary's focus on grammar echoes the kind of approach that Lea and Street (1998) call the skills model, which they propose 'has assumed that literacy is a set of atomised skills which students have to learn and which are then transferable to other contexts' (p. 158). The skills model is grounded in a view that language is a transparent medium with which to convey pre-existing thought (Turner, 1999). Its use of discrete activities, such as exercises that highlight particular aspects of grammar, lexis, punctuation, and spelling, is based on the belief that students need to master these skills before they can begin to write discursively.

Along these lines, Cleary asked students to do grammar activities separately from written assignments, rather than focusing on grammar in the context of making meaning in writing. Cleary's writing assignments centered on paragraphs rather than full essays. As a result, students wrote less text and thus created less writing for Cleary to mark, which was important in his work life as he was not compensated for time he spent out of the classroom. The following are the writing assignments he made during the semester:

- Write one paragraph on:
  - a description of your room or house
  - a dynamic description
  - your country/hometown
  - a 100-word synopsis of a textbook article on divorce
  - a description of your native language
  - a recipe from your country
  - a childhood remembrance
  - what is the computer to you?
- In-class essay on topic of choice.
- Research paper, three to five pages, on topic of student's choice.

These assignments did little to introduce students to Academic Writing. Their brevity precluded students from gaining practice in structuring and developing extended ideas or arguments, creating transitions between sections of an essay, or sustaining the task of writing over time. In fact, during the class as he gave students' work back to them, Cleary sometimes chided students who wrote texts that were longer than he requested. However, in one instance Katarina responded to Cleary's admonitions to keep her essays short by asking, 'How can I express my thoughts there on a small paper?' (Classroom transcript, 4 February 1999).

The quantity of writing Cleary assigned students to do was considerably less than students would be required to do in university-level writing courses. However, he believed that students would be able to move from writing short texts to writing longer pieces. In discussing his approach to teaching, Cleary used this metaphor for writing: 'The paragraph is the brick that builds the building of writing. And if you can produce a good paragraph you can produce any length of document' (Interview, 9 February 1999). For students in Basic Writing 3 who did not hold the goal of continuing in higher education, such as the retired Russians, these activities provided enjoyable writing practice in English. But for students preparing for degree courses in higher education, writing short pieces on topics such as providing 'a recipe from your country' gave them practice that was only loosely related to academic work.

In the same way that writing isolated paragraphs does little to help students to learn to write extended discourse, Cleary's unrelated assignments did not support students in building toward a larger academic project, which is a common progression in US writing courses. In the middle of the semester students were assigned a three-to-five-page research paper on a topic of their choice. By this time only seven students remained in the course, most of whom planned to go to university. Most students wrote descriptive texts characteristic of types of writing assignments at a much lower level – indeed, even of primary-school assignments. For instance, one student described the solar system while another discussed the advantages and disadvantages of various US states as tourist destinations. Only one student, Minji, wrote a paper approximating what she might need to do at university. Her topic, 'Effective Teaching of Musical Instruments for Preschoolers', was related to her goal of earning a second Bachelor's degree and becoming a music teacher. Minji was one of the students who had previously taken BW3 with another teacher; in addition her husband was a research sociologist at the university who helped her with her English writing.

▶ Tutor feedback on student writing

Besides making these brief assignments, Cleary's feedback on students' writing did not support them into more complex and developed Academic Writing. He provided little formative written or spoken commentary on students' writing; his feedback came at the level of corrections to surface-level features of their texts. Extract 1 exemplifies his spoken, in-class feedback.

> *Cleary:*   I have the papers from last time and I am going to spend a little bit of time with you right now, just a second, okay, not much time. . . . Suk-yu, uh just no spaces right here, like that. Make sure this is the same kind of letters as down here, okay. Now let me see, what else. Yeah, I want you to recopy this with these corrections, okay, but I don't think you should have a problem to understand. They're suggested corrections, they're not exactly, you know, as it should be done. . . . Now, when I give you the papers back, I want you to correct these papers for me, okay? Make sure that you go through them and correct them.   (Classroom transcript, 4 February 1999)

This extract demonstrates how, in offering students feedback on their writing, Cleary directed his attention to mechanical issues such as capitalization rather than to the writing process as meaning-making. Although he asks students to 'correct' their papers, his notion of students returning to work on their writing seems to be limited to superficial aspects of presentation. Indeed, Cleary focused heavily on the tidying up of students' first drafts. He explained that a cleaned-up typescript allowed him to 'read the meaning':

> That's really good, because you went back and took something and corrected it and gave me a copy. Now I can read the meaning. I don't have to think too much about all the mistakes. I can just read it and go, ooh, that's nice, yeah. Then I can appreciate your writing more. (Classroom transcript, 25 February 1999)

In this example, instead of using the revision of drafts of essays to help students develop meaning and clarify their thinking, Cleary conveys the notion that meaning is fixed in the students' first drafts and obscured by their linguistic errors rather than an ongoing process of development. Further, research has demonstrated that students sometimes respond to repeated correction of error by writing simpler rather than more complex sentences, thus limiting their possibilities for expressing complicated ideas in complex prose. As Rose (1983, p. 115) points out, 'Just about the only rhetorical connection the correctness model establishes is the negative sociolinguistic one: don't err lest ye be judged.'

▶ Analysis of the curricular shift

My analysis of this case study ultimately centered on understanding the events of the semester, as the data I gathered did not support my initial interest in how students engage with academic argumentation. As noted, 75 per cent of the students dropped out, in perhaps a manifestation of agency in face of instruction that was not tailored to their needs, goals, or abilities. The four students who continued longest in the course, Minji and the three siblings from a middle-class family from the United Arab Emirates, continued on to universities the next year (where they were all required to take additional preparatory ESOL writing courses).

I concluded that one of the factors in the shift in Basic Writing 3 from a writing curriculum to an English-language course was the tutor's lack of training in teaching writing, particularly to ELLs. Cleary's extensive experience and training in teaching English as a foreign/second language did not seem to transfer to teaching writing to ELLs (nor should we expect that transition to occur without training). Early in the term, Cleary explained what he planned to highlight in the course: 'The most important things for me right away are the sentence fragments and the run-on sentences' (Interview, 9 February 1999). He thus adopted a skills approach from the start. He seemed not to recognize that many of his students were heading for more advanced courses where they would do extended analytic forms of writing. Late in the semester he set the remaining students to work on hyphenating compound adjectives, as in Extract 2, from the workbook he was writing:

6.1	an East Asian war	6.6	North Indian desert
6.2	gold and ivory ornaments	6.7	a trust me smile
6.3	a don't lie to me expression	6.8	the car is well made
6.4	a thirty two inch nail	6.9	a glass lid kettle
6.5	cherry and blackberry filling	6.10	an eleven year old victim

This exercise exemplifies Cleary's focus on decontextualized examples of linguistic usage. Activities of this nature could certainly be used to help students edit a final draft of a paper. But to make such activities the foundation of a writing course distorts the message to students of what writing in academic contexts entails, moving the focus away from making meaning as a consequence of engaging with academic readings, ideas, and discussions related to particular disciplines, to focus on surface-level features of writing such as hyphenation.

A second factor in the course's shift to a skills curriculum was that Cleary had learned little about his students' backgrounds and purposes for taking the course. Information was not provided to him, for example, about students' educational attainment levels or future goals. He therefore was not able to draw on students' strengths or weaknesses in designing and implementing the curriculum. Connected to this lack of specific knowledge about the students, their identities as ELLs were a third factor that drew the focus of the curriculum toward English-language skills. Perhaps because of Cleary's experience teaching English abroad, his notion of his students' identities seemed coloured by their status as ELLs (for more discussion, see Curry, 2002). Cleary explained the academic level at which he saw his students:

> Most of these students are pretty elementary. Because obviously an American by this time has seen twelve or thirteen years of continually reading, writing English, and these people coming from a second language have a lot to overcome. They have all the concepts down, they're wonderfully agile mentally, but they have a real problem converting all of those into standard English writing. It's a real skill.   (Interview, 9 February 1999)

Cleary seems not to distinguish between being a native speaker of a language and acquiring proficiency in Academic Writing, which resonates with his allegiance to a skills model. The idea of 'converting' concepts into English hearkens back to a translation model of teaching English (Khanna et al., 1998) that recapitulates the view of language as a transparent lens onto thought. Cleary's view that an American secondary school graduate would be automatically able to 'convert [concepts] into standard English writing' perhaps represents a misplaced faith in the Academic Writing abilities of US high school graduates, one belied by the history of basic writing and first-year Composition courses. It also demonstrates a lack of understanding that writing in a second language demands more than linguistic proficiency; it also requires a knowledge of the specific writing context, including aspects such as the author's purpose, the audience, appropriate style, and linguistic register.

▶ The institutional context

It may be tempting to see the almost 'worst-case' scenario of Basic Writing 3 as idiosyncratic, a case of bad luck for a group of students in a poorly taught course. However, the extent to which the instructor alone was responsible for the shift of Basic Writing 3 to a skills course is arguable. Like Cleary, others at Monroe Community College also saw ELLs as requiring different kinds of academic work than native English speakers. Dean Ricardo Garcia explained this occurrence as common in the Alternative Learning Division:

> The philosophy that we've had is that at a certain point you break out of ESL and then you go into the basic ed. When we offer the writing class they tend to be filled by ESL, ex-ESL students, and then we tend to treat it as an ESL class. I mean, we shouldn't. It should be a writing class. (Interview, 22 October 1999)

The institutional environment thus supported the shift in the curriculum from writing to grammar on the basis of the students' identities as different from 'traditional' students. The dean's familiarity with this trend was indicative of other failures of the administration to support BW3. For instance, few students had been offered the opportunity to create a Personal Learning Plan, which was division policy; nor were they offered much other academic advising. Cleary was hired three weeks after the term had begun, and was given little orientation, training, or support throughout it. As a new tutor in the Alternative Learning Division, Cleary was never observed in his teaching, whether for formative or evaluative purposes. Likewise, students were not asked to complete questionnaires about the course and Cleary's teaching, a common practice in US tertiary education and in other divisions of Monroe Community College. Further, as a part-time tutor working on an hourly basis, Cleary suffered from a shortage of (paid) time to plan the course, respond to student writing, and meet with students. He lacked an office and keys to classrooms. After the semester Cleary identified the kind of support he would have wanted:

> One of the major improvements I would say in this whole teaching business is give a specific outline of a course and pass it on, pass on maybe a syllabus, a completed syllabus from previous semesters. And keep refining that syllabus with a couple of focal points. Just give me a general outline of what's expected by a certain date, make it sequential, make it realizable, [with] goals and objectives.   (Interview, 19 June 1999)[9]

In the US system, part-time adjunct instructors like Cleary are in a double bind. Traditionally, lecturers maintain almost complete control over the syllabus and content of their courses, operating with few constraints whether from internal or external assessors. This practice has contributed to academic freedom, yet it assumes that the instructor has the appropriate content knowledge as well as time to plan the course. In the case of adjunct instructors like Cleary, however, such freewheeling practices can translate into a lack of support, as he indicates, which then affects the quality of instruction.

▶ Replacing the skills model

Having critiqued the skills model for teaching writing, the question remains of what more appropriate approaches might be successful in contexts like Basic Writing 3. In Lea and Street's (1998) tripartite taxonomy, the academic socialization model is proposed as some improvement over the skills model, with a focus on the 'acculturation of students into academic discourse' (Lea and Street, 1998, p. 172). Beginning academic writers are seen gradually to gain experience with the types of writing they will need to undertake in their disciplinary courses, in a process of being 'scaffolded' by the tutor, who is seen as more expert (Bruner, 1978; Lave and Wenger, 1991). The socialization model assumes that students are uniformly aiming toward a common goal, that of learning academic discourses. Basic Writing 3, however, was heterogeneous in terms of students' backgrounds and future goals – and the particular combinations of these embodied in each student.

The course encompassed students with low educational attainment levels but high aspirations, such as the immigrants from Laos and Sierra Leone, who wanted to be a police officer and a lawyer respectively. It included students with high educational attainment and low aspirations, as in the case of the retired Russians. In between these poles fell the students who persisted the longest in the course and subsequently entered university programs, as well as other students who dropped out. This diversity in BW3 carried through to the types of writing that interested the students. For example, Olga, the student who wrote about US states as tourist destinations, was a retired Russian with a PhD; she was comparing Texas and California in order to plan her vacation. In this way the basic writing context involved non-academic types of writing, with which some students were satisfied.

It is possible to build, however, from non-Academic Writing tasks to more extended analytic and argumentative texts (Curry, 1996; Kutz et al., 1992). Lea (1998) distinguishes between the 'reformulation' and 'challenge' approaches that students may take toward academic literacy. She describes adult Open University undergraduates who brought their life experiences to bear on literacy activities on courses students had frequently selected especially for their relevance to their life situations. If the use of students' life experiences is carefully built into curricular tasks, a course between 'reformulation' and 'challenge' can be navigated.

The Academic Literacies approach comprises the third aspect of Lea and Street's (1998) taxonomy. Academic Literacies concentrates on the 'student's negotiation of conflicting literacy practices' (p. 172). By drawing on students' experiences and backgrounds, the Academic Literacies approach offers students the possibility of engaging with the dominant discourse practices of the academy by examining and challenging the ideologies and values they represent. It may require, however, that tutors possess a level of awareness of the functions of academic discourse that will enable them to subject such discourse to critical scrutiny by students at the same time as they are attempting to learn it. It is not obvious that BW3 tutor Cleary, for example, possessed this knowledge or awareness.

▶ Conclusion

This case study raises a number of issues to consider in providing Academic Writing tuition to 'non-traditional' students. In classrooms such as Basic Writing 3, where students bring great variation not only in linguistic and cultural backgrounds but also in educational attainment levels, teachers are presented with greater challenges than with more homogeneous groups of students. A prime concern is the quality of the teaching, one that Kennedy

(1997) echoes in discussing widening participation in the UK (for a discussion of US community college teaching, see Grubb et al., 1999):

> Sadly, the quality of teaching for new learners is not of universally good quality. . . . The reasons for this include the recruitment of inexperienced teachers, a lack of support for the expanding number of part-time teachers, and insufficient sharing of learning materials amongst teachers. A high proportion of classes are taught by staff who do not possess specialist qualifications in teaching basic skills or teaching English for speakers of other languages. (pp. 80–1)

The factors that Kennedy cites here are strikingly similar to those I have identified in the BW3 case study. With increasing numbers of 'non-traditional' students in higher education, the training of their tutors in methods of teaching Academic Writing, including issues specific to teaching ELLs and of multicultural pedagogy (Nieto, 2002), thus becomes increasingly important. Knowing one's students is also crucial: tutors need the time and resources to learn about students' educational backgrounds, career or vocational objectives, and reasons for study (Lillis, 2001; Rose, 1989). This information can enable tutors to design and build a curriculum not only to respond to students' needs and interests, but also to draw upon students' strengths. As the goal of widening participation often results in larger class sizes and the increased casualization of labour, however, this goal may be even more difficult to attain than previously (Grubb et al., 1999).

The improvements I am advocating, based on this case study of BW3 and my teaching experiences, accord with the recommendations of the UK's Working Group on English for Speakers of Other Languages.[10] The issues that have emerged here may be useful in contemplating the provision of dedicated writing courses for students entering tertiary educational institutions: teacher training and support, student-based curriculum development, and institutional practices including hiring. If the goals of widening participation are to be met – for more, and more diverse, students not only to enter but to stay and succeed in tertiary education – better educational provision based on a fuller understanding of the students themselves and the communicative demands they face in higher education is required.

As I have tried to demonstrate, the skills model of teaching Academic Writing was insufficient to meet this goal in Basic Writing 3. The assumption that students must first master discrete skills and will then transfer this atomistic knowledge into their Academic Writing is unwarranted. In fact, research in international contexts suggests that few of these types of skills-based activities provide gains in learners' understandings (Hillocks, 1984; Wyse, 2001). Instead, the skills model highlights student error rather than building on students' existing competences (Kutz et al., 1992). This approach contributes to the deficit model of certain types of students (Nieto, 2002) and can undermine students' confidence, creativity, and comfort with their own identities (Doloughan, 2001; Lea, 1998). I am not taking a position against the teaching of features of 'linguistic accuracy' such as grammar, spelling, and punctuation (Coffin et al., 2003), but advocating for these concerns to be the final focus of editing specific texts rather than the primary focus of academic literacy instruction.

In addition to speaking to the skills discourse in current circulation, these conclusions respond to the current debates about basic education. Rather than abolish basic education or other institutional structures designed to support students new to the practices of higher education, improvements should be made to instruction in academic literacy practices by hiring well-prepared teachers and providing them with working conditions that will enable them to know their students and to teach them appropriately. As widening participation initiatives continue around the world, these issues are likely to remain salient in many contexts.[11]

NOTES

1 Stereotypically, 'traditional' students are considered white, male, Christian, middle-class, and native-English speaking; whereas the 'non-traditional' category encompasses students of colour, more women, non-native speakers of English, students with disabilities, students of various religious affiliations, and those in the first generation of their families to enter tertiary education.

2 See www.dfes.gov.uk/curriculum_literacy/intro/nqf/ on key skills and the national curriculum.

3 Community colleges enable students to earn secondary school equivalence qualifications in adult basic education, lifelong learning, vocational training programs, and general education courses that count toward an Associate's (two-year) degree, transferable to four-year institutions. However, less than 25 per cent of community college students make the transfer into four-year institutions (Dougherty, 1994).

4 The US system does not distinguish between 'further' and 'higher' education; community colleges are considered a (low-status) part of higher education.

5 These figures are simplified representations of complex and fluid structures that are difficult to map given the range of degrees and qualifications available, and overlap between institutions. My focus here is on the access function of US community colleges, which are most comparable to UK FE colleges.

6 See www.lifelonglearning.co.uk/esol/front.htm

7 Because there are more than 3,000 institutions of higher education in the US and very little standardization in programs, it is difficult to generalize across institutions.

8 Institutions and participants in this study have been given pseudonyms.

9   In US institutions of higher education, there is little systematic external checking of course syllabi, exams, and so on; individual lecturers/tutors are usually left on their own to design and deliver courses.
10   Again, see www.lifelonglearning.co.uk/esol/front.htm
11   Thanks to the instructor, and to the students and administrators who participated in the study, as well as to Julia Clarke, Lisa Ganobcsik-Williams, Anna Magyar and Theresa Lillis for their comments, and to Sarah P. North for designing the figures.

14 Peering Across the Pond: the Role of Students in Developing Other Students' Writing in the US and UK

Bonnie Devet, Susan Orr, Margo Blythman and Celia Bishop

▶ Introduction

This chapter focuses on the one-to-one writing tutorial and the role students play in supporting other students in their writing. Although peer tutoring in writing is an integral part of writing pedagogy in US universities, this model has never been popular in UK higher education. This chapter examines US models of peer tutoring and assesses their implications for developing student writing in UK higher education.

This study arose from a conversation between two of the chapter's authors, Bonnie Devet and Margo Blythman, at the 2000 National Writing Centers Association conference in the US. Discussions about staffing foregrounded differences between US and UK approaches to supporting student writing at university level, and both sides realised the value of doing comparative work. Cross-cultural comparisons enable us to challenge our fundamental assumptions and to recognise the socially constructed nature of ideas we might otherwise have regarded as universal. As Jane Nelson and Kathy Evertz caution, we as educators must be aware of what we are *not* thinking about (2001, p. xv); in other words, our methodology is one Delamont and Atkinson call 'fighting familiarity' (1995).

The UK authors of this chapter are Susan Orr, Principal Lecturer in Quality Management and Enhancement at York St John College; and Margo Blythman, Teaching and Learning Co-ordinator, and Celia Bishop, Study Support Co-ordinator, at the London College of Communication, University of the Arts London.[1] For this chapter we interviewed 12 Study Support Tutors at the London College of Communication, University of the Arts London. The Study Support Service, offering small-group and one-to-one academic support to students, is staffed by qualified lecturers with specialist knowledge in the areas of language, literacy and EFL. As well as supporting student writing, the team works with students on all aspects of learning, including study skills and research techniques. The team includes both hourly-paid and salaried staff on academic contracts.

The Writing Lab at the College of Charleston, South Carolina, directed by Bonnie Devet, is staffed by undergraduate students paid by the hour and trained to be peer tutors. At the College of Charleston we surveyed departmental academic staff, peer tutors and students who had had writing support. These perspectives inform our analysis of the differences in structural/cultural factors and epistemology in the two institutions and education systems.

In Section One of this chapter, Devet outlines the origins and theories for using students as peer consultants in writing centres and explains why American educators view this model positively. In Section Two, Orr, Blythman and Bishop discuss implications of moving such a model into UK higher education.

▶ ## Section One: an American model

It's 9 a.m. The college Writing Lab, offering free individualized help on any part of the writing process, has just opened. In walks a student, or 'client'. Looking worried about an essay due tomorrow, the client signs in, saunters over to an empty table, and excavates his assignment sheet from his book bag. 'Perhaps', he thinks, 'this place can help me.' Like so many of his fellow students, this student has sought the help of a writing lab.

In an American university or college, this scene is repeated myriad times. It is, in fact, reported that '90 per cent of the institutions of higher education in the United States have developed writing centers or learning centers where writing is taught' (Wallace and Simpson, 1991, p. ix). So, who will walk over to the table to help the client? In universities across the US, no one pattern of staffing exists; some labs, such as the Writing Workshop at Bates College (Lewiston, Maine), employ professional writers, while many universities, like the University of South Carolina, assign graduate students pursuing a Master's or doctorate in English to work in labs. In spite of the variations, however, the chances are that undergraduate peer consultants will assist student-clients. These peer consultants usually range from sophomores (second-year students) to seniors (fourth-year students), majoring in fields as varied as Biology, English, or Sociology.

Writing labs have not always been staffed by peers. The earliest history of labs, in Minnesota during the 1930s and in Denver, Colorado, during the 1940s, shows no undergraduate peer tutors but only selected academic staff (Carino, 1995, p. 18). However, in the 1960s, with the rise of open enrollment, or the admission of all high school graduates at many public colleges and universities, there emerged the need for more labs and more staff. In all likelihood, it was then that undergraduates began to be employed as consultants (Murphy, 2002).

Why do many American colleges and universities use undergraduate students to help other students develop their writing? Employing peers lessens costs because fewer academic staff are needed (Bruffee, 1980, p. 144), and institutions save money by not paying for the more expensive graduate students. It is also easier to find a ready supply of peer tutors since more undergraduates are available than graduate students. Because of convenience, then, writing labs can hire more workers and offer more services to a greater number of students (Cobb, 1982).

But, if saving money and tapping into a large supply of workers were the only rationales for using peer consultants, US writing labs would not be thriving. Labs also use peer consultants because of the power of peer influence and process approaches for teaching writing.

The pedagogy of peer influence

Since the 1970s, American educators have suggested that colleges and universities mobilize peer influence as a pedagogy to help students. Citing a 1973 Presidential Commission report, *Youth: Transition to Adulthood*, Kenneth Bruffee explained that if educators could tap into the power peers exert over each other, a new form of education could be developed which would 'involve students in each other's intellectual, academic, and social development, an involvement which can benefit both tutors and their students' (1978, p. 447). Peer influence helps students develop because peers sway each other in making judgements or assessments (p. 453). As two students discuss a paper, the desire to fit in with peers leads student-writers and peer consultants to talk, negotiate, and question each other (p. 459). The dynamic of peer pressure means clients defend and modify their ideas accordingly so that they 'develop and express new ideas and make judgements based on a wider perspective than on their own teacher's' (Hawkins, 1985, p. 8). This talk with each other is, certainly, not alien to students. Study groups and gossip sessions in dorm rooms pervade student culture, so it seems fitting to extend the concept to peer consultants' working with students (Hobson, 2001, p. 171; Kail and Trimbur, 1987, p. 206).

Such talk leading to negotiated meanings implies that education does not always have to be based on a banking model where professors make deposits as students move through the system. Knowledge is not just 'out there', ready to be retrieved (Freire, 1970). Instead, knowledge is 'an artefact created by a community of knowledgeable peers and . . . learning is a social process not an individual one' (Bruffee, 1984). Knowledge and reality are seen 'as mediated or constructed through language in social use, as socially constructed, contextualized, as, in short, the product of *collaboration*' (Lunsford, 1991, p. 110). Thus, at the heart of the pedagogy of peer-group influence is another theory of learning – collaboration.

Collaboration may take place in groups where a peer consultant asks each student to read aloud a paper and then asks all to respond. The writing lab at the College of Charleston, though – like many writing labs – does not relegate clients to a group. Seeing the writing process as being emotional and writers as being vulnerable, a consultant in our lab sits next to the client-writer, becoming for the student a 'ready auditor' (North, 1984, p. 78) who asks questions as the student talks through ideas or reads a draft, allowing consultants to adjust to each student's needs. As clients and consultants talk, they arrive at knowledge, especially because the setting is personal and peer-influenced.

Process theories of Composition

Process approaches for teaching Composition (prevalent since the 1970s) also vindicate using peer consultants. One theory of process, 'expressionism', views student writers as individuals learning how to discover ideas, to adjust to an audience, and to develop persuasive skills (Faigley, 1986; Murray, 1985; Elbow, 1981). Peer consultants readily help student writers to talk through ideas, to develop a voice, and to work through invention strategies (Burnham, 2001). Peer consultants are ideally suited for this procedure, offering encouragement without the intimidating authority of teachers.

Cognition, a second theory of process, stresses how students learn to think and how they put those thoughts down on paper (Flower and Hayes, 1981; Lindemann, 1995). Peer consultants ask questions about the paper's argument or development, in effect, modelling procedures for thinking.

Peer consultants play a role in yet another process theory, 'social construction', in which writing instruction focuses on the 'socio-cultural and historical settings [where] writers develop their understanding of language and knowledge' (Murphy and Sherwood, 1995, p. 3). Social systems shape and control writers, who should understand that they are part of a larger discourse community whose dictates they follow. What is considered as proof in a History paper, for instance, may not be considered convincing evidence in a scientific lab report. So, student writers come to understand how a type of discourse reflects the values, beliefs, and assumptions of a discipline's traditions. Social construction underpins the work of writing labs, with consultants' showing clients the demands of academic discourse and introducing them to writing within different disciplines so that when writing a History paper, for instance, clients see what evidence and assumptions historians use, or when writing for a Literature class, students learn the organization and proofs considered valid and proper to write about poetry or plays.

Advantages of using peer consultants to support students' writing

As helpful as a theoretical underpinning is, no sense of the reality of peer-tutoring is possible without referring to the advantages of using undergraduates to play the part of an audience, provide an alternative way to learn, set up the talk, and establish a nurturing environment.

Although academic staff meet with students to discuss ideas for papers or to see or hear part of a draft, peer consultants offer a different take on this role of audience. Peers serve as 'true' readers of papers. In a recent session in the College of Charleston Writing Lab, a consultant role-modeled a reader's reaction and showed the client how to be her own audience for future papers. While listening to a client read a paper aloud, the consultant asked, 'Why did you break that paragraph from this one?' The client replied, 'This paragraph talks about natural resources while this one focuses on the economy.' The consultant, acting as a reader needing more help with the structure, said, 'That's good. But could the essay use a transition, or link, to explain that point further?' Such audience-playing is invaluable. As one faculty member commented, 'The Writing Lab helps students to think, re-examine their ideas by providing them with an immediate audience. The questions arising when students read their work to a real audience – they never seem to envision their professors in this way – create an awareness of the communication process and of their choices as writers'.

Beyond being an audience, consultants also offer an alternative way of learning by the very fact that they are not academic staff. In classrooms, students try to discern what professors or lecturers want in an ideal paper. In writing labs, though, students – with the guidance of a peer – write, re-write, and evaluate so they arrive at what students themselves want to create. Heather Richie, a former peer tutor, characterizes this alternative way of learning: 'It is leading clients to a productive frame of mind where they begin to answer their own questions and define their own writing styles' (Richie, 2001).

More times than not, the peer consultants' advice is what academic staff have already stressed in class; however, because the advice comes dressed in the peers' dialect and demeanour, students more readily retain the information. Not having taught before, consultants do not use a classroom approach. In our lab, a peer said to a client who was reading aloud a paper on settlers coming to Brazil, 'Right there, I'd use *immigrate* not *migrate* because *migrate* sounds like birds.' I, as a faculty consultant, would have explained the etymology of both words; the peer consultant, however, used terms the client would readily absorb.

Besides being direct, tutors' talk also contains advice that academic staff would not use, but because this phrasing arises from a peer to a peer, the credibility is powerful, forceful, effective. One consultant recounted a session where a client complained about his professor, saying the teacher bragged about never giving a grade above a C; the student felt frustrated. The peer consultant, as probably only a peer could do, replied, 'Well, wouldn't you rather work with a hard teacher and learn something than have an easy one and just get an A?' With clients, such tutor talk has unimpeachable authority.

There also seems to be less intimidation in labs staffed by peers. Richie (2001) explains:

> Faculty as consultants may be feared because of their academic standing and authoritative role. Students who are insecure about their performance with one professor may find little comfort in looking to another, equally intimidating professor for help. They may have an unrealistic sense that the institution as a whole is 'sizing' them up.

Peer consultants, trained to create a non-threatening, neutral environment, welcome clients to use open, casual communication (Harris, 1988) so that clients feel free to place ideas on the table, to discuss them, to revise them, to reshape them. Nothing has to be polished or perfect. Less intimidation leads to more freedom to grow as a writer and thinker.

Overcoming objections to using peer consultants

Employing undergraduate students can lead to problems arising from the age of peer consultants, from academics' and student clients' misunderstandings of how writing labs operate, and from the emotional engagement between consultants and clients. But these problems, ironically, can also be strengths.

The first disadvantage stems from the inherent nature of peers: their age. Clients working with someone their own age or with someone with whom they may have taken a class may feel inadequate. My survey of peer consultants reveals that the same-age factor poses other disadvantages. Clients may not, as one peer consultant explained, 'take us so seriously since we are the same age. They may try to buddy up with us instead of working.' International students, too, may not want to work with young tutors. If their home culture values age over youth, international clients often prefer a faculty consultant. Finally, older students (in the US, the 'non-traditional' undergraduate student is defined as 25 years or older) might under-estimate the quality of the consultation, thinking younger peer consultants do not know enough or cannot relate to the many responsibilities of families and jobs faced by non-traditional students. Besides age and inexperience, student clients sometimes think peer consultants lack the knowledge to help them so they worry that consultants will not find errors in papers or will not know what professors want in essays. In even the best of conditions, as one faculty member noted, consultants do not always give the best advice: 'Consultants [may] make a suggestion that contradicts or disagrees in some way with the professor's approach to essay writing.'

It is true that peer consultants will not find every error in a paper or know what every professor is looking for. The job of consultants, however, is not to be correctors of errors (Welsch, 2001), and not even a faculty consultant can be aware of each professor's or lecturer's desires for an assignment. Nor should we have to know. A writing lab's goal is to develop writers' independence. So, it is neither feasible nor part of the lab's mission to expect peer consultants to make corrections or to have ready knowledge about every professorial desire or quirk. Should clients, then, feel cheated when they work with a peer? No, students are accustomed to working with peers since 'peer review' is a common classroom activity in US universities. And two and a half years of surveys of our writing lab's clients reveal that they feel peer consultants to be 'competent'.[2]

What if peer consultants do not possess background on the subject matter of clients' essays? Lack of background can be beneficial. Without content knowledge, consultants ask clients to explain the topic so that the dynamic shifts, with clients becoming the experts, seeing how much they already know and observing how much background the paper should provide.

Other disadvantages can arise because the consultants' role is misperceived. Although some professors erroneously believe that peers should act like teachers, the teaching function is only one of several obligations consultants carry out. Consultants can be student-centered (the clients do most of the talking, thereby discovering for themselves what they want to say), collaboratively-centered (clients and consultants 'share equally in the conversation' (p. 31), or teacher-centered (consultants answer questions directly) (Reigstad and McAndrew, 1984). Consultants, then, become mini-teachers only when clients need to learn about a specific point, such as when students ask, 'What is a thesis?' or 'How can I recognize a comma splice in my paper?' Most of the time, though, peer consultants shift roles throughout the session, depending on the client's needs.

Although faculty sometimes worry that consultants are trying to replace them, the work of peer consultants complements that of professors. When students are offered conference time with their teachers, there is usually no time for them to do any writing in the office; students come to professors with 'an outline, a first draft, a statement of purpose with bibliography and note cards' (North, 1984, p. 80), primarily for reassurance that they are on the right track. Peer consultants, though, work with clients at whatever stage their papers may be, beginning 'where the writers are . . . [so that] going to the writing center is a means of getting started, or a way to keep going' (pp. 80–1). Although such consultations may not be so 'efficient' (p. 80) as in the professors' offices, they are centered on student-writers, and on the writing itself. Peer consultants also work with the faculty's assignments, helping clients to read and understand them. As North explains: 'In all instances the students must understand that [writing labs] support the teacher's position completely. . . . In practice, this rule means that we never evaluate or second-guess any teacher's syllabus, assignments, comments, or grades. If students are unclear about any of those, we send them back to the teacher' (p. 79). Peer consultants are trained never to take the side of students against professors; professors and peer consultants are 'fellow professionals' (p. 79). This sense of professionalism is vital to a lab's image. Although students provide the tutoring, academics respect a lab so staffed if they have a hand in the staffing. At the College of Charelston, professors nominate students they feel would be good consultants. When these students are hired, faculty have become woven into the web of the lab, staffed by their own choices. Professional respect is also achieved in another way. Labs can participate in an international certification program offered by the College Reading and Learning Association (CRLA). A lab director provides training which meets the CRLA criteria, letting a director demonstrate the professionalism of the student workers.

As faculty often misunderstand the peer consultants' work, so, too, do the clients misperceive labs, assuming consultants write, edit, and proofread papers. One consultant sums up how this misunderstanding affects the consultation process: 'Students are not too eager to learn because they often see us as proofreaders.' To make sure clients do, indeed, retain ownership of their papers, peer consultants explain to clients what they can and cannot do, offering 'informed suggestions' (Richie, 2001), and reinforcing the clients' ownership of essays by who holds the pen, how the paper is turned, and how silence is used to foster talk so that responsibility remains with clients. A faculty member in the English department sums up the consultants' role: 'My students seem to understand that . . . they are being taught how to fish and are not simply given fish.'

Another potential problem for peer tutors stems from the emotional load clients sometimes impose on peer consultants. When a consultation ends, clients often seek a stamp of approval for the paper ('Do you think I can make at least a B'?), a judgement no consultant would ever make. Consultants are trained to say that only professors are qualified to grade, so that clients focus less on grades and more on their development as writers.

Peer tutors and US higher education

What does the staffing of labs with peer consultants indicate about US higher education? I believe using peers reflects a theory of education, has an impact on classroom methodology, and influences the careers of future teachers.

Peer staffing shows an emphasis on liberal arts, defined as acquiring a wide exposure in one's discipline and to other fields. Reading papers from different disciplines, meeting students from all levels and social classes, seeing how others grapple with writing processes, and gaining new perspectives on writing procedures mean consultants and clients learn from each other, reflecting the broad-based curriculum of a liberal arts education. Using peer consultants emphasizes other key features of a liberal arts education: developing critical thinking skills, re-examining where authority lies in education, and seeing how an idea comes to life. Unlike in a classroom, where students find it easy to accept a professor's opinion because of the faculty member's academic status, writing lab clients are more likely to judge or evaluate suggestions simply because the consultants are *not* identified as possessing absolute knowledge (Richie, 2001). Engaging in such talk, clients learn how to be critical. By working together, clients and peer consultants also comprehend how an idea is born and shaped and reshaped and refined, realizing that 'ideas [are] not artificial entities fully formed into an abstract and completed state' (Bruffee, 1978, p. 462) but are subject to alteration, debate, and defence.

Peer tutoring also has an impact on classroom pedagogy and influences the careers of future teachers. In many disciplines, professors devote some class meetings to peer review, where students exchange papers in order to offer comments. Many of the details for carrying out such work have been developed in writing labs (Harris, 1986; I. Clark, 1992). Although writing labs are not the only source for effective questioning strategies, teachers once trained as peer consultants find that their practice of using open-ended questions with clients works well in classrooms, too (I. Clark, 1988, p. 350). Because consultants see first-hand how writers struggle with words, thoughts, and organization, peer-consultants-turned-teachers often gain 'a fuller sense of how to relate to students' (Murphy, 2002). Former consultants who are now teaching have seen the weaknesses and strengths in many assignments, so they are more aware of how to construct effective assignments (Rottenberg, 1988); they also become aware of how hard it can be to interpret teachers' comments in papers' margins, and therefore see the need to provide more thoughtful criticisms (Gadbow, 1989). Thus, methodology and insights gained as peer consultants cross over into classrooms and enrich teaching.

▶ **Section Two: peering into the UK context**

Devet identifies, in Section One, above, that the use of students as peer tutors in US writing centres is almost universal, and argues that it is an appropriate and widely accepted model of support for students' writing in US higher education. In this section we contextualise this debate by briefly looking at the UK higher education traditions of curricular specialisation and elitism. These traditions, we argue, help to explain why student peers are not an established part of the emerging writing-development field in the UK. We also examine the benefits and problems of using a peer model to develop student writing, and suggest that the challenge is not about whether or not we import this peer model of writing support; instead, the central challenge is to identify the aims of writing development in the UK and to select pedagogies that will achieve these aims. Only at this point is it necessary for each institution to identify the people (students *or* academic staff) who will support those aims.

Specialist curricula

A feature of the UK educational system is early specialisation. In spite of recent government attempts to broaden the post-16 curricula, students at the age of 16 still continue to reduce substantially the range of subjects they study. Many are able to start undergraduate studies at 19, having already carried out in-depth study in cognate subjects for two years prior to entering higher education. This system has, in turn, enabled higher education curricula to be very specialised; indeed, it is widely recognised that A Level exams were designed explicitly to prepare young people for higher education study. Specialisation has meant that, until fairly recently, if a student studied History, it was likely that he or she studied *only* History for the full three years of undergraduate study. This amount of specialism is now being lessened by a number of factors affecting the university system. For example, students are now encouraged to sit five to six AS Level exams in their first year of A Level study. The students will then select three of these subjects to complete to A2 standard. This has increased the breadth of post-16 study, and many students now are able to pursue subjects across the Arts and Sciences for at least one year of A Level study. In addition, within universities themselves, curricular changes are eroding the level of specialisation. In many universities, particularly the 'new' universities created since 1992, there has been a massive increase in the numbers of modular degrees offered. Modular degrees are primarily designed to increase access but these courses also enable students to study across a range of subjects. The interdisciplinary nature of the programmes that are studied within modular schemes has led to a breaking down of the narrow specialism of single-subject degrees. Indeed, even within single-subject degrees, it is increasingly common to be able to choose subsidiary subjects from a wide range of disciplines.

Essentially, the broader liberal arts curricula and open admissions system that form an integral part of the US education system are not part of the UK tradition. As a result, one could argue that, in the UK, higher education has traditionally privileged educational depth whilst in the US it has privileged educational breadth. One consequence of this breadth of study and open admissions is the assumption that all students need to be taught how to write, and as John Heyda details in Chapter 11, this means that all first-year undergraduate students study writing in a required general course, often referred to as 'freshman composition'. In fact, many US educationalists assume that 'freshman comp' is universal, so they are surprised that it is an entire disciplinary area of higher education curricula unheard of in the UK. The first question many from the US ask, then, is 'How do British students learn to write'? It is, indeed, an interesting area to be explored.

Whilst we recognise that higher education is diverse and that answers to this question are multifaceted and complex, we speculate that traditionally students learnt to write tacitly as part of the higher education experience. In the 1960s when only 8 per cent of all young people were allowed into the academy, strong writers would have been selected into the system and students with average writing profiles would not have got past the gatekeepers (NCIHE, 1997). Thus, the vast majority of students who experienced any kind of difficulty with writing would have been excluded at the point of selection. We suggest that within the traditional UK higher education model there was an assumption that students developed their writing through their subject.

Prior to the expansion of UK higher education in the 1990s, students would have had access to small study groups and seminar situations that allowed for timely and in-depth feedback on written work. There would have been opportunities for students to get feedback on drafts of writing, and the feedback offered would have meant that writing would have developed tacitly in tandem with the development of the academic subject.

An illustration of this tacit approach occurred when one of the UK authors of this chapter was at university in the early 1980s; she learnt how to hedge, learnt about transitions and about writing a thesis statement, but she only learnt the labels for these features of her writing when she started studying writing research literature years later. Thus, she was not able to name what she knew about writing structures until at least ten years after she learnt it.

In this context there was no need to have paid academic staff developing student writing in an explicit way, and students as peer tutors would not have been utilised. To summarise, we argue that the absence of peer tutoring (or indeed academic staff tutoring) to support student writing has been a consequence of the specialised curricula, the elitism and the selectivity of traditional higher education. However, current developments in higher education mean that these factors have been superseded by a move from elitism to inclusion, massification, widening participation, the concept of graduateness and the key skills agenda. As a result, UK universities are now developing learning-support units, programmes and initiatives for teaching writing and writing centres to address student writing in an explicit way. For these reasons it is timely to identify the strengths and weaknesses of using students as peer tutors in the UK context.

Peer learning in the UK

The model of students supporting or teaching other students is used in a variety of ways in UK higher education.[3] The use of peers has extended, enhanced and diversified approaches to learning in a range of contexts. Supplementary instruction and mentoring projects are widely accepted and a range of peer projects have been funded by HEFCE.[4] The focus in this section is not a critique of the use of peers *per se*, because we recognise the value of peer approaches (Blythman and Hampton, 2001). Instead, we want to focus on the use of peers specifically in the context of developing student writing.

We recognise that there are a number of advantages inherent in a peer model of writing development. Clearly, as Devet has identified, a peer model can reach large numbers of students who need support, and the staffing costs are lower than employing full-time lecturers. The study support units in the University of the Arts London, are used by 10 per cent of the total student body. If we were to train up students to work as peer tutors, we would be able to extend our offer to a greater number of students. In addition, with peer tutors in situ our academic Study Support colleagues would be able to spend more time developing Writing in the Disciplines (WID) initiatives across our institution. The current arrangements mean that our academic staff spend most of their time in one-to-one support with students, to the detriment of a wider developmental role.

Employing students in this way in our institution would have an added advantage because it would enable us to provide work for our students. Before the abolition of means-tested grants and the introduction of tuition fees, student employment was not an issue. Because university education was free and there were maintenance grants, it was unusual for any student to need to take paid employment during term time. This meant that institutions did not have a tradition of finding employment for their students. Because of the changes to students' financial position, however, it is now in our institution's interests to supply safe, valuable work opportunities for students.

We agree with Devet's suggestion that there are explicit benefits arising from peer tutors' and students' shared educational experience. Indeed, research has shown that in certain cases high-quality learning happens when the teacher is close to the experience of the student (Brookfield, 1998). The Study Support Lecturers interviewed at the University of the Arts London, shared this belief when they were asked to speculate about the benefits of a peer model: '[The peer tutors] have got vivid memories of what it is all about and how it feels and the struggles and so on'; peer tutors and students are '[a]ble to bond because of the similarity in age'; 'People see me looking rather elderly and it's rather nice to be helped by someone closer to your age and a peer.'

Although these tutors see the benefits of a peer model, they also raise several areas of concern. We would like to explore these further and develop our own critique of the peer approach. First, we recognise that peer tutoring is cheaper and that it would employ students in a productive way, but we believe that one cannot look at the issue of student employment without addressing the wider issue of lecturers' pay, status and morale. If we were to introduce a peer model at the University of the Arts London, we would want to be confident that doing so would not threaten the livelihood of currently employed staff. We are aware that even if student-tutors were introduced for sound pedagogical reasons, there would be a degree of cynicism amongst staff that this was simply a money-saving exercise.

Within our own institution, Study Support Lecturers are on academic rates of pay, but nationally the situation is not so clear cut. Writing development is an emerging field and staff who support students' writing find themselves on a range of academic and non-academic pay scales depending on where and how their jobs are located – for example, in student services, teaching and learning units, or in academic departments. In the UK, teaching is increasingly stratified, with new grades of teaching assistants, learning assistants and technician teachers. The gap between the academic and non-academic is less categorical than it has been in the past and this is particularly true in the area of writing tuition. Linda Shamoon and Deborah Burns raise what for us is an additional concern: 'Writing centre work could be done by a wide array of individuals including the tenured professor, in the modern Fordist university it will be done by the lowest paid and least skilled worker' (2001, p. 64).

We note that US writing centre literature shares a strong sense of being 'other' and being 'on the borderlines' of formal instruction,[5] and we speculate that the use of students as peer tutors has served to reinforce this borderland experience. Being on the borders can be a continued source of celebration *and* frustration. So on one hand, Jeanne Simpson argues that writing-centres should embrace institutional goals, whilst on the other hand, Steve Braye and Beth Boquet subscribe to the outlaw identity (Simpson et al., 1994, p. 8). The US writing-centre movement wants to move into the main-stream of university experience, but also wants to stress its independence from the mainstream.

We contrast this tension with what happens at the University of the Arts London, where study support is embedded in the fabric of the university. This centralised position is partly due to the status of the Study Support Unit's academic staff team, and the fact that these colleagues are repre-sented at all levels of the institutional hierarchy. We take the view that our work must be, and indeed is, mainstream (Blythman and Orr, 2002; Orr and Blythman, 2000). As academics on an academic contracts level of pay, we do not have the concerns about marginality that are so prevalent in American writing-centre literature. If students were trained up as part of the study support offer, however, there is a danger that our very centrality could be threatened. This is not to condone a view that students have less status than lecturers; it is simply a recognition that differential pay scales and concepts of professionalism are important in the eyes of many colleagues – a concern reportedly shared by American colleagues (Shamoon and Burns, 2001).

Writing support at the University of the Arts London

If we are to look at peer tutoring in depth, we need to explore our Study Support Lecturers' pedagogy at the University of the Arts London. When the study support team were asked to define what they offer to students, they often referred to the importance of their 'life experience'. This advantage is precisely what they felt peer tutors would not have. It was recognised that students have recent college experience, but most do not have the 'breadth' of experience that lecturers say they draw on to support their students.

When we explored the team's approaches to pedagogy, we noted that they are able to move from directive to non-directive approaches seamlessly, depending on the needs of each student. Significantly, we found examples of the Study Support Lecturers using the very pedagogies described by Devet above as being the sole preserve of peers. This led us to see that Devet dichotomises the work of peers and the work of academic staff. She writes from a position that assumes that academics 'intimidate' students and uphold banking models of education. This oppressive transmission model of teach-ing is then contrasted with a student-centred, collaborative peer approach. We disagree with this polarity and argue that Study Support Lecturers are able to have meaningful collaborative relationships with the students they support. Our research shows that the study support team interviewed does not use what Lyn Gow and David Kember refer to as transmission-based approaches to teaching (1993). An in-depth analysis of the team's approaches to pedagogy reveal that the lecturers subscribe to and employ a student-centred, learner-facilitation approach. Thus, we do not believe there are pedagogies that are the sole preserve of a peer any more than we would subscribe to the view that there are any pedagogies that are the sole preserve of lecturers; this is a false dichotomy. Peers and lecturers are not categorically different in their approaches to pedagogy, and student-centredness can emerge (or be absent) in both contexts.

Some peers are more peer than others

It is likely that peer tutors will feel more comfortable adopting a non-directive approach with students (Cogie, 2001). We are concerned that this would disadvantage some students who need to be explicitly introduced to the hidden practices of higher education. Activities that on the surface may seem very directive can provide the support students need to advance as writers (Cogie, 2001). Devet emphasises the peerness of a peer tutoring approach by saying that, for example, students 'share the same dialect'. We worry that this implies a view that students are homogeneous. However, students today are an increasingly heterogeneous group, who have different experiences in higher education due to differential access to power and social capital. Nancy Grimm argues that we need to recognise that peer tutors often have more social capital than those they support and they may be unaware of how this privileges them because much of what they know is tacit and seems 'natural' to them. Because a peer tutor is not supposed to tell a student what to do, this may preserve the status quo because peer tutors will 'withhold insider information' (Grimm, 1999, p. 18). This will not challenge inequality, but will merely replicate it. A working-class student may feel more 'equal' when working with a working-class academic than with a middle-class peer tutor. Thus, peers do not always have equal relations with their students. In problematising the peerness of a peer approach we are not implying that lecturers have equal relationships with their students. We merely want to point out that when lecturers work with students there is no assumption about peerness and using students as tutors may give the appearance of equality without it actually being experienced by students as a truly peer experience.

Several US writing centre directors have informed us that the process by which a student becomes a peer tutor is very selective and that many are rejected. We would like to explore this because if middle-class monolingual students form the majority of peer tutors we fear that this would replicate differences in status, rather than challenge these distinctions. Grimm (1999) suggests that the screening of peers helps ensure that peers that are selected are positioned 'within the culture of power' (p. 113). This concern was articulated by several of the Study Support team at the University of the Arts London, who stated that students would not like to be supported by students who somehow saw themselves as 'better than them'.

▶ Conclusion

It is probable that there will be contexts and situations in UK higher education where student writing can be developed by adopting a peer-tutoring model; however, it is important for universities to match staffing models to localised curricular, pedagogic and micro-political need. Additionally, we have to take account of national policy drivers and the ways in which these affect the local situation. For these reasons we argue that there are dangers in attempting to replicate the US peer-tutoring model in an unreconstructed form.

We agree with Grimm when she warns that 'we inadvertently create conditions for closure and misrepresentation when we emphasise the importance of the peer relationship in tutoring' (1999, p. 112). It is our conclusion that in the UK it is essential that we develop appropriate pedagogical approaches for writing development rather than focus on a particular model of staffing. We hope that our interrogation of the peer-tutoring model in this chapter will encourage readers to assess the appropriateness of peer tutoring for their own institutional contexts, and that it will also emphasise the need to think carefully before adopting or adapting models of Academic Writing provision.

NOTES

1   The University of the Arts London, was formerly the London Institute.
2   When clients were asked: 'With whom do you prefer to have consultations: professors, students, or no preference?' no one group was favoured.
3   See Beardon (1998), Boud (1995), Falchikov (2001), Rust and Wallace (1994) and Topping (1996a and 1996b).
4   For example, at Kingston University there is a well-established supplementary instruction programme in the Law department, and at the University of Leeds first-year Philosophy students have developed a subject-based peer support system.
5   See Riley (1994), Shamoon and Burns (2001), Summerfield (1988) and Trimbur (1987).

Bibliography

Andrews, R. (1995) *Teaching and Learning Argument* (London: Cassell).

Andrews, R. (2003) 'The End of the Essay?', *Teaching in Higher Education*, 8:1, 117–28.

Aronowitz, S. (1973) *False Promises: The Shaping of American Working Class Consciousness* (New York: McGraw-Hill).

Aronowitz, S. (1997) 'Academic Unionism and the Future of Higher Education', in C. Nelson (ed.), *Will Teach for Food: Academic Labor in Crisis* (Minneapolis: University of Minnesota Press), pp. 181–214.

Assessment Reform Group (1999) *Inside the Black Box* (Cambridge: University of Cambridge School of Education).

Assiter, A. (ed.) (1995) *Transferable Skills in Higher Education* (London: Kogan Page).

Avery, S. (ed.) (1998) *From Sixth Form to Higher Education: English Oral and Written Language Skills Explored* (Cambridge: Anglia Polytechnic University).

Bakhtin, M. (1981) 'Discourse in the Novel', in M. Holquist (ed.), *The Dialogic Imagination: Four Essays by M. Bakhtin*, trans. C. Emerson and M. Holquist (Austin: University of Texas Press), pp. 259–422.

Ballard, B. (1984) 'Improving Student Writing: An Integrated Approach to Culture Adjustment', in R. Williams, J. Swales and J. Kirkman (eds), *Common Ground: Shared Interests in ESP and Communication Studies* (Oxford: Pergaman Press) pp. 43–53.

Ballard, B. and Clanchy, J. (1988) 'Literacy in the University: An "Anthropological" Approach', in G. Taylor, B. Ballard, V. Beasley, H. Bock, J. Clanchy and P. Nightingale (eds), *Literacy by Degrees* (Milton Keynes: SRHE and Open University Press), pp. 7–23.

Barber, B. (1992) 'Jihad vs. McWorld', *Atlantic Monthly*, 3, 53–63.

Barnett, R. (1994) *The Limits of Competence: Knowledge, Higher Education and Society* (Buckingham: Open University Press).

Barnett, R. (2000) *Realising the University in an Age of Supercomplexity* (Buckingham: Open University Press).

Barnett, R. and Blumner, J. (1999) *Writing Centers and Writing Across the Curriculum Programs: Building Interdisciplinary Partnerships* (Westport, CT: Greenwood Press).

Bartholomae, D. (1986) 'Inventing the University', *Journal of Basic Writing*, 5:1, 4–22.

Barton, D., Hamilton, M. and Ivanič, R. (2000) *Situated Literacies: Reading and Writing in Context* (New York: Routledge).

Baskin, C., Barker, M. and Farr-Wharton, Y. (1997) 'Mediating Cognition and Culture: a Pilot Study of the Literacy and Academic Communication Skills of First Year Commerce Students', in Z. Golebiowski (ed.), *Selected Proceedings of the First National Conference on Tertiary Literacy: Research and Practice*, vol. 1: *Policy and Practice of Tertiary Literacy* (Melbourne: Victoria University of Technology), pp. 66–81.

Bauman, Z. (1998) *Globalization: The Human Consequences* (Cambridge: Polity Press).

Baynham, M. (1996) *Literacy Practices: Investigating Literacy in Social Contexts* (London: Longman).

Baynham, M. (2000) 'Academic Writing in New and Emergent Discipline Areas', in M. Lea and B. Stierer (eds), *Student Writing in Higher Education: New Contexts* (Buckingham: Open University Press), pp. 17–31.

Bazerman, C. and Russell, D. (eds) (1994) *Landmark Essays on Writing Across the Curriculum* (Davis, CA: Hermagoras Press).

Bazerman, C., Little, J., Bethel, L., Chavkin, T., Fouquette, D. and Garufis, J. (2005) *Reference Guide to Writing Across the Curriculum* (West Layfayette, IN: Parlor Press and the WAC Clearinghouse).

Bean, J. (2001) *Engaging Ideas* (San Francisco: Jossey Bass).

Beardon, L. (1998) 'Casting the Net: Peer Assisted Learning on the Internet', in S. Goodlad (ed.), *Mentoring and Tutoring by Students* (London: Kogan), 206–16.

Belcher, D. and Braine, G. (1995) *Academic Writing in a Second Language* (Norwood, NJ: Ablex).

Bennett, N., Dunne, E. and Carré, C. (2000) *Skills Development in Higher Education and Employment* (Buckingham: Open University Press).

Bergstrom, C. (2004) 'The Status of Writing in the University', *English Subject Centre Newsletter*, 6, 10–13.

Berkenkotter, C. and Huckin, T. (1995) *Genre Knowledge in Disciplinary Communication: Cognition/Culture/Power* (Mahwah, NJ: Lawrence Erlbaum).

Berlin, J. (1980) 'Current Traditional Rhetoric: Paradigm and Practice', *Freshman English News*, 8:3, 1–4, 13–19.

Berlin, J. (1982) 'Contemporary Composition: the Major Pedagogical Positions', *College English*, 44:8, 765–77.

Berlin, J. (1984) *Writing Instruction in Nineteenth-Century American Colleges* (Carbondale: Southern Illinois University Press).

Berlin, J. (1987) *Rhetoric and Reality: Writing Instruction in American Colleges, 1900–1985* (Carbondale: Southern Illinois University Press).

Beverley, J. (1978) 'Higher Education and Capitalist Crisis', *Socialist Review*, 42, 67–91.

Biggs, J. (1999) *Teaching for Quality Learning at University* (Buckingham: Open University Press).

Biggs, J. and Collis, K. (1982) *Evaluating the Quality of Learning: The SOLO Taxonomy* (New York: Academic Press).

Bizzell, P. (1982) 'Cognition, Convention, and Certainty: What We Need to Know about Writing', *PRE TEXT*, 3:3, 213–44.

Björk, L., Bräuer, G., Rienecker, L. and Jörgensen, P. (eds) (2003) *Teaching Academic Writing in European Higher Education* (Dordrecht: Kluwer).

Blythman, M. and Hampton, D. (2001) 'Informal Peer Tutoring in Study Support Networks Designed to Encourage Attendance', in N. Falchikov (ed.), *Learning Together: Peer Tutoring in Higher Education* (London: Routledge/Falmer), pp. 245–8.

Blythman, M. and Orr, S. (2002) 'A Joined Up Policy Approach to Student Support', in M. Peelo and T. Wareham (eds), *Failing Students in Higher Education* (Buckingham: Open University Press), pp. 45–55.

Boice, R. (1987) 'Is Released Time an Effective Component of Faculty Development Programs?', *Research in Higher Education*, 26:3, 311–26.

Bolton, G. (2001) *Reflective Practice: Writing and Professional Development* (London: Chapman).

Bonanno, H. and Jones, J. (1997) *Measuring the Academic Skills of University Students, the MASUS Procedure: A Diagnostic Assessment* (University of Sydney: Learning Assistance Centre Publications).

Boud, D. (1995) 'How Can Peers be Used in Self-Assessment?', in D. Boud (ed.), *Enhancing Learning through Self-Assessment* (London: Kogan), pp. 200–6.

Boud, D. (1999) 'Situating Development in Professional Work: Using Peer Learning', *International Journal for Academic Development*, 4:1, 3–10.

Bourdieu, P. and Passeron, J.-C. (1990) *Reproduction in Education, Culture and Society* (London: Sage).

Brandt, D. (2001) *Literacy in American Lives* (Cambridge: Cambridge University Press).

Branthwaite, A., Trueman, M. and Hartley, J. (1980) 'Writing Essays: the Actions and Strategies of Students', in J. Hartley (ed.), *The Psychology of Written Communication* (London: Kogan Page), pp. 98–112.

Braverman, H. (1974) *Labor and Monopoly Capital: The Degradation of Work in the Twentieth Century* (New York: Monthly Review Press).

Bright, M. (2004) ' "Degrees for Sale" at UK Universities', *Observer*, 1 August, accessed at http://education.guardian.co.uk/higher/news/story/0,,1273854,00.html on 11 August 2004.

Brill, H. (1999) 'False Promises of Higher Education: More Graduates, Fewer Jobs', *Against the Current*, 35, 34–9.

Brint, S. and Karabel, J. (1989) *The Diverted Dream: Community Colleges and the Promise of Educational Opportunity in America, 1900–1985* (New York: Oxford University Press).

Britton, J. (1982) 'Writing to Learn and Learning to Write', in G. Pradl (ed.), *Prospect and Retrospect: Selected Essays of James Britton* (Portsmouth, NH: Boynton/Cook), pp. 94–111.

Britton, J., Burgess, T., Martin, N., McCleod, A. and Rosen, H. (1975) *The Development of Writing Abilities (11–18)* (London: Macmillan Education).

Brodkey, L. (1989) 'On the Subjects of Class and Gender in "The Literacy Letters" ', *College English*, 51:2, 125–41.

Brookfield, S. (1998) 'On the Certainty of Public Shaming: Working with Students "Who Don't Get It" ', in C. Rust (ed.), *Improving Student Learning* (Oxford: Oxford Centre for Staff Development), pp. 17–32.

Brown, G. and Atkins, M. (1988) *Effective Teaching in Higher Education* (London: Methuen).

Bruffee, K. (1978) 'The Brooklyn Plan: Attaining Intellectual Growth through Peer-Group Tutoring', *Liberal Education*, 64, 447–68.

Bruffee, K. (1980) 'Staffing and Operating Peer Tutoring Writing Centres', in L. Kasden and D. Hoeber (eds), *Essays for Teachers, Researchers, and Administrators* (Urbana, IL: NCTE), pp. 141–9.

Bruffee, K. (1984) 'Peer Tutoring and the "Conversation of Mankind" ', reprinted in C. Murphy and J. Law (eds) (1995), *Landmark Essays on Writing Centres* (Davis, CA: Hermagoras Press), pp. 87–98.

Bruner, J. (1978) 'The Role of Dialogue in Language Acquisition', in A. Sinclair, R. Jarvella and W. Levelt (eds), *The Child's Conception of Language* (New York: Springer-Verlag), pp. 241–56.

Bryan, C. (1998) 'Raising Standards in English', in S. Avery (ed.), *From Sixth Form to Higher Education: English Oral and Written Language Skills Explored* (Cambridge: Anglia Polytechnic University), pp. 6–17.

Burnham, C. (2001) 'Expressive Pedagogy: Practice/Theory, Theory/Practice', in G. Tate, A. Rupiper and K. Schick (eds), *A Guide to Composition Pedagogies* (New York, Oxford University Press), pp. 19–35.

Cameron, D. (1995) *Verbal Hygiene* (London: Routledge).

Campbell, O. (1939) 'The Failure of Freshman English', *English Journal*, 28: 177–85.

Candlin, C. and Plum, G. (1999) 'Engaging with the Challenges of Interdiscursivity in Academic Writing: Researchers, Students and Tutors', in C. Candlin and K. Hyland (eds), *Writing: Texts, Processes and Practices* (London: Longman), pp. 193–217.

Carey, A. (1995) 'Goals, Guidance, Grades, and Gift-Giving', *Teaching English in the Two-Year College*, 22:2, 129–35.

Carino, P. (1995) 'Early Writing Centers: Toward a History', reprinted in R. Barnett and J. Blumner (eds) (2001), *The Allyn and Bacon Guide to Writing Center Theory and Practice* (Boston: Allyn and Bacon), pp. 10–21.

Clamp, P. and Gregory, G. (1988) 'Study Course Provision in Higher Education: a Case Study', *Assessment and Evaluation in Higher Education*, 13:3, 242–52.

Clark, I. (1988) 'Preparing Future Composition Teachers in the Writing Center', *College Composition and Communication*, 39:3, 347–50.

Clark, I. (1992) *Writing in the Center: Teaching in a Writing Center Setting*, 2nd edn (Dubuque, Iowa: Kendall/Hunt).

Clark, I. (1993) 'Portfolio Evaluation, Collaboration, and Writing Centers', *College Composition and Communication*, 44:4, 515–24.

Clark, I. (1997) *Writing about Diversity*, 2nd edn (New York: Harcourt Brace).

Clark, R. (1992) 'Principles and Practice of CLA in the Classroom', in N. Fairclough (ed.), *Critical Language Awareness* (London: Longman), pp. 117–40.

Clark, R. and Ivanič, R. (1997) *The Politics of Writing* (London: Routledge).

Clark, R. and Ivanič, R. (eds) (1999) *Critical Language Awareness,* Special Issue of *Language Awareness*, 8:2, 63–70.

Clarke, J. (2002) 'A New Kind of Symmetry: Actor-Network Theories and the New Literacy Studies', *Studies in the Education of Adults*, 34:2, 107–22.

Clerehan, R. (2003) 'Transitions to Tertiary Education in the Arts and Humanities: Some Academic Initiatives from Australia', *Arts and Humanities in Higher Education*, 2:1, 72–89.

Cobb, L. (1982) 'Overcoming a Financial Obstacle: Undergraduate Staffing in the Composition Lab', *Writing Lab Newsletter*, 7:4, 1–4.

Coffield, F. (1999) 'Breaking the Consensus: Lifelong Learning as Social Control', *British Educational Research Journal*, 24:4, 479–500.

Coffin, C., Curry, M. J., Goodman, S., Hewings, A., Lillis, T. and Swann, J. (2003) *Teaching Academic Writing: A Toolkit for Higher Education* (London: Routledge).

Cogie, J. (2001) 'Keeping the Contradiction Productive', in J. Nelson and K. Evertz (eds), *The Politics of Writing Centres* (Portsmouth, NH: Boyton/Cook), pp. 37–49.

Coles, W. (1969) 'Freshman Composition: the Circle of Unbelief', *College English*, 31, 134–42.

College Reading and Learning Association, accessed at www.crla.net on 10 June 2004.

Collins Dictionary of the English Language (1979) (London: Collins).

Connors, R. (1989) 'Rhetorical History as a Component of Composition Studies', *Rhetoric Review*, 7, 230–40.

Connors, R. (1996) 'The Abolition Debate in Composition: a Short History', in L. Bloom, D. Daiker and E. White (eds), *Composition in the Twenty-First Century: Crisis and Change* (Carbondale: Southern Illinois University Press), pp. 47–63.

Construction Task Force (1998) *Rethinking Construction* [The Egan Report] (London: Department of the Environment, Transport and the Regions), accessed at www.rethinkingconstruction.org.uk on 8 February 2005.

Copperman, P. (1978) *The Literacy Hoax: The Decline of Reading, Writing, and Learning in the Public Schools and What We Can Do About It* (New York: William Morrow).

Corbett, E. (1965) *Classical Rhetoric for the Modern Student* (New York: Oxford University Press).

Cottrell, S. (2003) 'About Personal Development Planning', accessed at www.palgrave.com/skills4study/html/pdp/about_pdp.htm on 2 September 2005.

Council for College and University English (1997) *The English Curriculum: Diversity and Standards* (London: QAA).

Crème, P. and Lea, M. (2003) *Writing at University: A Guide for Students*, 2nd edn (Maidenhead: Open University Press).

Crowley, S. (1990) *The Methodical Memory: Invention in Current-Traditional Rhetoric* (Carbondale: Southern Illinois University Press).

Crowley, S. (1998) *Composition in the University: Historical and Polemical Essays* (Pittsburgh: University of Pittsburgh Press).

Crowley, S. (1999) 'The Universal Requirement in First-Year Composition', *Basic Writing e-Journal*, 1:2, accessed at www.asu.edu/clas/english/composition/cbw/bwe_fall_1999.htm#sharon on 12 June 2004.

Crowley, S. (2000) 'Composition in the University Revisited: Sharon Crowley Responds to Raul Sanchez', *JAC Online*, accessed at www.cas.usf.edu/JAC/194/rereview.html#crowley on 12 June 2004.

Crowley, T. (2003) *Standard English and the Politics of Language* (Basingstoke: Palgrave Macmillan).

Crystal, D. (1995) *The Cambridge Encyclopaedia of the English Language* (Cambridge: Cambridge University Press).

Curry, M. J. (1996) 'Teaching Managerial Communications to Native and Nonnative Speakers of English', *Business Communication Quarterly*, 59:1, 27–35.

Curry, M. J. (2001) 'Preparing to be Privatized: the Hidden Curriculum of a Community College ESL Writing Class', in E. Margolis (ed.), *The Hidden Curriculum in Higher Education* (New York: Routledge), pp. 175–92.

Curry, M. (2002) 'Cultural Models in the US Writing Classroom: Matches and Mismatches', in M. Graal and R. Clark (eds), *Writing Development in Higher Education: Changing Contexts for Teaching and Learning* (Leicester: University of Leicester), pp. 45–61.

Davidson, C. (1999) 'Outlaw Cultures, Hybrid Identities, and Joyful Designs: Links between Creative Writing and Composition', paper presented at the *Second Conference on Creative Writing in Higher Education*, Sheffield Hallam University.

Davidson, C. (2000) 'Teaching Writing Theory as Liberatory Practice: Helping Students Chart the Dangerous Waters of Academic Discourse Across the Disciplines in Higher Education', in S. Mitchell and R. Andrews (eds), *Learning to Argue in Higher Education* (Portsmouth, NH: Boynton/Cook), pp. 118–28.

Davidson, C. and Tomic, A. (1994) 'Removing Computer Phobia from the Writing Classroom', *English Language Teaching Journal*, 48:3, 205–13.

Davidson, C. and Tomic, A. (1999) 'Inventing Academic Literacy: an American Perspective', in C. Jones, J. Turner and B. Street (eds), *Students Writing in the University: Cultural and Epistemological Issues* (Amsterdam: John Benjamins), pp. 161–70.

Davidson, G. and Lea, M. (1994) 'Modularity', Technical Issues Paper (London: Further Education Unit).

Davies, S. (2004) *Royal Literary Fund Fellowships: The Human Exchange* (London: Royal Literary Fund).

Davies, S., Swinburne, D. and Williams, G. (2006) *Writing Matters: The Royal Literary Fund Report on Higher Education* (London: Royal Literary Fund).

Day, G. (2004a) 'Opinion Column', *The Times Higher Education Supplement*, 30 January, p. 15.

Day, G. (2004b) 'Opinion Column', *The Times Higher Education Supplement*, 16 July, p. 13.

Delamont, S. and Atkinson, P. (1995) *Fighting Familiarity: Essays on Education and Ethnography* (Cresskill, NJ: Hampton Press).

Delanty, G. (2001) *Challenging Knowledge: The University in the Knowledge Society* (Buckingham: Open University Press).

Department for Education and Employment (2000) *Opportunity for All: Skills for the New Economy* (Sudbury: DfEE).

Department for Education and Skills (2003) *The Future of Higher Education* (London: HMSO).

Dias, P., Freedman, A., Medway P. and Paré, A. (1999) *Worlds Apart: Acting and Writing in Academic and Workplace Contexts* (Mahwah, NJ: Lawrence Erlbaum).

Dillon, G. (1991) *Contending Rhetorics: Writing in the Academic Disciplines* (Bloomington: Indiana University Press).

Dobbs, M. (2005) 'Scorers of New SAT Get Ready for Essays', *Washington Post*, 16 January, A01.

Dolan, J. and Castley, A. (1998) *Students Supporting Students*, SEDA Paper, 105 (Birmingham: SEDA).

Doloughan, F. (2001) *Communication Skills and the Knowledge Economy: Language, Literacy, and the Production of Meaning* (London: Institute of Education).

Donald, J. (1992) 'The Development of Thinking Processes in Postsecondary Education: the Application of a Working Model', *Higher Education*, 24:4, 413–30.

Donaldson, A. and Topping, K. (1996) *Promoting Peer-Assisted Learning amongst Students in Higher and Further Education*, SEDA Paper, 96 (Birmingham: SEDA).

Dougherty, K. (1994) *The Contradictory College: The Conflicting Origins, Impacts, and Futures of the Community College* (Albany: State University of New York Press).

Drew, S. (1998) *Key Skills in Higher Education: Background and Rationale*, SEDA Special Report no. 6 (Birmingham: SEDA).

Dysthe, O. (2001) 'The Mutual Challenge of Writing Research and the Teaching of Writing', accessed at www.uib.no/plf/ansatte/olga/mutual.rtf on 3 October 2005.

Edwards, D. and Mercer, N. (1987) *Common Knowledge: The Development of Understanding in the Classroom* (London: Methuen).

Elbow, P. (1981) *Writing with Power* (New York: Oxford University Press).

Elbow, P. (1998) *Writing without Teachers*, 2nd edn (New York: Oxford University Press).

Eliot, T. S. (1963) *Collected Poems, 1909–1962* (London: Faber & Faber).

Ellsworth, E. (1989) 'Why Doesn't This Feel Empowering? Working Through the Repressive Myths of Critical Pedagogy', reprinted in L. Stone (ed.) (1994), *The Education Feminism Reader* (London: Routledge), pp. 300–27.

English, F. (1999) 'What do Students Really Say in their Essays? Towards a Descriptive Framework for Analysing Student Writing', in C. Jones, J. Turner and B. Street (eds), *Students Writing in the University: Cultural and Epistemological Issues* (Amsterdam: John Benjamins), pp. 17–27.

Faigley, L. (1986) 'Competing Theories of Process: a Critique and a Proposal', *College English*, 48, 527–42.

Falchikov, N. (ed.) (2001) *Learning Together: Peer Tutoring in Higher Education* (London: Routledge/Falmer).

Fernandez, J. A. and Marsh, J. (2002) 'From Frustration to Fun', *Thinking Writing: News from the Writing in the Disciplines Project*, 1, 3–4.

Flower, L. (1994) *The Construction of Negotiated Meaning: A Social Cognitive Theory of Writing* (Carbondale: Southern Illinois University Press).

Flower, L. and Hayes, J. (1981) 'A Cognitive Process Theory of Writing', *College Composition and Communication*, 32, 365–87.

Francis, B., Robson, J. and Read, B. (2001) 'An Analysis of Undergraduate Writing Styles in the Context of Gender and Achievement', *Studies in Higher Education*, 26:3, 313–26.

Freedman, A. (1993) 'Show and Tell? The Role of Explicit Teaching in the Learning of New Genres', *Research in the Teaching of English*, 27:3, 222–51.

Freire, P. (1970) *Pedagogy of the Oppressed* (New York: Continuum).

Freire, P. (1974) *Education for Critical Consciousness* (London: Sheed and Ward).

Fulwiler, T. (1980) 'Journals Across the Disciplines', *English Journal*, 69:9, 14–19.

Fulwiler, T. (1984) 'How Well does Writing Across the Curriculum Work?', *College English*, 46, 113–25.

Fulwiler, T. (1987) *Teaching with Writing* (Portsmouth, NH: Boynton/Cook).

Gadbow, K. (1989) 'Teachers as Writing Center Tutors: Release from the Red Pen', *Writing Lab Newsletter*, 14:4, 13–15.

Ganobcsik-Williams, L. (2003) ' "Is this Freshman Composition?" Teaching General Studies Writing in Europe', in *Proceedings of the Second Conference of the European Association for the Teaching of Academic Writing*, CD-ROM.

Ganobcsik-Williams, L. (2004) *A Report on the Teaching of Academic Writing in UK Higher Education* (London: Royal Literary Fund).

Garner, M. and Edwards, H. (1995) 'Integrating Academic Discourse: What Else Can We Learn from Experience?' in K. Chanock (ed.), *Proceedings of the National Language and Academic Skills Conference: Integrating the Teaching of Academic Discourse into Courses in the Disciplines* (Melbourne: La Trobe University).

Garner, R. (2004) 'Students "Cannot Write Essays" ', *Independent* 6 March, accessed at http://education.independent.co.uk/news/article72401.ece on 11 August 2004.

Gee, J. (1996) *Social Linguistics and Literacies: Ideology in Discourses*, 2nd edn (London: Falmer).

Gibbs, G. (1992) *Improving the Quality of Student Learning* (Bristol: Technical and Educational Services).

Gibson, R. (2005) Personal email to Lisa Ganobcsik-Williams, 19 September.

Giddens, A. (1999) *Reith Lectures* (London: BBC).

Giltrow, J. (2000) ' "Argument" as a Term in Talk about Student Writing', in S. Mitchell and R. Andrews (eds), *Learning to Argue in Higher Education* (Portsmouth, NH: Boynton/Cook), pp. 129–45.

Giltrow, J. and Valiquette, M. (1994) 'Genres and Knowledge: Students Writing in the Disciplines', in A. Freedman and P. Medway (eds), *Learning and Teaching Genre* (Portsmouth, NH: Boynton/Cook), pp. 3, 47–62.

Giroux, H. (1993) 'Literacy and the Politics of Difference', in C. Lankshear and P. McLaren (eds), *Critical Literacy: Politics, Praxis and the Postmodern* (Albany: State University of New York Press), pp. 367–77.

Glaser, R. (1999) 'Expert Knowledge and Processes of Thinking', in R. McCormick and C. Paechter (eds), *Learning and Knowledge* (London: Paul Chapman), pp. 88–102.

Goggin, M. and Miller, S. (2000) 'What is New about the "New Abolitionists": Continuities and Discontinuities in the Great Debate', *Composition Studies*, 28, 85–112.

Gonzalez Arnal, S. and Burwood, S. (2003) 'Tacit Knowledge and Public Accounts', *Journal of Philosophy of Education*, 37, 377–91.

Gottschalk, K. and Hjortshoj, K. (2004) *The Elements of Teaching Writing* (Boston, MA: Bedford/St Martin's).

Gow, L. and Kember, D. (1993) 'Conceptions of Teaching and their Relationship to Student Learning', *British Journal of Educational Psychology*, 63:1, 20–33.

Grabe, W. and Kaplan, R. (1996) *Theory and Practice of Writing* (London: Longman).

Graff, G. (1990) 'Teach the Conflicts', *South Atlantic Quarterly*, 89, 51–67.

Great Britain Committee of Inquiry into the Engineering Profession (1980) *Engineering Our Future* [the Finniston Report] (London: HMSO).

Green, C. and Klug, H. (1990) 'Teaching Critical Thinking and Writing through Debates: an Experimental Evaluation', *Teaching Sociology*, 18, 462–71.

Greenbaum, L. (1969) 'The Tradition of Complaint', *College English*, 31, 174–87.

Greenberg, K. (1997) 'A Response to Ira Shor's "Our Apartheid: Writing Instruction and Inequality" ', *Journal of Basic Writing*, 16:2, 90–4.

Grimm, N. (1996) 'Rearticulating the Work of the Writing Center', *College Composition and Communication*, 47:4, 523–48.

Grimm, N. (1999) *Good Intentions: Writing Center Work for Postmodern Times* (Portsmouth, NH: Boyton/Cook).

Groom, N. (2000) '"A Workable Balance": Self and Sources in Argumentative Writing', in S. Mitchell and R. Andrews (eds), *Learning to Argue in Higher Education* (Portsmouth, NH: Boynton/Cook), pp. 65–73.

Grubb, W. and Associates (1999) *Honored But Invisible: An Inside Look at Teaching in the Community College* (New York: Routledge).

Gunner, J. and Frankel, E. (1997) *The Course of Ideas*, 2nd edn (Reading, MA: Addison-Wesley).

Hacker, D. (2005) 'Language Debates', accessed at www.dianahacker.com/writersref/subpages_language/comseries.html on 20 September 2005.

Halliday, M. (1994) *An Introduction to Functional Grammar*, 2nd edn (London: Edward Arnold).

Hampton, G. (2002) 'Improving First Year Transition and Retention through Faculty Development', paper presented at the *Fifteenth International Conference on the First-Year Experience*, University of Bath.

Hampton, G., Russell, W., Skillen, J., Rodgerson, L., Robinson, S. and Trivett, N. (2003) 'Integrating Tertiary Literacy into the Curriculum: Effects on Performance and Retention', in *Proceedings of the Uniserve Science Symposium: Improving Learning Outcomes* (University of Sydney), pp. 25–30.

Harre, R. (1983) *Personal Being* (Oxford: Basil Blackwell).

Harris, J. (1997) *A Teaching Subject: Composition since 1966* (Upper Saddle River, NJ: Prentice Hall).

Harris, M. (1986) *Teaching One to One: The Writing Conference* (Urbana, IL: NCTE).

Harris, M. (1988) *Writing Centers* (Urbana, IL: NCTE).

Hartley, J. (ed.) (1980) *The Psychology of Written Communication* (London: Kogan Page)

Hartley, J. (1998) 'Students, Writing and Computers', in R. Lonsdale (ed.), *Writing in Higher Education: Perspectives in Theory and Practice* (Aberystwyth: University of Wales), pp. 2–5.

Haswell, R. (2005) WPA listserv, accessed at http://listserv.muohio.edu/scripts/wa.exe?A0=wpa on 17 May 2005.

Hawkins, N. (1985) 'An Introduction to the History and Theory of Peer Tutoring in Writing', in T. Haring, N. Hawkins, E. Morrison, L. Stern and R. Tatu (eds), *A Guide to Writing Programs: Writing Centers, Peer Tutoring Programs, and Writing Across the Curriculum* (Glenview, IL: Scott, Foresman), pp. 7–18.

Hayes, J. and Flower, L. (1980) 'Writing as Problem Solving', *Visible Language*, 14, 388–422.

Haynes, C. (1996) 'Social Construction', in P. Heilker and P. Vandenberg (eds), *Keywords in Composition Studies* (Portsmouth, NH: Boynton/Cook), pp. 221–24.

Heath, S. (1983) *Ways with Words* (Cambridge: Cambridge University Press).

Hebron, C. (1984) 'Newcastle Polytechnic's Writing Centre and its Origins: a Description of an Innovation', in R. Williams, J. Swales and J. Kirkman (eds), *Common Ground: Shared Interests in ESP and Communication Studies* (Oxford: Pergamon Press), pp. 87–98.

HEFCE (2001) 'Supply and Demand in Higher Education', *Consultation Paper 01/62* (Bristol).

HEFCE (2003) 'Building Capacity for Change: Research on the Scholarship of Teaching', accessed at www.hefce.ac.uk/ on 1 November 2005.

Heilker, P. and Vandenberg, P. (eds) (1996) *Keywords in Composition Studies* (Portsmouth, NH: Boynton/Cook).

Herrington, A. (1981) 'Writing to Learn: Writing Across the Disciplines', *College English*, 43:4, 379–87.

Hicks, M., Irons, E. and Zeegers, P. (1995) 'Academic and Communication Skills Taught in Science and Engineering Courses', in K. Chanock (ed.), *Proceedings of the National Language and Academic Skills Conference: Integrating the Teaching of Academic Discourse into Courses in the Disciplines* (Melbourne: La Trobe University).

Higher Education Statistics Agency, accessed at www.hesa.ac.uk on 5 September 2004.

Hillocks, G. (1984) 'What Works in Teaching Composition: a Meta-Analysis of Experimental Treatment Studies', *American Journal of Education*, 93:1, 133–70.

Hillocks, G. (2002) *The Testing Trap: How State Writing Assessments Control Learning* (New York: Teachers College Press).

Hoadley-Maidment, E. (1997) 'From "Story" to Argument: the Acquisition of Academic Writing Skills in an Open-Learning Context', *Language in Education*, 11:1, 55–68.

Hobson, E. (2001) 'Writing Center Pedagogy', in G. Tate, A. Rupiper and K. Schick (eds), *A Guide to Composition Pedagogies* (New York: Oxford University Press), pp. 165–82.

Hodges, W. (2004) 'An Experimental Course in Mathematical Writing', *MSOR Connections*, 4:3, 29–31.

Hodginson, L. (1996) *Changing the Higher Education Curriculum Towards a Systematic Approach to Skills Development* (Milton Keynes: Open University Vocational Qualifications Centre).

hooks, b. (1988) *Talking Back: Thinking Feminist, Thinking Black* (Boston, MA: South End Press).

Hounsell, D. (1984a) 'Learning and Essay Writing', in F. Marton, D. Hounsell and N. Entwistle (eds) *The Experience of Learning* (Edinburgh, Scottish Academic Press), pp. 103–23.

Hounsell, D. (1984b) 'Essay Planning and Essay Writing', *Higher Education Research and Development*, 3:1, 13–31.

Hounsell, D. (1987) 'Essay Writing and the Quality of Feedback', in J. Richardson, M. Eysenck and D. Piper (eds), *Student Learning: Research in Education and Cognitive Psychology* (Buckingham: Open University Press), pp. 109–19.

Hounsell, D. (1988) 'Towards an Anatomy of Academic Discourse: Meaning and Context in the Undergraduate Essay', in R. Säljö (ed.), *The Written World: Studies in Literate Thought and Action* (Berlin: Springer-Verlag), pp. 161–77.

Hounsell, D. (2003) 'Student Feedback, Learning and Development', in M. Slowey and D. Watson (eds), *Higher Education and the Lifecourse* (Maidenhead: Open University Press/McGraw-Hill), pp. 67–78.

Hull, G. (1997) *Changing Work, Changing Writers: Critical Perspectives on Language, Literacy, and Skills* (Albany: State University of New York Press).

Ivanič, R. (1998) *Writing and Identity: The Discoursal Construction of Identity in Academic Writing* (Amsterdam: John Benjamins).

Ivanič, R. (1999) 'A Framework for Thinking about Writing, and Learning to Write', paper presented at *Discourses and Learning Conference*, Lancaster University.

Jackson, M. (1991) 'Writing as Learning: Reflections on Developing Students' Writing Strategies', *Higher Education Research and Development*, 10:1, pp. 41–52.

James, B., Skillen, J., Percy, A., Tootell, H. and Irvine, H. (2004) 'From Integration to Transformation', in K. Deller-Evans and P. Zeegers (eds), *Language and Academic Skills in Higher Education*, pp. 37–47, accessed at http://www.flinders.edu.au/SLC/LASpapers.HTM on 20 December 2005.

Jones, C., Turner, J. and Street, B. (eds) (1999) *Students Writing in the University: Cultural and Epistemological Issues* (Amsterdam: John Benjamins).

Jones, J. (2004) 'Learning to Write in the Disciplines: the Application of Systemic Functional Linguistic Theory to the Teaching and Research of Student Writing', in L. Ravelli and R. Ellis (eds), *Analysing Academic Writing: Contextualized Frameworks* (London: Continuum), pp. 254–73.

Kail, H. and Trimbur, J. (1987) 'The Politics of Peer Tutoring', reprinted in C. Murphy and J. Law (eds), (1995), *Landmark Essays on Writing Centres* (Davis, CA: Hermagoras Press), pp. 203–9.

Kaufer, D. and Geisler, C. (1989) 'Novelty in Academic Writing', *Written Communication*, 6:3, 286–311.

Kemp, F. WPA Listserv, accessed at http://listserv.muohio.edu/scripts/wa.exe?A0=wpa on 28 December 2004.

Kennedy, H. (1997) *Learning Works: Widening Participation in Further Education* (Coventry: Further Education Funding Council).

Kent, T. (1993) *Paralogic Rhetoric: A Theory of Communicative Interaction* (Lewisburg: Bucknell University Press).

Kent, T. (ed.) (1999) *Post-Process Theory: Beyond the Writing Process Paradigm* (Carbondale, IL: Southern Illinois University Press).

Khanna, A., Verma, M., Agnihotri, R. and Sinha, S. (1998) *Adult ESOL Learners in Britain* (Clevedon: Multilingual Matters).

Kidasa (2005) 'Gantt Charts', accessed at www.ganttchart.com/ on 18 December 2005.

Kinneavy, J. (1984) 'Translating Theory into Practice in Teaching Composition: a Historical View and a Contemporary View', in R. Connors, L. Ede and A. Lunsford (eds), *Essays on Classical Rhetoric and Modern Discourse* (Carbondale, IL: Southern Illinois University Press), pp. 69–81.

Kitzhaber, A. (1953) 'Rhetoric in American Colleges, 1850–1900', unpublished doctoral dissertation (University of Washington).

Kolb, D. (1984) *Experiential Learning* (Englewood Cliffs, NJ: Prentice-Hall).

Kress, G. (1998) 'Visual and Verbal Modes of Representation in Electronically Mediated Communication: the Potentials of New Forms of Text', in I. Snyder (ed.), *Page to Screen: Taking Literacy into the Electronic Era* (London: Routledge), pp. 53–79.

Kress, G. (2000) 'Multimodality', in B. Cope and M. Kalantzis (eds), *Multiliteracies: Literacy Learning and the Design of Social Futures* (London: Routledge), pp. 182–202.

Kutz, E., Groden, S. and Zamel, V. (1992) *The Discovery of Competence: Teaching and Learning with Diverse Students* (Portsmouth, NH: Boynton/Cook).

Kynell, T. (1996) *Writing in a Milieu of Utility: The Move to Technical Communication in American Engineering Programs, 1850–1950* (Norwood, NJ: Ablex).

Lamb, B. (1992) *A National Survey of UK Undergraduates' Standards of English* (London: The Queen's English Society).

Larson, R. (1994) 'Enlarging the Context: from Teaching Just Writing, to Teaching Academic Subjects *with* Writing', in R. Winterowd and V.

Gillespie (eds), *Composition in Context: Essays in Honor of Donald C. Stewart* (Carbondale, IL: Southern Illinois University Press), pp. 109–25.

Latham, M. (1994) *Constructing the Team* (London: HMSO).

Lave, J. and Wenger, E. (1991) *Situated Learning: Legitimate Peripheral Participation* (Cambridge: Cambridge University Press).

Lea, M. (1994) ' "I Thought I Could Write Until I Came Here": Student Writing in Higher Education', in G. Gibbs (ed.), *Improving Student Learning: Theory and Practice* (Oxford: Oxford Centre for Staff Development), pp. 216–26.

Lea, M. (1998) 'Academic Literacies and Learning in Higher Education: Constructing Knowledge through Texts and Experience', *Studies in the Education of Adults*, 30:2, 156–71.

Lea, M. and Stierer, B. (eds) (2000) *Student Writing in Higher Education: New Contexts* (Buckingham: Open University Press).

Lea, M. and Street, B. (1996) 'Academic Literacies', *Learning Matters*, 3, 2–4.

Lea, M. and Street, B. (1998) 'Student Writing in Higher Education: an Academic Literacies Approach', *Studies in Higher Education*, 23:2, 157–72.

Lea, M. and Street, B. (1999) 'Writing as Academic Literacies: Understanding Textual Practices in Higher Education', in C. Candlin and K. Hyland (eds), *Writing: Texts, Processes and Practices* (London: Longman), pp. 62–81.

Lefoe, G., Skillen, J. and James, B. (2001) *A Discussion Paper on Team Teaching* (Wollongong: University of Wollongong, Centre for Educational Development and Interactive Research).

Lillis, T. (1997) 'New Voices in Academia? The Regulative Nature of Academic Writing Conventions', *Language and Education*, 11:3, 182–99.

Lillis, T. (1999) 'Whose "Common Sense"? Essayist Literacy and the Institutional Practice of Mystery', in C. Jones, J. Turner and B. Street (eds), *Students Writing in the University: Cultural and Epistemological Issues* (Amsterdam: John Benjamins), pp. 127–47.

Lillis, T. (2001) *Student Writing: Access, Regulation, Desire* (London: Routledge).

Lillis, T. (2003) 'Student Writing as "Academic Literacies": Drawing on Bakhtin to Move from Critique to Design', *Language and Education*, 17:3, 192–207.

Lillis, T. and Turner, J. (2001) 'Student Writing in Higher Education: Contemporary Confusion, Traditional Concerns', *Teaching in Higher Education*, 6:1, 57–68.

Lindemann, E. (1995) *A Rhetoric for Writing Teachers*, 3rd edn (New York: Oxford University Press).

Losey, K. (1997) *Listen to the Silence: Mexican American Interaction in the Composition Classroom and the Community* (Norwood, NJ: Ablex).

Lunsford, A. (1991) 'Collaboration, Control, and the Idea of a Writing Center', reprinted in C. Murphy and J. Law (eds), *Landmark Essays on Writing Centres* (Davis, CA: Hermagoras Press), pp. 109–15.

Lunsford, A. and Ede, L. (1990) *Singular Texts/Plural Authors: Perspectives on Collaborative Writing* (Carbondale, IL: Southern Illinois University Press).

Lunsford, A. and Ruszkiewicz, J. (2004) *Everything's an Argument*, 3rd edn (Boston, MA: Bedford/St Martin's).

Macrorie, K. (1970) *Telling Writing* (New York: Hayden Book Company).

Malcolm, J. (2000) 'Joining, Invading, Reconstructing: Participation for a Change?', in J. Thompson (ed.), *Stretching the Academy: The Politics and Practice of Widening Participation in Higher Education* (Leicester: NIACE), pp. 12–22.

Marshall, B. (2000) 'The Ice Age Stunneth', *The Times Higher Education Supplement*, 1 December, 15.

Marton, F. and Säljö, R. (1976) 'On Qualitative Differences in Learning. I: Outcome and Process', *British Journal of Educational Psychology*, 46: 4–11.

Marton, F., Hounsell, D. and Entwistle, N. (eds) (1997) *The Experience of Learning* (Edinburgh: Scottish Academic Press).

Mason, J. and Washington, P. (1992) *The Future of Thinking: Rhetoric and Liberal Arts Teaching* (London: Routledge).

Mathieson, M. (1975) *The Preachers of Culture: A Study of English and its Teachers* (Towata, NJ: Rowan and Littlefield).

Mauk, J. and Metz, J. (2004) *The Composition of Everyday Life: A Guide to Writing* (Boston, MA: Thomson Wadsworth).

Maxwell, C. (2004) 'Teaching Nineteenth-Century Aesthetic Prose: a Writing Intensive Course', paper presented at the *Seventh National WAC Conference*, St Louis, Missouri.

McGivney, V. (2001) *Fixing or Changing the Pattern? Reflections on Widening Adult Participation in Learning* (Leicester: NIACE).

McKinney, C. (2003) 'Developing Critical Literacy in a Changing Context: the Challenges of "Critique" in South Africa', in S. Goodman, T. Lillis, J. Maybin and N. Mercer (eds), *Language, Literacy and Education: A Reader* (Stoke: Trentham Books), pp. 189–202.

McLean, P., Surtie, F., Elphinstone, L. and Devlin, M. (1995) 'Models of Learning Support in Victorian Universities: Issues and Implications', *Higher Education Research and Development*, 14:1, 75–86.

McLeod, S. (ed.) (2002) Special Issue on *WAC in International Contexts*, *Language and Learning Across the Disciplines*, 5:3.

McLeod, S., Miraglia, E., Soven, M. and Thaiss, C. (eds) (2001) *WAC for the New Millennium: Strategies for Continuing Writing-Across-the-Curriculum Programs* (Urbana, IL: NCTE).

McMahon, K. (2004) *What's Going On with Student Writing?* (London: Royal Literary Fund).

McQuade, D. and Atwan, R. (1997) *Thinking in Writing*, 4th edn (London: McGraw-Hill).

McVeigh, T. (2002) 'Generation Blighted by Exam Meddling', *Guardian*, 22 September, accessed at http://education.guardian.co.uk/alevels2002/story/0,,796843,00.html on 12 August 2004.

Mehan, H. (1979) *Learning Lessons: Social Organisation in the Classroom* (Cambridge: Cambridge University Press).

Mercer, N. (1995) *The Guided Construction of Knowledge* (Clevedon: Multilingual Matters).

Miller, R. (1997) *The Informed Argument*, 5th edn (London: Harcourt Brace Jovanovich).

Mitchell, S. (1994) *The Teaching and Learning of Argument in Sixth Forms and Higher Education: Final Report* (University of Hull: School of Education).

Mitchell, S. and Andrews, R. (eds) (2000) *Learning to Argue in Higher Education* (Portsmouth, NH: Boynton/Cook).

Mitchell, S. and Riddle, M. (2000) *Improving the Quality of Argument in Higher Education: Final Report* (London: Middlesex University, School of Education).

Mitchell, S., Marks-Fisher, V., Hale, L. and Harding, J. (2000) 'Making Dances, Making Essays: Academic Writing in the Study of Dance', in M. Lea and B. Stierer (eds), *Student Writing in Higher Education: New Contexts* (Buckingham: Open University Press), pp. 86–96.

Moghtader, M., Cotch, A. and Hague, K. (2001) 'The First-Year Composition Requirement Revisited: a Survey', *College Composition and Communication*, 52: 455–61.

Monroe, J. (2002) 'Global Cultures, Local Writing: Collaborative Contexts: the Cornell Consortium for Writing in the Disciplines', in S. McLeod (ed.), Special Issue on *WAC in International Contexts, Language and Learning Across Disciplines*, 5:3, pp. 11–27.

Monroe, J. (2003a) 'Writing and the Disciplines', *Peer Review*, 6:1, 4–7.

Monroe, J. (2003b) *Local Knowledges, Local Practices: Cultures of Writing at Cornell* (Pittsburgh: University of Pittsburgh Press).

Moses, I. (1985) *Supervising Postgraduates*, HERDSA Green Guide no. 3 (Campbelltown, NSW: HERDSA).

Muchiri, M., Mulama, N., Myers, G. and Ndoloi, D. (1995) 'Importing Composition: Teaching and Researching Academic Writing Beyond

North America', *College Composition and Communication*, 46:2, 175–98.

Mullin, J. (2001) 'Writing Centers and WAC', in S. McLeod, E. Miraglia, M. Soven and C. Thaiss (eds), *WAC for the New Millennium: Strategies for Continuing Writing-Across-the-Curriculum Programs* (Urbana, IL: NCTE), pp. 179–99.

Murphy, C. (2002) Personal email to Bonnie Devet, 3 January.

Murphy, C. and Law, J. (eds) (1995) *Landmark Essays on Writing Centres* (Davis, CA: Hermagoras Press).

Murphy, C. and Sherwood, S. (1995) 'The Tutoring Process: Exploring Paradigms and Practices', in C. Murphy and S. Sherwood (eds), *The St. Martin's Sourcebook for Writing Tutors* (New York: St Martin's Press), pp. 1–17.

Murray, D. (1985) *A Writer Teaches Writing*, 2nd edn (Boston, MA: Houghton Mifflin).

Murray, D. (2005) *Write to Learn*, 8th edn (Boston, MA: Thomson Wadsworth).

Murray, R. (2001) 'Integrating Teaching and Research through Writing Development for Students and Staff', *Active Learning in Higher Education*, 2:1, 31–45.

Murray, R. and MacKay, G. (1998) *Writers' Groups for Researchers and How to Run Them*, Universities' and Colleges' Staff Development Agency Briefing Paper, 60 (Sheffield: UCSDA).

National Center for Education Statistics (2002) 'Digest of Education Statistics, 2002, Chapter 3: Postsecondary Education', accessed at http://nces.ed.gov/programs/digest/d02/lt3.asp on 6 October 2004.

National Center for Education Statistics (2003) 'Projections of Education Statistics to 2013, Section 2: Enrollment in Degree-Granting Institutions', accessed at http://nces.ed.gov/programs/projections/ch_2.asp on 6 October 2004.

National Commission on Writing in America's Schools and Colleges (2003) *The Neglected 'R': The Need for a Writing Revolution*, accessed at www.writingcommission.org/ on 15 December 2004.

National Commission on Writing in America's Schools and Colleges (2004) *Writing: A Ticket to Work . . . Or a Ticket Out*, accessed at www.writingcommission.org/ on 15 December 2004.

NCIHE (1997) *Higher Education in the Learning Society: Report of the National Committee of Inquiry into Higher Education* [The Dearing Report] (London: HMSO).

Nelson, J. and Evertz, K. (eds) (2001) *The Politics of Writing Centers* (Portsmouth, NH: Boyton/Cook).

Newkirk, T. (1995) 'The Writing Conference as Performance', *Research in the Teaching of English*, 29:2, 193–215.

Newport, E. (1990) 'Maturational Constraints on Language Learning', reprinted in P. Bloom (ed.) (1994), *Language Acquisition* (Cambridge, MA: MIT), pp. 543–60.

Nieto, S. (2002) *Language, Culture, and Teaching: Critical Perspectives for a New Century* (Mahwah, NJ: Lawrence Erlbaum).

Nightingale, P. (1988) 'Understanding Processes and Problems in Student Writing', *Studies in Higher Education*, 13:3, 263–83.

Nightingale, P. (1991) 'Speaking of Student Writing . . .', *Journal of Geography in Higher Education*, 15:1, 3–13.

North, S. (1984) 'The Idea of a Writing Center', reprinted in C. Murphy and J. Law (eds) (1995), *Landmark Essays on Writing Centres* (Davis, CA: Harmagoras Press), pp. 71–85.

North, S. (1987) *The Making of Knowledge in Composition: Portrait of an Emerging Field* (Upper Montclair, NJ: Boynton/Cook).

O'Brien, T. (1995) 'Rhetorical Structure Analysis and the Case of the Inaccurate, Incoherent Source-Hopper', *Applied Linguistics*, 16:4, 442–82.

Ofsted (2000) *The Teaching of Writing in Primary Schools: Could Do Better*, HMI Discussion Paper (London: DfES).

Ohmann, R. (1976) *English in America: A Radical View of the Profession* (New York: Oxford University Press).

Olschner, L. (2004) Personal email to Sally Mitchell, 10 July.

Orr, S. and Blythman, M. (2000) 'Have You Got Ten Minutes? Can You Just Sort My Dissertation Out?', in M. Graal and R. Clark (eds), *Writing Development in Higher Education: Partnerships Across the Curriculum, Proceedings of the 6th Annual Writing Development in Higher Education Conference* (Leicester: University of Leicester), pp. 203–16.

Owen, G. (2003) 'Harder Exams will Teach Pupils How to Argue', *The Times*, 12 November.

Oxford (2005) 'What is the Oxford Comma?' accessed at www.askoxford.com/asktheexperts/faq/aboutother/oxfordcomma?view =uk on 20 September 2005.

Pardoe, S. (1994) 'Writing in Another Culture: the Value of Students' KAL in Writing Pedagogy', in D. Graddol and J. Swann (eds), *Evaluating Language* (Clevedon: Multilingual Matters), pp. 37–51.

Peck, J. and Coyle, M. (1999) *The Student's Guide to Writing: Grammar, Punctuation and Spelling* (Basingstoke: Macmillan).

Petelin, R. (2002) 'Another Whack at WAC: Reprising WAC in Australia', in S. McCleod (ed.), Special Issue on *WAC in International Contexts, Language and Learning Across the Disciplines*, 5:3, pp. 98–109.

Peterson, L. (1992) *The Norton Reader*, 11th edn (New York: W. W. Norton).

Piolat, A. and Roussey, J-Y. (1996) 'Students' Drafting Strategies and Text Quality', in Quality Assurance Agency for Higher Education (2000), *Academic Standards: Chemistry, Computing, Law* (Gloucester: QAA).

Poskitt, J. (2002) 'National Consultation on Exemplars: What Difference Does it Make for Teachers?', accessed at www.tki.org.nz/r/assessment/research/research1_e.php on 16 June 2004.

Pratt, J. (1997) *The Polytechnic Experiment: 1965–1992* (Buckingham: Open University Press).

Prior, P. (1998) *Writing/Disciplinarity: A Sociohistoric Account of Literate Activity in the Academy* (Mahwah, NJ: Lawrence Erlbaum).

Quality Assurance Agency for Higher Education (2000) *The English Benchmarking Statement* (Gloucester: QAA).

Quality Assurance Agency for Higher Education (2001) *Guidelines for HE Progress Files*, accessed at www.qaa.ac.uk/academicinfrastructure/progressFiles/default.asp on 2 September 2005.

Ramsden, P. (1992) *Learning to Teach in Higher Education* (London: Routledge).

Read, B., Francis, B. and Robson, J. (2001) ' "Playing Safe": Undergraduate Essay Writing and the Presentation of the Student "Voice" ', *British Journal of Sociology of Education*, 22:3, 387–99.

Reid, I. (ed.) (1987) *The Place of Genre in Learning: Current Debates* (Geelong: Deakin University Press).

Reigstad, T. and McAndrew, D. (1984) *Training Tutors for Writing Conferences* (Urbana, IL: NCTE).

Richie, H. (2001) Personal interview with Bonnie Devet, 22 March.

Rickford J. (1998) 'The Ebonics Controversy in My Backyard: a Sociolinguist's Experiences and Reflections', accessed at www.stanford.edu/~rickford/papers/EbonicsInMyBackyard.html on 4 January 2005.

Ridley, T. M. (1996) *Whither Civil Engineering?* (London: Institution of Civil Engineers).

Riley, T. (1994) 'The Unpromising Future of Writing Centers', *The Writing Center Journal*, 15:1, 20–34.

Roemer, M., Schultz, L. and Durst, R. (1999) 'Reframing the Great Debate on First-Year Writing', *College Composition and Communication*, 50, 377–92.

Rose, M. (1983) 'Remedial Writing Courses: a Critique and a Proposal', *College English*, 45:2, 109–28.

Rose, M. (1985) 'The Language of Exclusion: Writing Instruction at the University', *College English*, 47:4, 341–59.

Rose, M. (1989) *Lives on the Boundary* (New York: Penguin).

Rose, M. (2004) *The Mind at Work: Valuing the Intelligence of the American Worker* (New York: Viking).

Rottenberg, A. (1988) 'Learning to Teach by Tutoring', *Writing Lab Newsletter*, 12:10, 11–12.

Rowland, S. (2004) 'Academics Should Not Lead Unexamined Lives', *The Times Higher Education Supplement*, 30 July 2004, p. 12.

Russell, D. (1994) 'American Origins of the Writing-Across-the-Curriculum Movement', in C. Bazerman and D. Russell (eds), *Landmark Essays in Writing Across the Curriculum* (Davis, CA: Hermagoras Press), pp. 3–22.

Russell, D. (2001) 'Where do the Naturalistic Studies of WAC/WID Point? A Research Review', in S. McLeod, E. Miraglia, M. Soven and C. Thaiss (eds) (2001), *WAC for the New Millennium: Strategies for Continuing Writing-Across-the-Curriculum Programs* (Urbana, IL: NCTE), pp. 259–298.

Russell, D. (2002) *Writing in the Academic Disciplines: A Curricular History*, 2nd edn (Carbondale, IL: Southern Illinois University Press).

Russell, D. and Foster, D. (2002) *Writing and Learning in Cross-National Perspective: Transitions from Secondary to Higher Education* (Urbana, IL: NCTE).

Rust, C. and Wallace, J. (eds) (1994) *Helping Students Learn from Each Other: Supplemental Instruction*, SEDA Paper, no. 86 (Birmingham: SEDA).

Scardamalia, M. and Bereiter, C. (1994) 'Development of Dialectical Processes in Composition', in B. Stierer, and J. Maybin (eds), *Language, Literacy and Learning in Educational Practice* (Clevedon: Multilingual Matters), pp. 295–309.

Scarry, J. and Scarry, S. (eds) (2003) *The Holt Reader* (New York: Holt Rinehart-Winston).

Schell, E. (1998) *Gypsy Academics and Mother-Teachers: Gender, Contingent Labor, and Writing Instruction* (Portsmouth, NH, Boynton/Cook).

Scollon, R. and Scollon, S. (1981) *Narrative, Literacy and Face in Interethnic Communication* (Norwood, NJ: Ablex).

Scott, M. (2000) 'Writing in Postgraduate Teacher Training: a Question of Identity', in M. Lea and B. Stierer (eds), *Student Writing in Higher Education: New Contexts* (Buckingham: Open University Press, pp. 112–24.

Scott, M. (2001) 'Written English, Word-Processors and Meaning Making: a Semiotic Perspective on the Development of Adult Students' Academic Writing', in L. Tolchinsky (ed.), *Developmental Aspects in Learning to Write* (Dordrecht: Kluwer), pp. 163–76.

Scott, M. (2002) 'Cracking the Codes Anew: Writing about Literature in England', in D. Russell and D. Foster (eds), *Writing and Learning in Cross-National Perspective: Transitions from Secondary to Higher Education* (Urbana, IL: NCTE), 88–133.

Scott, P. (1995) *The Meanings of Mass Higher Education* (Buckingham: Open University Press).

Seshachari, N. (1994) 'Instructor-Mediated Journals: Raised Critical Thinking and Discourse Levels', *College Teaching*, 42:1, 7–11.

Shamoon, L. and Burns, D. (2001) 'Labor Pains: a Political Analysis of Writing Center Tutoring', in J. Nelson and K. Evertz (eds), *The Politics of Writing Centers* (Portsmouth, NH: Boyton/Cook), pp. 62–73.

Sharples, M. (1999) *How We Write: Writing as Creative Design* (London: Routledge).

Shaughnessy, M. (1977) *Errors and Expectations: A Guide for the Teacher of Basic Writing* (New York: Oxford University Press).

Shor, I. (1997) 'Our Apartheid: Writing Instruction and Inequality', *Journal of Basic Writing*, 16:1, 91–104.

Simpson, J., Braye, S. and Boquet, B. (1994) 'War, Peace, and Writing Center Administration', *Composition Studies/Freshman English News*, 22:1, 65–95.

Sinclair, J. and Coulthard, M. (1975) *Towards an Analysis of Discourse: The English Used by Teachers and Pupils* (Oxford: Oxford University Press).

Skillen, J. and Mahony, M. (1997) 'Literacy and Learning Development in Higher Education: an Issue of Institutional Change', accessed at www.swin.edu.au/aare/conf97.htm on 1 March 2005.

Skillen, J. and Trivett, N. (2001) 'Explicit Teaching of Genre Conventions in Tertiary Education: an Example from Biology', *Academic Exchange Quarterly*, 113.

Skillen, J., Merten, M., Percy, A. and Trivett, N. (1999) 'Integrating the Instruction of Generic and Discipline-Specific Skills into the Curriculum: a Case Study', in R. James et al. (eds), *Proceedings of the Higher Education Research and Development Society of Australasia International Conference*, accessed at www.herdsa.org.au/branches/vic/Cornerstones/authorframeset.html on 6 March 2004.

Skillen, J., Percy, A., Trivett, N. and James, B. (2001) 'Creating Partnerships in Supporting Student Learning: a Paradigm Shift in Learning Support', in P. Little, J. Conway, K. Cleary, S. Bourke, J. Archer and A. Kingsland (eds), *Learning Partnerships: Proceedings of the Annual HERDSA Conference 2001*, CD-ROM.

Smithers, R. (2003) 'Student Spelling and Grammar at "Crisis" Levels', *Guardian*, 1 March, accessed at http://education.guardian.co.uk/students/news/story/0,,906649,00.html on 11 August 2004.

Smoke, T. (1999) 'Preparing Students for Higher Education', *ESL Magazine*, 2:5, 20–3.

Soven, M. (2001) 'Curriculum-Based Peer Tutors and WAC', in S. McLeod, E. Miraglia, M. Soven and C. Thaiss (eds), *WAC for the New Millennium: Strategices for Continuing Writing-Across-the-Curriculum Programs* (Urbana, IL: NCTE), pp. 200–32.

Speak–Write unpublished research data (1999) (Cambridge: Anglia Polytechnic University).

Sternglass, M. (1997) *Time to Know Them: A Longitudinal Study of Writing and Learning at the College Level* (Mahwah, NJ: Lawrence Erlbaum).

Stierer, B. (1997) *Mastering Education: A Preliminary Analysis of Academic Literacy Practices within Master-Level Courses* (Milton Keynes: Centre for Language and Communications, Open University).

Stierer, B. and Maybin, J. (eds) (1994) *Language, Literacy and Learning in Educational Practice* (Clevedon: Multilingual Matters).

Stoodt, B. and Balbo, E. (1979) 'Integrating Study Skills Instruction with Content in a Secondary Classroom', *Reading World*, 18, 247–52.

Stott, R. and Avery, S. (eds) (2001) *Writing with Style* (London: Longman).

Stott, R. and Chapman, P. (eds) (2001) *Grammar and Writing* (London: Longman).

Stott, R., Rylance, R. and Snaith, A. (eds) (2001) *Making Your Case: A Practical Guide to Essay Writing* (London: Longman).

Stott, R., Young, T. and Bryan, C. (eds) (2001) *Speaking Your Mind* (London: Longman).

Street, B. (1998) ' "Hobbesian Fears" and Galilean Struggles: Response to Peter Freebody', *Literacy and Numeracy Studies*, 8:2.

Summerfield, J. (1988) 'Writing Centers: a Long View', reprinted in C. Murphy and J. Law (eds) (1995), *Landmark Essays on Writing Centres* (Davis, CA: Hermagoras Press), pp. 63–8.

Swales, J. (1990) *Genre Analysis: English in Academic and Research Settings* (Cambridge: Cambridge University Press).

Tapper, J. (2000) 'Partnerships in Writing Development: Communication Across the Curriculum and the Disciplines', in M. Graal and R. Clark (eds), *Writing Development in Higher Education: Partnerships Across the Curriculum: Proceedings of the 6th Annual Writing Development in Higher Education Conference* (Leicester: University of Leicester), pp. 33–45.

Tapper, J. (2003) 'Communication Across the Curriculum: from Tertiary Literacy to Graduate Outcomes', Abstract for paper presented at the *Second EATAW/EWCA Conference: Tutoring and Teaching Academic Writing*, Central European University, accessed at www.ceu.hu/eataw/abstract.htm#T on 14 August 2005.

Taylor, G., Beasley, V., Bock, H., Clanchy, J. and Nightingale, P. (eds) (1988) *Literacy by Degrees* (Buckingham: Open University Press).

Thesen, L. (1994) 'Voices in Discourse: Re-thinking Shared Meaning in Academic Writing', unpublished MPhil dissertation (Cape Town: University of Cape Town).

Thesen, L. (2001) 'Modes, Literacies and Power: a University Case Study', *Language and Education*, 15:2 and 3, 132–45.

Thow, M. and Murray, R. (2001) 'Enabling Student Writing for Undergraduate Projects: a Practical Approach', *Physiotherapy*, 87:3, 134–9.

Thurlow C., Lengel, L. and Tomic, A. (2004) *Computer Mediated Communication: Social Interaction on the Internet* (London: Sage).

Tomic, A. (1996) 'Challenges and Rewards in the Mixed Culture Classroom', *College Teaching*, 44:2, 69–73.

Topping, K. (1996a) 'Effective Peer Tutoring in Further and Higher Education: a Typology and Review of the Literature', *Higher Education*, 32, 321–45.

Topping, K. (1996b) *Effective Peer Tutoring in Further and Higher Education*, SEDA Paper, no. 95 (Birmingham: SEDA).

Torrance, M., Thomas, G. and Robinson, E. (1992) 'The Writing Experiences of Social Science Research Students', *Studies in Higher Education*, 17:2, pp. 155–67.

Torrance, M., Thomas, G. and Robinson, E. (1994) 'The Writing Strategies of Graduate Research Students in the Social Sciences', *Higher Education*, 27, 379–92.

Torrance, M., Thomas, G. and Robinson, E. (1999) 'Individual Differences in the Writing Behaviour of Undergraduate Students', *British Journal of Educational Psychology*, 69, 189–99.

Trimbur, J. (1987) 'Peer Tutoring: a Contradiction in Terms?', *Writing Center Journal,* 7:2, 21–8.

Trimmer, J. (2003) *Writing with a Purpose*, 13th edn (Boston: Houghton Mifflin).

Trivett, N. and Skillen, J. (1998) 'Using Computer Technology to Integrate Instruction in Discipline-specific Literacy Skills into the Curriculum: a Case Study', *Proceedings of the 1998 ASCILITE Conference*, accessed at http://www.ascilite.org.au/conferences/wollongong98/asc98-pdf/trivettskillen.pdf on 20 December 2004.

Truss, L. (2003) *Eats, Shoots and Leaves* (London: Profile Books).

Turner, J. (1999) 'Academic Literacy and the Discourse of Transparency', in C. Jones, J. Turner and B. Street (eds), *Students Writing in the University: Cultural and Epistemological Issues* (Amsterdam: John Benjamins), pp. 149–69.

Turner, J. (2004) 'Language as Academic Purpose', *Journal of English for Academic Purposes*, 3:2, 95–109.

United States National Commission on Excellence in Education (1984) *A Nation at Risk: The Full Account* (Cambridge, MA: USA Research).

University of Derby (2003) *Corporate Planning Statement* (Derby: University of Derby).

Vardi, I. (2000) 'How Do First-Year Lecturers Help Students Develop Writing Skills?', *Flexible Learning for a Flexible Society* (Toowoomba: HERDSA).

Varnum, R. (1996) 'Composition Studies', in P. Heilker and P. Vandenberg (eds), *Keywords in Composition Studies* (Portsmouth, NH: Boynton/Cook), pp. 44–8.

Vygotsky, L. (1986) *Thought and Language* (Cambridge, MA: MIT Press).

WAC Clearinghouse (2005), accessed at http://wac.colostate.edu/ on 10 October 2005.

Wallace, R. and Simpson, J. (1991) 'Preface', *The Writing Center: New Directions* (New York: Garland), pp. ix–x.

Walvoord, B., Hunt, L., Dowling, H. and McMahon, J. (1997) *In the Long Run: A Study of Faculty in Three Writing-Across-the-Curriculum Programs* (Urbana, IL: NCTE).

Warren, D. (2002) 'Curriculum Design in a Context of Widening Participation in Higher Education', *Arts and Humanities in Higher Education*, 1:1, 85–99.

Wason, P. (1980) 'Conformity and Commitment in Writing', *Visible Language*, 14:4, 351–63.

Webb, C. (2002) 'Language and Academic Skills Advisers: Professional Ontogenesis', *Proceedings of the 2001 Australian Language and Academic Skills Conference*, accessed at http://learning.uow.edu.au/LAS2001 on 26 February 2005.

Welsch, K. (2001) 'The Writing Conference and "Correction" Interference', *Writing Lab Newsletter*, 26:4, 4–7.

Whyte, W. (1956) *The Organization Man* (New York: Simon & Schuster).

Winch, C. and Wells, P. (1994) 'The Quality of Student Writing in Higher Education: A Cause for Concern', *British Journal of Educational Studies*, 43:1, 75–87.

Winter, R., Parker, J. and Ovens, P. (2003) 'The Patchwork Text: a Radical Re-Assessment of Coursework Assignments', *Innovations in Education and Teaching International*, 40:2, entire issue.

Womack, P. (1993) 'What are Essays For?', *English in Education*, 27:2, 42–8.

Woodrow, M. (2002) *Pyramids or Spiders? Cross-Sector Collaboration to Widen Participation: Learning from International Experiences*, Report to

Scottish Funding Councils for Further and Higher Education, accessed at www.sfc.ac.uk/library/06854fc203db2fbd000000f44901dccb/ he2502a.pdf accessed on 21 June 2002.

Writing Institute Network for Success, accessed at http://ohiowins.uc.edu/ on 14 December 2004.

Wyse, D. (2001) 'Grammar for Writing? A Critical Review of Empirical Evidence', *British Journal of Educational Studies*, 49:4, 411–27.

Young, A. (2002) *Teaching Writing Across the Curriculum* WAC Clearinghouse Landmark Publications in Writing Studies, accessed http://wac.colostate.edu/books/young_teaching/ an 3 January 2000.

Young, R. (1980) 'Arts, Crafts, Gifts, and Knacks: Some Disharmonies in the New Rhetoric', *Visible Language*, 14:4, 341–50.

Young, T. (2004) 'Humanities Degrees in Writing-Intensive Professions', *English Subject Centre Newsletter*, 6, 4–9.

Young, T., Price, K. and Williamson, V. (eds) (forthcoming, 2007) *Writing at Work: Advanced Writing Skills for Graduate Professionals* (London: Longman).

Zamel, V. and Spack, R. (1998) *Negotiating Academic Literacies: Teaching and Learning Across Languages and Cultures* (Mahwah, NJ: Lawrence Erlbaum).

Index